Tradition and Crisis

Tradition and Crisis

Jewish Society
at the End of the Middle Ages

By Jacob Katz

The Hebrew University, Jerusalem

Schocken Books · New York

First published in Hebrew in 1958
First edition in English in 1961

First SCHOCKEN PAPERBACK edition 1971

Copyright © 1961 by The Free Press of Glencoe, Inc.
Library of Congress Catalog Card No. 61-9168
Manufactured in the United States of America

Third Printing, 1977

Preface

This book is the English version of the Hebrew original, which appeared in Jerusalem in 1958. It was published by the Bialik Institute.

The text has remained substantially unchanged. The notes, however, have been omitted, because most of the sources for the book are Hebrew. Those readers who have a command of that language will be able to refer to the Hebrew version. For the non-Hebraists the footnotes would not have added to the text, as they are mostly interwoven with the interpretation of the sources. Nevertheless, I should like to give the reader an idea of the kind of sources on which the presentation of this work is built.

Jewish communities and super-communities had their own by-laws, many of which have been preserved and published in part. In respect to some of them, we also possess the records of proceedings of their councils. Throughout the ages, outstanding rabbis have beeen approached on ritual and legalistic questions, and their responses have been handed down in what has become known as *responsa* (questions and answers) literature. These questions and answers affected social life in all its aspects.

The same applies to the legalistic literature, such as the religious codices which, while based on talmudic tradition, illustrate changes of approach to social problems through the modifications and variations found in each new version. The period from the sixteenth to the eighteenth centuries was most prolific in terms of the output of moralistic literature and homiletics. Although repetitive, these, too, are valuable historical sources when collated with older versions.

More direct sources are the pamphlets on subjects of controversy—especially on sectarian movements—and memoirs, the first of which appear in this period. These kinds of sources are much more useful in writing the social rather than the narrative

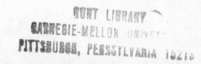

history, the method which has been used most frequently in dealing with the Jewish history of this period.

I have appended a selected bibliography of books in English and German for the reader who wishes to pursue the subject in greater detail.

J. KATZ

Eliezer Kaplan School
The Hebrew University
July, 1961

Selected Bibliography

Abrahams, I., Jewish Life in the Middle Ages, Philadelphia, 1896.

Baer, J. F., Galut, New York, 1947.

Baron, S. W., The Jewish Community, 3 vols., Philadelphia, 1942.

Caro, G., Sozial- und Wirtschaftsgeschichte der Juden im Mittelalter und der Neuzeit, 2 vols., Leipzig, 1908–20.

Dubnow, S., Weltgeschichte des Juedischen Volkes, vols. 8–10, Berlin, 1925–9.

————, History of the Jews in Russia and Poland, from the Earliest Times until the Present Day, Philadelphia, 1916.

Graetz, H., Geschichte der Juden, vols. 9–11, Leipzig, 1891–1908.

Katz, J., Die Entstehung der Judenassimilation in Deutschland und deren Ideologie, Frankfurt a.M., 1935.

————, Exclusiveness and Tolerance, Studies in Jewish Gentile Relations in Medieval and Modern Times, Oxford, 1961.

Parkes, J., The Jew in the Medieval Community, London, 1938.

Scholem, G., Major Trends of Jewish Mysticism, New York, 1954.

Schnee, H., Die Hoffinanz und der Moderne Staat, 3 vols., Berlin, 1953–5.

Sombart, W., The Jews in Modern Capitalism, Glencoe, Ill., 1951.

Stern, S., Der Preussische Staat und die Juden, 2 vols., Berlin, 1925.

————, The Court Jew, Philadelphia, 1950.

Wiener, M., Judische Religion im Zeitalter der Emancipation, Berlin, 1933.

Contents

PART THREE   DISINTEGRATION

PART ONE

Foundations

I

Definition of the Subject

*T*HE CONCEPT "TRADITIONAL SOCIETY" IS EM-
ployed in this book to denote a type of society which regards
its existence as based upon a common body of knowledge and
values handed down from the past. This concept accurately de-
scribes the whole of world Jewry, at least from the talmudic era
(200 C.E.) up to the age of European Emancipation (during
the first half of the nineteenth century), and it applies to some
part of Jewish society even in more recent times. We shall, however, confine our discussion to one particular period. We propose
to describe, in terms of a socio-historical analysis, traditional
Jewish society in the stage prior to its dissolution, i.e., from the
sixteenth to the second half of the eighteenth century. This dis-

solution itself, the transition to Hasidism in eastern Europe and to Enlightenment and Emancipation in the West, forms the epilogue to our subject. We shall deal with antecedent periods only insofar as we need to trace the traditions and values that came down to the period of study to their source.

In Jewish history, the sixteenth, seventeenth, and eighteenth centuries are regarded as a particularly eventful and significant period. From the ecological point of view, we see that Polish Jewry rose in importance beyond any previous time. German Jewry also regained its vitality by the end of the seventeenth century. During this period, Jews settled again in Holland and England, countries that had been closed to them for many centuries. Even resettlement in the Holy Land, though subject to many fluctuations, made its mark on the history of the period. The literary output in the fields of halakha, cabala, and homiletics was prolific. We find documents reflecting contemporary reactions to the great events of the period, the most outstanding of which are the pogroms of 1648 and the appearance of Sabbatai Zevi in 1665–66 in Turkey. About one hundred years after Sabbatai Zevi, two new movements appeared on the Jewish scene—Hasidism and Haskala—each of which constitute a turning point in the social history of the community.

According to the routine historical method which traces events and processes in chronological sequence, any one of these events and processes would present a separate subject. Our social historical method limits our terms of reference. First, we are circumscribed geographically. The area with which we deal embraces Lithuania, Poland, Hungary, and the Germanic lands— including Moravia and Bohemia in the East and Alsace in the West; in brief, we shall be concerned with the region populated by Ashkenazi Jewry in its broader sense. These countries were affected by the transition to Hasidism, on the one hand, and the social disintegration in the wake of civic emancipation, on the other. In other countries, like England, France, Italy, the Balkans,

North Africa, and elsewhere, different factors and circumstances intervened.

Social history differs from narrative history. The former is concerned not with the single occurrence, but with the social reality prevailing at a given time. Social history leaves no sphere outside its terms of reference. Economic, political, cultural, social, and religious activities must all be described and analyzed. Data from all these spheres are assembled to provide clues relating to the norms prevailing in every field during a given period. In other words, social history is not concerned with particular historical events, but with describing the institutions within the framework of which these events took place. Accordingly, when we come to describe economic activity, in-group and out-group social relations, community administration, family life, and the like, we shall not ask: how did this particular individual conduct himself in any one of these fields? We shall rather pose the questions: What was the accepted way of conduct? How did the average member of the society act?

The first task of social history is therefore to determine what is typical and accepted within the framework of various social institutions. This aim can be achieved so long as we confine our study to institutions, like the family, of which many exist simultaneously within a single society. No one will deny that the study of certain family histories—genealogical research—calls for a consideration of their social history as well. This implies describing the traits characteristic to most of the families of this society and tracing the variations in the archetypal pattern. Admittedly, the family described by the social historian has no actual reality; it is merely an abstraction conjured up by the scholar who has reconstructed its picture from the records of the many families he investigated. Nevertheless, this generalizing approach constitutes the most rewarding method of describing the evolution and development of the family in its social context.

This method, however, does not lend itself so easily to the

study of social institutions of a broader and more formal nature
—institutions such as the *kehilla* or super-*kehilla* organizations.
In this context, another method has received wide acceptance.
The history of each *kehilla* and super-*kehilla* organization is
presented separately. In fact, however, there is no difference in
principle between the family and the community. Both lend themselves equally to investigation and description in their specific
and typical aspects. Everything depends on the aim in mind. The
history of one *kehilla* may have to be presented as an individual,
specific case, a faithful, factual record of its existence; whereas
that of another may have to be reconstructed through a process of
abstract generalization.

It is the aim of the present work to depict the average Jewish
social institutions during the period under discussion. This objective imposes a geographical limitation. Although the different
Jewish communities throughout the Diaspora were united during
this period, by a common historical consciousness, as we shall
presently demonstrate, this in no way forged them into components of one single society. The Jews of Poland and Yemen, of
Holland and Palestine, regarded themselves as belonging to the
same people. They even maintained institutions of an educational
and religious character which embodied one common tradition.
But even these institutions differed in many respects from country
to country. We can note these differences even more clearly in economic, political-communal, family, and social institutions. Indeed,
the latter vary from country to country to an extent that makes
them incompatible for common treatment. The social structure can
only really be fathomed by treating Jewish history according to
geographic regions or "centers." Each center, therefore, enjoys a
kind of historiographic autonomy which is a projection of the
autonomy obtaining in real life. An area governed by one uniform pattern of life justifies separate socio-historical treatment.
Where several regions share a similar normative pattern, this
may be accepted as evidence of actual contact between them.

Areas distant from each other would not betray these similarities unless there existed actual contact between them. The Jewish communities in Poland, Bohemia, Moravia, Germany, and western Hungary were undoubtedly socially akin, justifying their treatment as one area for the purposes of this study. The ultimate separation of these countries from each other into autonomous and even contrasting and mutually exclusive categories symptomatizes the historical turning point towards which our description of this society will lead us in the concluding phase of our study.

Hence, it becomes obvious that our regional subdivision of Jewish history is purely a matter of method, in no way calling into question the underlying national unity of the Jewish people in the lands of their dispersion. This unity is an indisputable fact, as we shall presently demonstrate. A proper evaluation of this unity will indicate how far it can serve as a basis for uniform historical treatment.

A common religion, nationhood, and messianic hope may be said to form the bonds that unite the Jewish people in the various countries to which they were dispersed. We shall show, Chapter III, how far these characteristics separated the Jew from his non-Jewish environment. But the separateness of each Jewish community in every locality does not itself forge all communities into one single social entity. Only to the extent that these characteristics constitute active and effectual forces of consciousness leading to a living relationship can one justifiably speak of social unity. It goes without saying that the various sections of Jewry were linked by many bonds. Communities which were far apart expressed their kinship in many ways, ranging from mutual aid to interest in and deep concern for each other's fate. In comparison with other periods of Jewish history, we shall see that the sixteenth to eighteenth centuries produced a strengthening of the bonds between the various widely separated sections of the Jewish people. It is doubtful whether there ever was a time since the decline of the Roman Empire when Jewry's political organization was still centralized, in which contact among Jewish groups was as intensive as in the period under discussion.

The improved means of communication and intensified commercial ties which characterize this era in the history of European and Mediterranean nations had its repercussions, too, upon the Jewish people. The society was particularly dependent on good communications for maintaining contact with its widely scattered communities. The intensification of contact is evident in various spheres. Mutual aid was practiced by Jewish communities in different countries. Jewish notables of central Europe organized to avert the expulsion of their brethren from Prague in 1745. Jewish communities, from Constantinople to Amsterdam, co-operated in ransoming Jewish captives, victims of the eastern European pogroms of 1648–49. The Holy Land grew in increasing importance as an object of pilgrimage and, to an even larger extent, as a place for permanent settlement. Emigration to the Holy Land fortified consciousness of a common origin and strengthened the belief in a messianic future. Palestine became the meeting place for Jews from different countries who then returned to their respective communities. Diaspora Jews rallied to help their brethren in the Holy Land.

All these factors served to strengthen the links between world Jewry. During this period, emissaries were despatched from the Holy Land to all the Jewish communities throughout the Diaspora to solicit funds for the support of the settlers. These itinerant emissaries promoted contact between Jewries and acted as a unifying factor. The mobility of the Jewish community facilitated the dissemination of ideas that were being developed at the centers of Jewish learning. Contemporary halakhic codification, methods of talmudic study, cabalistic and homiletic theories were rapidly publicised and reached a much wider circle than in previous epochs. The success of Sabbatai Zevi's activities can only be explained on the basis of the wide currency of the Messianic ideas contained in the Lurianic Cabala. That Sabbatai Zevi could alert a whole people scattered far and wide in many countries to be ready for the very moment of redemption, is eloquent testimony to the unity of the Jewish people in this era.

The recognition of the "organic" unity of the entire Jewish people constitutes sufficient grounds for writing its history on a comprehensive, national scale. This approach suffers from one drawback. Such a record would merely present those processes and events common to the Jewish people as a whole, i.e. those that determine its religious, historical, and messianic consciousness. However, any writing of history—not only social history—which does not wish to ignore any phase and manifestation of human endeavor—political, economic, institutional, and the like —must confine itself to a smaller historical canvas. We find that Jewish history to some extent repeats itself, not only in the temporal dimension, but primarily in spatial dimensions. The history of various Jewish communities, though they still possess their own unique ingredients, read like variations of the same theme.

By describing Jewish traditional society in one of its historical manifestations, we shall achieve two objectives simultaneously. First, we present what happened to a given community in one specific historical setting. Second, we generalize from this example and regard it as an archetype for Jewish traditional society. Only in the concluding stage of our study, when dealing with the transition to Hasidism and Enlightenment, would it appear that we are confronted with a unique historical phenomenon from which no conclusions applicable elsewhere can be drawn. The twin movements of Hasidism and Haskala seem to have no parallel elsewhere in Jewish history.

Yet even these two unique movements reveal typical traits. They exemplify two disintegrating tendencies that affect traditional society and its institutions: religious charisma and rationalism. Religious charisma springs from consciousness of immediate religious destiny, whereas rationalism is grounded in the belief of the intellect's unlimited validity. Religious charisma and rationalism are opposites in essence and may conflict with each other when met in one historical situation. But they form a common front against a third phenomenon, the traditional society. Their common denominator is their tendency to claim a self-derived authority in opposition to the acknowledged validity of tradition. These two sources of challenge to traditional authority are not without parallel in earlier periods of Jewish history. More than once, traditional Jewish society was imperiled by shafts of criticism speaking in the name of reason or a superior religious communion. Why was the traditional social structure spared the realization of this danger until the first half of the eighteenth century, and how was it spared? The fact that these two forces sent forth their challenge simultaneously bears double evidence that Jewish traditional society reached a turning point during the latter part of the eighteenth century.

II   *Jewish Society and the General Setting*

IN THE INTRODUCTORY CHAPTER, WE AC-
cepted the premise that the widely scattered sections of the
Jewish people represent a uniform social entity. The very fact of
dispersion implies, on the other hand, that each section is simultaneously a part of a different society, i.e. the non-Jewish community of its respective environment. The Jewish community
belongs, first ecologically, to the surrounding non-Jewish milieu.
Jews constitute a segment of the society around them. They
perform some definite functions within this society, and many
of their needs are supplied by it. Sociologically speaking, the
Jewish community may be termed a "subgroup" of the society-
at-large. Though as a subgroup it does not share many of the

features of the dominant environment, it is integrated into the over-all pattern, since it could not exist otherwise. In the following chapters, we shall dwell on the nature of this integration, as well as on the divergent features distinguishing the two societies from each other. We start with the description of those data which determine the place of Jewish society in the general setting. These involve demographic, ecological, religio-cultural, and political aspects.

The total number of Ashkenazi Jews in the first half of the period under discussion (1648) has been estimated by demographers at about three quarters of a million, one third of them living in central European countries, the remainder in the East (in Poland and Lithuania). This figure represents approximately one half of the total Jewish population at that time. By the end of this period, the European Jewish population had doubled, and included about one million and a half souls at the close of the eighteenth century. This figure does not represent more than 2 to 3 per cent of the general population of the respective countries of Poland, Lithuania, Germany, and Austro-Hungary; although in Poland in the seventeenth century, the Jewish community may have attained a proportion of from 6 to 7 per cent of the total. At any rate, even the Jews in Poland regarded themselves as constituting a tiny minority.

The size of Jewish communities during this period ranged from isolated individuals in non-Jewish settlements to 10,000 and more in the Prague community of the seventeenth and eighteenth centuries. The density of Jewish settlement also varied considerably in each region. In central and western Germany, the Jewish communities were widely separated so that contact was maintained only between the more mobile upper strata of the respective communities. In other areas, such as Poland, Moravia, and Alsace, where Jewish settlement was much denser, the closer and more frequent contact created a deeper and broader sense of community and a richer pattern of mass Jewish living. We shall see, moreover, that even the widest dispersion did not undermine the basic Jewish community feeling. On the other hand, the minority status of the Jews seems to have been accepted as natural and permanent, expressing the qualitative distinctions between them and the autochthonous population. Their status and fundamental aspirations remained unchanged even in cases where they happened to constitute the majority of the population.

Besides the numerical relationship, the peculiar status of the Jews found its ecological expression in the separate neighborhoods they inhabited. During our period, the ghetto was a feature of Jewish settlement in Germany and Poland. The Jews were restricted to certain streets by government ordinance—except in hamlets and villages where the Jewish population was too small to warrant the establishment of a special quarter for them. Similarly, some towns in Germany, like Hanover and Dresden, formed an exception because Jews settled in them when this segregational policy was losing its hold and the local authorities no longer insisted on separate neighborhoods for the Jewish and Christian populations. However, even in such places, Jews concentrated around their communal institutions, the synagogue, *be'th hamidrash,* etc. These Jewish neighborhoods were far more attractive than the cramped, enclosed ghettos. But they reflected, in their spontaneous emergence, Jewish segregative tendencies.

A further symptom of social segregation was reflected in the outward appearance of the Jew. In the period under discussion, he was no longer required to wear the medieval badge of identity. In most places, this practice no longer had even theoretical legal force. Yet his dress differed, to a larger or smaller extent, from that of his neighbors. Other distinctive features were the men's beards and sidelocks, the married women's covered hair, and perhaps their physiognomy, which was somehow more distinctive than during periods of social rapprochement. All these distinguished and set the Jew apart from the rest of the population, which in itself presented a diversity of trades and classes.

Language represents the third distinctive characteristic. Yiddish was spoken by Ashkenazic-Polish Jewry of this period, and each country and locality had its own distinctive dialect. What matters here is the fact that Jews communicated with each other in a language different from that of their neighbors. The linguistic differentiation varied with each locality. The language barrier was a formidable one in Poland and Lithuania where the vernacular was very far removed from Yiddish. The local population did not understand it at all—except for individuals who made it their business to master the language or who picked it up through their Jewish contacts—just as the Jews became conversant with the language of their environment to meet their needs. The Judeo-German speech of the Jews in Germanic countries, in spite of its linguistic kinship with the vernacular, was markedly different in pronunciation, syntax, and vocabulary. Judeo-German, like the Yiddish of eastern Europe, had absorbed hundreds of words and idioms from Hebrew and Talmudic-Aramaic, especially loan words and phrases from popular Jewish literary sources. This absorption of fundamental concepts and idioms from traditional thought imparted to Yiddish and Judeo-German a peculiar Jewish flavor. Hence, both Jew and non-Jew considered the Jewish vernacular to be a strong racial barrier. As long as the Jews maintained their religio-cultural autonomy and exclusiveness, Yiddish and Judeo-German served appropriate vehicles of expression for the inner Jewish world.

The foregoing distinctive characteristics may be traced historically to the religious schism that separated Judaism and Christianity in the remote past. To them may be added the ever-present differences in religious fundamentals, the mutually exclusive doctrines and creeds, the separate institutions of Divine worship, divergent rites and customs, all of which set the pattern for a distinct Jewish and Christian way of life. We shall yet see how social contact between these two religious communities was established—in spite of the confessional barrier. At any rate, this

attachment of the faithful to their mutually hostile creeds constituted the most serious and immediately perceptible barrier separating two groups living in constant physical proximity to one
another.

So it seems superficially. Closer scrutiny indicates, however,
that the Jews' peculiar status is not directly traceable to religious
differentiation. We find many places in the world where adherents
of different religions, no less hostile to each other, live side by
side without the reduction of one of the parties to a status similar
to that of the Jew in the Christian world. This status is exempli-
fied by the denial of residential rights, except through a special
political and legal dispensation to both the native born and domi-
ciliating Jew. It was, then, not the religious divergence only,
but the socio-political conclusion drawn from it which determined
the place of the Jew in the Christian world after the second half
of the Middle Ages. The teachings of the Church, in conjunction
with other complicated political and legal factors, were responsible for the process which slowly reduced the European Jew from
a citizen of his place of residence to an alien whose right of
domicile was dependent upon special governmental dispensation.
This concept of status found expression in the term *servi camerae*
(chamber serfdom), the legal validity of which remained unchallenged throughout this period. Controversy arose only as to whose
serfs they were at a given time—whether they belonged to the
emperor or the municipality in Germany, the king or the landed
nobility in Poland. Their servile status, the dependency of their
residential rights on the powers-that-be, remained undisputed.

The Jews themselves did not question this concept during the
period under discussion. Judaism itself lent color to it by pictur-
ing the fate of the Jew in exile, dependent on the whim and fancy
of his hosts. Even when residential rights were not imminently
threatened, Jews would add a mental rider: "Until the King of
Kings will show his mercy and send his redeemer to redeem us!"
The hope of ultimate redemption lent force to the individual Jew's

consciousness of his status as a temporary resident, as he was indeed considered by the citizens of countries which played his host. The Christians, too, cited this attachment of the Jews to their historical homeland in support of their refusal to grant them indigent rights. This completes in two directions the ideological circle which determined the alien status of the Jews in society, a status tolerated *de facto* rather than accepted *de jure*.

The temporary nature of Jewish residential rights was reflected in the frequent negotiations conducted between Jews and the authorities over the granting or withholding of such privilege. In some cases, the bargaining concerned the renewal of Jewish rights of domicile in a particular place. In any case, we find that, at least formally, the agreements under discussion between the two parties delineated Jewish rights, their legal status, their trades and occupations, their duties, including taxes and other commitments. In fact, it would be difficult to term these agreements as having been reached by free consent of the parties concerned. Jewish participation could be said to have been on a free and more or less equal basis only when it involved a notable of means, who would have been welcome in many other countries. But where a whole community petitioned for or negotiated for the renewal of a residential permit, the two parties were far from meeting on the same level. In addition to physical force, the authorities had well-established legal precedent to fall back on in their expulsion of Jews from their territory. Some expulsions were actually enforced, as the Vienna expulsion of 1670 and the Prague expulsion of 1745. It is evident from the negotiations conducted to avert the execution of these edicts and from the general reaction of the Jews to these calamities, that they did not question their legality. Rather, they argued against the motive for the expulsion and sought to discredit it either by maintaining that the Jews were the victims of a libel, or that such action was economically unprofitable and a violation of religious and humanitarian concepts. But we do not find them complaining of injustice or illegality—as we do find in the Middle Ages when the Jews rose to defend their rights, though this approach was reverted to at the close of our period.

There were respites of serenity and relative security in Poland prior to the catastrophe of 1648 and in Germany for the Court Jews. In such instances, the consciousness of exile in the sense of the lack of absolute security were blunted occasionally. However, even this relative sense of security emerged from the psychological impact on the influence and power wielded temporarily by certain sections of Jewish society rather than as a result of a more favorable legal status. As soon as this situation deteriorated, the Jews' sense of security, which had never been based on a feeling of real attachment to their place of residence, evaporated. The Jews always interpreted the calamities and sufferings that descended upon them in the wake of political and social upheavals as the scourge of the Diaspora. This conviction was intensified by the fact that it was the Jews who suffered most even when the calamity was of a general nature, when the country as a whole was in a turmoil, and particularly when forced conversions were part of the pattern.

The interplay of three factors determined whether or not the Jews would be awarded residential permit: expectation of profit; fear of adverse repercussions; and the strength of local religious fanaticism. These factors operated against a background which, as described earlier, deprived Jews of any claim to residence without resort to special pleading. Their commonly accepted legal status put the onus of proof on them if they wished to gain residential admission. It is not a listing of the number of expulsions, whether few or many, which sums up the period, but rather the ever-present dread and possibility of eviction. One of the main tasks of the Jewish communities and their supra-communal organizations remained to anticipate any threat of expulsion, and, in the event of its materializing, to take speedy steps to have the edict revoked.

III

The Barrier against the Outside World

*T*HE DEMOGRAPHIC, ECOLOGICAL, RELIGIO-CUL-tural, and political data described in the previous chapter are objective data that determined the existential framework of the Jewish community. They, together with a well-defined tradition, moulded the thought and practice of individuals in their relationship to the non-Jewish world. Tradition sets a pattern, a hierarchy of concepts, accepted norms, and mores, which guide the individual in thought and action. These now require definition and qualification.

The first fundamental question in connection with this topic is: How does Judaism regard itself in relation to the gentile world? In other words, in what elements did Jewry see the essential difference between itself and the world from which it dissociated itself? Talmudical tradition applies a uniformly negative term to all religions outside of Judaism: *avoda zara* ("strange worship" i.e., paganism). In halakhic discussions and in moralistic and homiletic literature, this term is applied to Christianity as a matter of course.

This distinction obviously laid a firm foundation to guide the Jew in his conduct towards his environment. The traditional sources contain an entire code of prescriptions and injunctions affecting all spheres of contact with the non-Jewish world, ranging from dining to commerce. But precisely in this sector of the relationships with non-Jews we find a wide discrepancy between principles and practice. In theory, the religious exclusiveness promulgated in the Talmud remained in force. In practice, however, the acknowledgement of the validity of talmudic law constituted a formality only.

Even in the early Middle Ages, conditions of life had radically changed from those obtaining in talmudic times. From a majority group, self-supporting with respect to its basic economic requirements, Jewish society had been reduced by the medieval era into a minority group that merely formed an appendage to the general economic structure. Under these altered circumstances, it was no longer possible to apply rules for dissociation which had been designed to preclude Jewish contact with pagan worship and its followers. Even in the early Middle Ages, such talmudic regulations as those prohibiting the trading between Jew and non-Jew "three days prior to their religious holy days" and the like were no longer applied. Such questions, however, were still the subject of discussion. In our period, however, their general obsolescence was taken for granted. Only trade with actual sacramental items like incense still remained prohibited since no valid grounds could be found for a dispensation. But now a general tendency to relax the segregative rules in all their spheres of contacts with the non-Jewish world was prevalent. The best example of this is afforded by the Jews' trading in gentile wine. Jewish law forbids any dealing with wine with which a gentile has come in contact. The prohibition is ultimately derived from the idolatrous and sacramental association of wine. During the Middle Ages, the prohibition was still honored. It was only with the greatest reluctance that a dispensation was evolved permitting a Jew to dispose of wine which had become prohibited by gentile contact or to accept gentile wine in lieu of payment of a debt. In our period, however, this dispensation was increasingly taken for granted mainly in Polish towns bordering on Hungary and in Moravian communities, where wine-trading constituted a characteristic occupation. At the beginning, the stricter religious authorities opposed this practice, but they had to bow to increasing economic pressure. In the course of time, this prohibition became obsolete and wine-trading became a typical Jewish occupation in many regions of eastern and western Europe.

Although in this as in many other instances economic pressure played a decisive role, it did not constitute the sole factor influencing the suspension of religious prohibitions. Such suspension required adequate grounding in halakhic sources, and it would certainly not be correct to state that religious law was ready to issue any dispensation demanded on grounds of ever-changing economic necessity. But the way of adjustment to the changing circumstances had already been paved during the Middle Ages. The recognized halakhic authorities of the eleventh and twelfth centuries justified certain dispensations by resorting to a distinction between the heathens of the talmudic era and the gentiles of "the present age," i.e., medieval Christians. On the basis of this distinction ("gentiles of the present age are not versed in idol worship"), they confirmed the dispensation allowing trading on the Christian religious holy days, and the acceptance of a gentile's oath. This distinction was not originally applied generally but merely constituted a theoretical argument in the halakhic repertoire invoked in special cases. During the medieval period, such distinctions remained formal and more or less theoretical owing to the competitive tension existing between Judaism and Christianity. But the reorientation that subsequently took place in the relationship between the two religions charged these formulae with immediate fundamental significance.

The competitive tension relaxed. Christian missionary zeal abated somewhat, and Jewish interest in converts ceased almost entirely. Though some cases of conversion occurred, the proselytizing fervor often displayed by the medieval Jew in Germany was a thing of the past. The relaxation of inter-faith tension betokened no rapprochement, no glossing over of religious differences or devaluation of their social significance, as was implied during the period of the dissolution of traditional society. On the contrary, the erection of social barriers, ecological and cultural distinctions, led to a clear line of demarcation completely setting apart the bearers of the two religions.

We shall subsequently see how this social seclusion produced an ideology that determined the place of Israel among the nations. This insulation also led to a more relaxed and composed approach to Christianity, viewing it no longer as a dangerous rival but rather as the legitimate creed of those nations amongst whom they happened to be domiciled. The formulae which were invoked to disprove the idolatrous character of Christianity, were now accompanied by positive appraisals of the dominant faith: "These nations, in whose midst we, the people of Israel, are exiled, uphold the belief in *creatio ex nihilo*, the Exodus, and other essential tenets of religion; their worship is directed to the Creator of the heavens and the earth." Such statements recur continually in various contexts. The tolerant view thus taken of Christianity reinforced the religio-legal distinction originating in the halakhic field. On the basis of the broader implication of this definition, the prohibition of non-sacramental gentile wine was eased. Similar considerations prompted Moses Isserles (1510–1572) to permit trade in sacramental objects such as rosaries. Even when halakhic argumentation accepted the premise that Christian worship came under the category of idolatry—as another authority does in dealing with the case of lending festive apparel to Christians for wearing in church—there was no tendency to apply the letter of the law in all its severity. Dispensations were issued without difficulty on the basis of dialectical distinctions and with a view to promoting better neighborly relations—in halakhic terminology, "to prevent resentment" and to "promote peaceful relations."

Although considerations of "good neighborliness" were often cited in justification of various types of everyday contacts with gentiles, these should not be construed as representing any tendency towards social rapprochement. Such concepts had been employed both in medieval and talmudic periods. Jewish physicians or midwives were permitted to treat non-Jews "to prevent resentment"—in other words, for the sake of creating an atmosphere of good will in mutually unavoidable intercourse. However, it was taken for granted that contacts remained strictly businesslike, that no encouragement whatsoever was given to sociability as such, to cultivation of personal attachments, entertainment, and fraternization.

In this sphere there was no relaxation of the strict rules. They tended to become even more intensely enforced. Regular social contact between Jew and gentile was precluded by the dietary restrictions. The latter would not prevent entertaining a gentile in a Jewish home, but they stood in the way of mutual social intercourse. Only on rare formal occasions did Jew and gentile invite each other. Religious authorities inveighed against even these occurrences, however exceptional. The halakhic authorities and moralists exercised unremitting vigilance to ensure that existing conditions and the dispensations allowed in the economic field should not lead to a breakdown of the social barriers.

The everyday conditions of life compelled the Jews to enter gentile homes frequently. This in itself was not objectionable from the Jewish point of view. This practice, however, became very questionable by moralistic and halakhic standards when peddling involved Jewish women entering gentile homes to offer their wares. Here religious and social requirements clashed. On the one hand, the business trips of unaccompanied women in pursuit of their livelihood already constituted a serious breach of the traditional norms of propriety and the social function of the Jewish woman. Her stay in a gentile home even violated formally the halakhic rules prohibiting a Jewish woman to be alone with any man other than her husband. On the other hand, the process of occupational differentiation during this period, which will be discussed later, made it imperative for women to help in earning the family's living. It is easy to see the interaction of these factors and the solutions that were prompted by the social pressures, varying with each locality. At first peddling was prohibited to women or their engaging in it was regulated by laws rendering it impossible to implement (e.g., they had to be accompanied by chaperons!). In eighteenth-century Lithuania, when some social strata still saw their economic interests menaced by peddling, much was made by the threatened groups of the religious and moral scruples. In western Germany, however, where peddling constituted an essential means of eking out a livelihood, the religious authorities displayed leniency. A dispensation was evolved to allow women to peddle, though it was issued only to legalize established practice and as an emergency measure.

No such fundamental objections were raised with respect to the menfolk entering a gentile home. But it was still necessary to give them religious guidance on how to conduct themselves at prayers and mealtimes in these special circumstances. These instructions were unequivocally designed to direct the Jew to observe the religio-social barrier even in the course of his unavoidable business contacts. How to reconcile this religious and social separatism with the necessity of not giving offense to the gentile host remained a delicate problem in theory and practice.

The conflict between the tendency to facilitate economic integration and the necessity of preserving the social and religious barriers can be detected in many discussions by halakhic and moralistic authors. The danger that these barriers would be undermined originated not only from the increasing contact in the economic sphere, but came indirectly from a looser application of the very principles invoked in the granting of the dispensations in the economic sphere.

What happened in the case of non-sacramental gentile wine affords an instructive example. We have noticed that the dispensation allowing Jews to trade in such wine became increasingly widespread. Simultaneously, in the social context, the scruples against partaking of such wine evaporated. Disregard of this prohibition was usually prevalent in countries like Italy and Moravia where wine was the local beverage. However, the difficulty of enforcing this prohibition did not constitute the sole factor that led to violation. Other dietary restrictions, too, made life extremely complicated, and could only be observed by supreme effort and self-denial. In this case, however, there was another consideration. The principle invoked in permitting trade in non-Jewish wine could also be applied with equal logic to its consumption. Trade in gentile wine was permitted because Christians were no longer considered idolaters, whose very touch ritually contaminated. Consumption of the wine should also be permitted on that score. The practice of drinking non-Jewish wine gained the quasi-acceptance even of some halakhic authorities.

Social pressure combined with logic to invalidate a traditional taboo. But these two factors came up against a third one: the anxiety that the disappearance of this restriction would dangerously facilitate social intercourse. The Talmud alludes to this danger in its dictum that "gentile wine is prohibited on account of their daughters" (i.e., illicit relationships). As long as the restriction against trading remained in force, religious authority had no reason to resort to the anti-fraternization argument, since it applied particularly to convivial drinking. After the trading restrictions were relaxed, however, this argument was employed not merely formally, but as an expression of well-founded anxiety over the effects of such a dispensation in undermining religious and social barriers.

It is significant to observe how the advocates of this argument succeeded in restoring and reinforcing the restrictions by making use of a new aspect. The proponent of this trend was the outstanding authority of the generation after Isserles, Rabbi Judah Loew of Prague, toward the close of the sixteenth century. Judah Loew conducted widespread propaganda for the restrictions against partaking of gentile wine and used every form of public pressure to restore the prohibition to its former force and validity. To him, this restriction meant the maintenance of the social barrier between Jew and gentile. He did not content himself with the practical reinstatement of the restriction, but provided it with a fresh ideological basis. For this purpose, he resorted to a cabalistic train of thought. Wine prepared exclusively by Jewish hands symbolized for him the metaphysical essence of Judaism, whereas wine that had come into gentile contact stood for the opposite. The partaking of such wine was no longer regarded merely as a minor ritual offense of rabbinical non-biblical ordination, but became a fundamental violation in the metaphysical sense, the perpetrator of which would thereby exclude himself from the celestial Israel. Such an interpretation could originate only with an author who believed that acts in the world of reality, religious ones in particular, had repercussions in the spiritual realm. Indeed, Judah Loew was of a mystic turn of mind, his outlook very closely akin to the world of the Zohar and its initiates. Little wonder, therefore, that the Cabalists of his generation responded to these ideas and disseminated his views forbidding the consumption of gentile wine.

This change in the motivation of the prohibition reflected a trend of general significance. The distinction between Judaism and Christianity had been transferred from the purely religio-legal realm to the metaphysical. Christianity had ceased to be regarded as an idolatrous cult thus weakening the force of the prohibition against gentile wine. But this development was combatted by the emergence of an ideology stressing the symbolical implications of the wine banquet that reinforced the original prohibition. What had happened was that distinctions on theological grounds were superseded by those based on differences in kind and essence—a characteristic trend in contemporary thinking on the role of the Jew in the gentile world.

These two concepts, the one tracing the antagonism between Israel and the nations to a mere divergence in articles of creed, the other, to a difference in essence, were both reflected in the Midrashic and philosophical literature of the ancient and medieval period. Both the Midrash and philosophers like Yehuda Halevy traced religious and historical differences to the dissimilar character of Jew and non-Jew respectively. It is irrelevant whether they traced these differences to a biological or racial source—the Jews being the descendants of Abraham, Isaac, and Jacob; the gentiles, Esau—or to divergent reactions to a particular historical and metaphysical event—the former's acceptance of the Torah at Sinai and the latter's rejection. In any event, a qualitative difference was involved for which the individual was not responsible and which he could not change. Hence, the theological divergences were to be traced to a deep-seated, essential distinction of a meta-biological and meta-historical nature between the two camps. This naturalistic orientation developed during this period first of all under the impact of cabalistic literature, particularly the Zohar. According to the Zohar, Israel's singularity was to be traced to its derivation from the sphere of holiness in the hierarchy of the Divine spheres, whereas the nations were correspondingly connected with the sphere of defilement.

These ideas were propagated in various forms through moralist and homiletic literature until they were more or less accepted as the basic premise of contemporary thinking. Their absorption was facilitated both by the ever-increasing cabalistic influence, and by the viewing of the distinction between Israel and the nations as an essential, metaphysical one, which aptly parallels the profound differences separating the two in the contemporary social scene. Despite the frequent business contacts and the temperate evaluation of Christianity as the legitimate creed of the nations, the gentile world loomed threateningly all around the Jew, perhaps more ominously than in the Middle Ages. It was hostile not as the competitive religion striving to lure the Jew from the true faith, but as a world totally strange and alien, the terrestial manifestation of the *sitra ahara* or forces of evil. The martyrs of this period who preferred death to apostasy were not as concerned with demonstrating the truth of their faith to those who would forcibly convert them in the name of false gods as were their counterparts in the crusades. They were, rather, desperately anxious to spare themselves from being devoured alive by the forces of evil and defilement epitomized by the dominant faith. Nothing in the utterances of these martyrs, as recorded and handed down by their contemporaries, savours of hatred for Christianity or a wish to demonstrate its utter futility, as one finds in the Middle Ages. Now they were inspired by resignation to the inscrutable ways of Divine providence. Their martyrdom spelt a tacitly accepted fatalism which lacked the compensatory element of personal decision and willing choice. For the victims of the Chmielnitzki pogroms of 1648, baptism represented nothing more than a means of physical survival. Unlike the martyrs of the crusades, these Jews held the prospect of conversion to represent no more than an attempt at compulsion from without rather than an insidious attraction from within.

The acknowledgement by Jewish thinkers of the period of Christian affinity with monotheism certainly did not penetrate deeply into the public consciousness. It is even doubtful whether the actual formulators of this approach were fully appreciative of its implications. We have noted how a new symbol of the alien world outside evolved out of the prohibition of gentile wine. The previously accepted age-old symbols of the Christian world retained their repelling force with even greater effectiveness. In spite of the dispensation permitting trade in objects with sacramental associations, the prohibition of any dealing with them when they were actually being used in Christian worship remained undisputedly in full force. The Jewish medieval attitude of deliberate hatred towards Christian religious emblems was replaced in this period by a dread and repulsion rooted in the collective consciousness. It seems to me that we are justified in seeing here the results of the slow but constant educational effect of historical circumstance which implanted a deep feeling of revulsion towards Christian symbols—just at a time when moderate and even tolerant intellectual concepts were gaining ground.

IV *Contacts between Jews and Gentiles*

SUMMING UP OUR ANALYSIS IN THE PREVIOUS
two chapters, we may say that although the Jewish community
represented a subgroup of society, its closely knit internal solidarity combined with its religious and social exclusiveness to create a
specific social entity warranting the description "a world of its
own." This definition reflects the contradictory situation of Jewry.
The existence of this separate "world" was predicated on the constant contact of its inhabitants with those of the world outside. The
ways and frequency of this contact depended on conditions which
varied with each locality and individual.

Let us take the two extremes in this context of interracial
contact. The most intimate contact is to be found in the case of

the solitary Jew settled with his family in a village, fort, or sometimes even town, plying the occupation of leaseholder, concessionaire of a distillery, trader, moneylender, tax-collector and the like. The extent to which he could supply his own needs out of his occupation was extremely limited, and he was, in large measure, dependent on direct exchange with his gentile neighbors for his products and services or their monetary value. Moreover, anybody in such a position maintained neighborly relations, giving and receiving help in case of need and the course of everyday contacts. Without this, such an individual could not exist, however much he considered himself an outsider and was so considered by his neighbors. There is no doubt that these isolated Jews were on close terms with their neighbors in times of peace just as we also find cases of mutual assistance wherever and whenever the need arose, particularly in cases of natural disasters. Sociologically speaking, this solitary Jew belonged to his non-Jewish environment as a member of the "accommodation group." On the other hand, he had social, cultural, and religious needs which he could not expect to satisfy from his contact with the members of his "accommodation group."

The manner in which such an isolated individual solved his problem depended on circumstances and on the extent of his religious attachment. There emerged diverse types of adjustment. At one end was complete submergence within the "accommodation group," the most extreme expression of which was acceptance of the dominant faith. At the other, was the strictest allegiance to the group of origin and the scrupulous observance of all the religious and social restrictions, all of which involved denying himself many benefits and liberties offered by social intercourse.

It was the clear policy of such remote individuals themselves, as well as that of Jewish institutions, communities, and super-communal organizations, to make every effort to combat this isolation. Individuals who made good in their isolated places of settlement always attracted other Jews. They would also engage a tutor for their children if they could afford it, and, if their business and wealth warranted, household retainers. In this way, whole communities developed from the step of a single Jewish pioneer. But even if he remained alone, he would periodically visit a Jewish center on a business trip or to spend a holiday. The home of the solitary Jew provided hospitality for itinerant co-religionists, wandering mendicants, and preachers. Even rabbis from the cities would call upon the lone Jewish settler. Whether the visitor came on an educational mission or in his own interest, these calls were effective in strengthening the bonds between the isolated individual and the Jewish world and its values.

Complete severance of ties with the original group was rare. However, even as a hypothetical case, the possibility clearly brings out the problem of dual affiliation to society and his own subgroup. The whole Jewish society shared this problem to a certain extent. However, just as there were isolated individuals who felt the full impact of this problem, so there were others who were left quite untouched. These were the individuals who lived in a large Jewish community and dealt exclusively with their co-religionists, the preacher of a particular synagogue (in contra-distinction to his itinerant counterpart), the Hebrew teacher, and the like. They seemed to be little bothered by the conflict. Theoretically speaking, even these sheltered individuals were linked on the economic level with the non-Jewish farmers whose produce they consumed. But there were intermediaries between the two: the merchant, the artisan, the peddler, etc. These spared him the direct contact with the world alien to him. In his case, the ac-commodation group and the original group were almost identical.

The majority of the community moved between the foregoing two extremes of contact between the larger society and the subgroup. The frequency of their personal contact with non-Jews and its social character varied according to their occupation. The moneylender, who waited at home for the non-Jew to come to borrow, repay, pawn, or redeem his pawn, merely maintained a formal contact with the Christian world. The conditions and terms of these transactions were more or less fixed, were subject to exact computation, and involved no protracted bargaining. The trader who offered his wares to shopkeepers or who sold them in the market place, had to bargain with his prospective customers. The ultimate agreement on the price reached represented a kind of reconciliation between two opponents who had previously haggled with and outsmarted each other. Despite the apparent opposing interests of Jew and gentile, this situation brought the two parties closer together. Peddling, which became very prevalent during this period, brought the Jew or Jewess directly into the gentile home. Other occupations also brought Jews into contact with their neighbors. Itinerant traders travelled in company with non-Jews in their wagons, and often had no choice but to lodge with them. Some individuals, particularly communal representatives, notables and professional intercessors at court (*shtadlan*) chanced upon towns and places where there were no Jews, so that they were accommodated in non-Jewish homes. In sixteenth-century Germany, we find that Jews, among them many a great scholar, frequented spas for their health and spent some time in Christian homes and environment.

There were, moreover, trades and occupations which brought Jews into constant contact with certain gentiles. The Jewish tenant farmer who had to pay his landlord in kind, and the court Jew who served his potentate in a variety of ways, had this kind of contact. An inversion of this social situation is represented by the relationship of the Jewish farm-manager to the non-Jewish hands, which led to the dependence of the latter on the former. Such a situation also obtained, where the government had not prohibited it, in wealthy Jewish homes which employed non-Jewish servants.

The social contact between Jewish physician and gentile patient or vice versa constituted a special kind of contact. The same was true of the relationship between teacher and pupil. Jews studied languages and sciences under Christian teachers; whereas Christians, particularly theologians, were dependent on Jewish instructors in their Hebrew studies. Medicine was learned through apprenticeship to an experienced physician, although Jewish medical students also attended the universities: at the local German universities from the last decades of the seventeenth century on, or at foreign universities. Thus, some Polish Jewish medical students attended Italian universities. Sometimes—though rarely—Jewish apprentices were accepted by gentile craftsmen.

In other words, Jewish social isolation did not imply lack of contact between the Jewish community and the non-Jewish world. Jewish residential segregation did not significantly curb contact with the gentile world. Separatism merely gave expression to its theoretical value—as if to say that had it been practically feasible, complete segregation from the outside world would have been desirable.

Moreover, even this relative seclusion created a separate Jewish domain which served for exclusively Jewish activity. The Jewish quarter lived a life of its own in which society-at-large had no part. Gentiles came to it only on business, and were excluded from its social life—most emphatically from ceremonies of a religious or ritual character. This separate domain of Jewish life set the standard even for the life outside its boundaries. Individual Jews who resided permanently outside the ghetto judged their lives by the internal parochial standards. They suffered a twofold sense of exile because of their distance from the focal points of Jewish life. Many of these isolated settlers had tasted intensive Jewish living in their youth when studying at one of the Torah centers. They repaired to remote spots only after they had failed to make good in the Jewish center. An ideological bond and consciousness in the superiority of life in the larger Jewish communities was preserved also by those Jews who had been born and bred in such isolation, although they were constantly exposed to the non-Jewish environment, practically knowing nothing else.

Their ecological dispersion among the gentiles was prompted only by unavoidable economic or political necessity and never favored for its own sake.

Jewish communal life was, in principle, based on a segregative tradition. We must distinguish, however, between those who looked to tradition to guide them in their everyday lives, and those who presented its theoretical formulation as reflected in halakhic, aggadic, and moralistic literature. The latter were the competent interpreters of religious law, applying its principles and restrictions to the ever-changing situation. They lived almost exclusively in the focal centers, usually belonging to the "protected" group which maintained only indirect contact with the non-Jewish world. It is no wonder, then, that the standards they put forth did not always suit the general Jewish public which was called upon to translate them into practice in daily dealings. The general public, and isolated Jewish settlers in particular, allowed themselves a certain latitude in their non-Jewish contacts and dispensations dictated by current necessity naturally evolved. The religious authorities either fought against these dispensations or attempted to legitimize them after the event, depending on the seriousness of the violation, the pressure of circumstances, and the personal predilections of the interpreter of the law. In any case, it is clear that these dispensations did not involve any basic reform of tradition. Those who actively observed the dictates of tradition—irrespective of whether their observance was consistent, partial, or otherwise—and those who formulated them on the basis of their mastery of the relevant literary sources shared alike the same reverence for its binding character. All agreed that no action could be justified unless its legitimacy had been established, before or after the event, by resort to precedents or principles implicit in tradition.

V   *The Attitude toward the Environment*

*W*E HAVE HITHERTO DEALT WITH PROBLEMS
of contact between Jew and non-Jew only insofar as the interests
of the Jewish community were concerned. Dispensations were
resorted to in order to enable the individual Jew to earn a decent
livelihood; cultural and religious restrictions were maintained in
order to safeguard the Jewishness of the community. But this
did not exhaust the problems involved. Jewish society had to
come to terms with the outside world in the sphere of their common interests. Relations between the two had to be governed by
recognized legal procedures and moral conventions.

The settling of legal problems between Jew and non-Jew
would seem to fall under the purview of the authorities to which

both were subject, i.e. the State. The privileges (*kiyummim*) granted to the Jews also laid down the legal institutions—usually the non-Jewish courts—competent to adjudicate between both parties. These legal institutions, however, were resorted to only for litigation. Ordinary daily intercourse and common business interests required an operative code of terms and moral conventions, a kind of unwritten law. The judicial institutions could contribute only indirectly towards the solution of this problem— which was sociological rather than legal—by fixing norms which were propagated through the publicity given to court decisions. However, when such rigid religious and social barriers separated the Jewish from the non-Jewish society, the courts of the state, whose jurisdiction Jews accepted only under duress, had little practical influence. Insofar as Jews were influenced by moral and legal scruples in their dealings with non-Jews, these were derived from concepts originating in internal Jewish sources.

Legal and moral concepts were imbibed by individuals in the process of their education from early childhood onward, as we shall see in the chapters on educational problems. The student was introduced into a dualistic legal and moral system embodying mutually exclusive concepts for Jews and non-Jews respectively. This situation was aptly summed up by a contemporary authority in the following dictum: "The Torah was designed specifically for Israel." Auxiliary legislation had been promulgated for governing relations between Jew and non-Jew. Such an approach was understood both where Jewish law reigned supreme in the Talmudic era and where it subsequently exercised only partial jurisdiction. The concept of a uniform code of law, regulating human affairs regardless of race and creed, never entered the picture. The double legal and moral standard was not merely a mental reservation but was the accepted practice in all sections of society. The respective Jewish and non-Jewish sections of society were governed by their own mutually exclusive laws. Each required a legal and moral code regulating their conduct towards outsiders. What were the nature and content of this code?

In this context, the main difficulty for the Jewish community lay in the fact that the laws and moral conventions of the Talmud enactments presupposed an indigenous Jewish settlement confronted with undesirable heathen aliens in their midst, contact with whom could lead to transgression. It was therefore regarded as a sacred duty to dislodge and even to destroy them. Talmudic discussion and disputation is conducted against such a background. The radical and extremist view condoned the appropriation of heathen goods and disapproved of extending any sort of assistance to idolators. The more moderate view was inspired by humane or proselytizing motives or by deference to public opinion. However, in the Diaspora, under the conditions of ghetto settlements from the sixteenth to the eighteenth century and also to a large extent at the beginning of the Middle Ages, conditions had changed. The Jews were now the minority; the gentiles, the dominant majority. The latter, too, could not be strictly classed as idolaters. The belief in the Trinity was not, in Jewish eyes, synonymous with the pagan cults of the ancient world. The former hostile inter-faith tension had relaxed. Jews were no longer eager to proselytize, nor Christians to indulge in forced conversions. These far-reaching changes would seem to have rendered the traditional rules obsolete. As we have already seen, however, it was characteristic of Jewish society to maintain the traditional fabric, theoretically at least, in its entirety.

Conflict between traditional rules and existing reality took place in the field of direct Jew-gentile relations. Jewish society had no alternative but to void all discriminatory rules governing their relations with gentiles which were liable to provoke dangerous repercussions. The rule condoning appropriation of gentile goods was unthinkable in the medieval and post-medieval period. Yet these rules could not be invalidated with one stroke. The traditional exegetical methods had to be resorted to, adjusting application of the law to the new situation. By these methods, in fact, medieval Jewish codifiers ruled that misappropriation of gentile goods was prohibited. Where *hillul hashem* (defamation of the name of the Lord, i.e. disgracing the Jewish religion) was involved, it was equally forbidden to take advantage of the gentile's errors in business transactions. Out of the same motives, it became mandatory for Jews to return gentiles' lost articles. But a condition limiting the foregoing decisions to cases resulting in *hillul hashem* where the gentile would find out indicated that the law had not been fundamentally changed. Only outright fraud was forbidden; the non-Jew's own error in calculation could be pocketed without compunction. Thus we still find discussion in both medieval and more recent responsa on who was entitled to pocket the proceeds of such an error where two Jewish parties were contesting for the same. Rulings such as these indicate that there was a limit to the modifying of these ancient discriminatory regulations on the basis of exegetical devices. No fundamental rescission took place.

As we have seen in Chapter III, there were, however, attempts to bring about a fundamental revision of enactments concerned with limiting contacts between the Jew and the outside world. Halakhic thought tended to distinguish between the ancient peoples, to whom certain discriminatory rules had originally applied in the Mishnah and Talmud, and the Christian peoples "among whom we are dwelling." This distinction was given philosophical and theological weight, perhaps under the influence of the humanistic movement, in the early sixteenth century. The term *goyim* or "gentiles" was no longer a suitable term to describe the adherents of Christianity. How, it was argued, could nations which acknowledge the authenticity of the Mosaic law and the prophets which believed in the miracles wrought for Israel be equated with the idolaters who lacked this faith? This train of thought grew firmly entrenched in certain circles during the sixteenth century and paved the way for the concept of a common basis shared by Judaism and Christianity. This viewing of Christian peoples in a special light formed the justification for exempting them from the talmudic restrictions governing "gentiles." To the Tosafist argument that non-Jews were no longer versed in idolatry, basically a negative argument, was now added the positive principle that stressed the Christian link with fundamental Jewish tenets. Some religious authorities injected an emotional appeal in this direction, and their call for fair play in dealings with non-Jews was based on the religious kinship of the two faiths.

Notices pointing out the difference between the pagan gentiles of ancient times and the Christian gentiles "of our day" or "in whose midst we are dwelling" appear, to be sure, on the title page of many a Hebrew book printed in central Europe from the sixteenth century onwards. These stereotyped declarations were ostensibly intended to satisfy the censorship which forbade the publication of anti-Christian sentiments. But the contents of the works took no notice of these declarations. Contemporary Christians were placed in the same category as the ancient idolaters in the ritual disquisitions inside the covers of these works. It would be wrong, however, to assume that these declarations were lacking in sincerity. The distinction was applied in full in the realm of practical ethics and commercial honesty. But the Jewish codifiers were bound by traditional casuistry and failed to see any necessity to apply this distinction consistently in all spheres.

The same inconsistency may be observed in the social context. The realization of a fundamental difference between the gentiles in biblical and talmudic sources and those among whom they lived was confined to a limited circle of scholars who themselves only barely sensed it. The wider public could not be expected to share this feeling. The depressing conditions of the Diaspora, on the one hand, and the strong hold of tradition on the other, militated against the emergence of a common standard of ethics and values grounded in shared humanistic religious beliefs.

A serious problem of social education faced Jewish leadership: at a time when existing conditions encouraged laxity, they had to enforce proper standards of conduct toward the outside world. Jewish governing institutions, the *kehilla* and the super-*kehilla,* maintained strict vigilance over the conduct of their individual members in all fields. They called for observance of the law of the land and honesty and equity in business dealing. Violators were prosecuted with all the means at their disposal: fines, corporal punishment, and excommunication. One very effective weapon was the threat to withdraw the community's protection from violators apprehended by the gentile authorities. Sometimes non-Jews were forewarned not to deal with shady individuals. In extreme cases, if a violator had been caught red-handed, the Jewish authorities would not hesitate even to hand the offender over to non-Jewish justice—the most serious punitive measure resorted to by the Jewish community.

However, these legal and disciplinary measures alone did not solve the problem. The question remained how to inculcate a sense of public responsibility and a level of conduct required to combat opportunistic impulses. Inner moral standards had to be inculcated which would preclude the Jew's quieting his conscience on the grounds of gentile persecution of his people. There was much natural and justifiable prejudice to be overcome. Gentile hatred of the Jews was the confirmed experience of the individual and the group; a feeling of Jewish superiority and a long tradition of dualistic concepts in the legal and ethical system also operated against such standards. Only the most powerful considerations could be expected to awaken the Jewish sense of fair play towards the outside world.

The all-important consideration in this connection was the Jewish community's isolation in a hostile world. The danger threatening the group as a result of individual misconduct operated as the most forceful check. Reiterated warnings and admonitions that were issued by public institutions and communal leaders stressed the fact that the life and death of the whole community rested in the hands of its individual members. The security of the Jewish community constituted a supreme and essential value, though it would appear to have been prompted by utilitarian consideration. The individual was called upon to forego personal advantages, the negative consequences of which he might himself escape. The demand was made on him in the interest of the community as a whole.

Another principle which imposed proper conduct upon the individual sprang from the desire to protect the good name of the Jew and, automatically, that of his faith. Judaism proclaimed standards of honesty binding on Jew and non-Jew alike. The traditional terms employed in this context were *hillul hashem*, defamation of the Divine name, and its converse *kiddush hashem*, consecration of the name. These terms of talmudic origin became widely current in the Middle Ages and later. But a change in connotation can be detected. Their positive undertones faded in an era which witnessed the forsaking of that religio-national concept which had hitherto manifested itself in a missionary zeal to swell the ranks of the faithful. During the Middle Ages, this missionary spirit acted as an incentive to the Jew to keep his conduct above reproach in order to attract gentiles to Judaism. Such considerations found no adherents in the atmosphere of indifference shared by Jews in our period toward the religious fate of the surrounding non-Jewish world. The terms *kiddush hashem* and *hillul hashem* no longer implied a call for positive action to demonstrate to the gentiles the purity and sanctity of the Jewish faith. Rather, they bore passive undertones, calling for refraining from any act which might bring Jewry into disrepute. Sometimes these terms merely served as warning signals of the danger facing the community from individual misconduct.

As has been mentioned above, there was a tendency to base

inter-community ethics on a common Judeo-Christian religious basis: belief in revelation and the Biblical tradition. In some instances, we also find attempts to establish autonomous ethical values. Defrauding gentiles was abhorrent for educational reasons, since it represents an unethical act which corrupts the perpetrator irrespective of the class of victim. However, even such considerations, cherished by the few, assumed that there existed a distinction between Jew and gentile, and that ethical norms applied basically only to one's own kind. Jewish isolation conditioned its ethical thought which attempted to escape the utilitarian motives of its postulates. There was evidently no other solution for this society but to show its realistic appraisal of its situation by imposing self-enforced legal curbs prompted by considerations of preserving its good name.

VI The Economic Basis of the Jewish Community

$\mathcal{A}$LL DEFINITIONS BY THE STATE DETERMINING the status of the Jews included permission to engage in some form of economic activity. Without this, the physical existence of the community would have been inconceivable and the grant of residential privileges meaningless. Indeed, the charters permitting Jewish residence invariably specified the occupations in which they might engage. In some cases, subsequent Jewish economic activity tended to exceed the bounds set by the authorities. There may have been various reasons for this. The authorities might subsequently have given their permission or turned a blind eye to violators of the terms of the charter, or the violators might have pursued their illegitimate activities unnoticed and therefore unchallenged.

Sociological analysis must, of course, deal with historical conditions as they really existed. Here we shall trace these in broad
outline. In Jewish economic history, the uniformity which
marked Jewish economic life in the Middle Ages gave way to
increasing occupational diversity during the sixteenth to eighteenth centuries. The main sources of livelihood for Jews in medieval Europe including Poland had been international trade and
moneylending. In the period under discussion, these two occupations continued to remain of major importance, but the financial
operations now found new outlets. Along with granting loans on
interest, in which the Jew was interested only in insuring re-
payment by taking some security, the Jew now began to invest
his capital in productive enterprises under direct Jewish management. The farming of tolls and excise for the government, the
administration of the mint under royal license, the exploitation
of mines, the operation of distilleries, and the manufacture of
potash, were all regarded as highly profitable undertakings. Similar opportunities for investment were available in agriculture.
The landed gentry in Poland and Lithuania would lease their
estates and their tenant farmers for unrestricted exploitation.
Commerce, too, became more diversified—primarily in the variety of commodities in which the Jews traded.

The methods of trade, too, became more ramified. Alongside
the itinerant merchant, making the rounds of his wealthier customers in their castles or setting up his stall at the fairs, the
storekeeper made his appearance, offering his wares throughout
the year. The hawking of goods at the prospective customer's
home extended to the poorer classes, and the peddler, bent under
his pack, plodding from village to village, became a familiar,
almost ubiquitous character. The top of this economic scale was
occupied by the royal purveying contractor, particularly for the
military, who undertook to finance entire campaigns for his
sovereign.

To complete the picture, mention must be made of Jewish

craftsmen who, in this period, were no longer rare phenomena. In Poland and Bohemia, during the seventeenth and eighteenth centuries, Jewish artisans formed a broad social stratum making a substantial contribution to Jewish economic enterprise. The most extensive occupational diversity was to be found in seventeenth century Poland and Lithuania. In the Germanic countries, in Alsace, and in Western Hungary, the practice of leasing estates was uncommon, though not unknown. Here, on the other hand, arose the royal purveying contractor, represented in the Court Jew, whose counterpart rarely existed in Poland and Lithuania.

The prime cause for this occupational ramification in the sixteenth to eighteenth centuries must not be sought in any change in their status within the framework of the state. They remained, as we have seen in Chapter II, aliens of the state, conditionally granted certain residential privileges. The cause lies rather in the changes that evolved in the political and economic life in Europe during this era. We must perforce confine ourselves to an account of the changes relevant only to Jewish economic activity.

First of all, there was the expanding area for the exchange of local produce. Another sign of the times was the increase of overseas imports. In return for these imports, the countries, particularly those not directly engaged in overseas traffic, had to pay in their own produce. The opportunity to obtain imported goods acted as an additional incentive for intensifying local production; now not only luxury goods imported from afar were the objects of interstate trade, but also local raw materials and surplus agricultural produce. The opening up and expansion of potential markets led to a search for surplus not absolutely required for local consumption. This expansion of commercial exchange involved increased and more efficient production through both old and new methods and the development of the economy.

Such development was facilitated only by a group of interlocking factors: improved communications, technical equipment, marketing facilities, such as storage, an increased efficiency on the part of the workers, and a keener initiative among both entrepreneurs and middlemen. The Jews, as active participants in the economy, could take some credit for progress in these fields. On the whole, however, their share was not particularly conspicuous, and certainly does not warrant ascribing to them a major historic responsibility for engineering this development. Their contribution was notable in one sphere, without which, it is true, the entire process of development was inconceivable: the provision and promotion of funds. Productive efficiency, the exchange of surplus goods facilitated by long-distance communications, would not have been possible without provision of the means to finance them.

Financing meant long-term advancement of money in expectation of profitable returns. In this sphere, indeed, Jews were active far in excess of their numerical proportion. This situation constituted a continuation from the previous era, when money-lending and interstate commerce formed the main sources of Jewish livelihood. Transactions of this kind had to rely on disposal of funds. The creation of new opportunities for investment diverted Jewish funds to these new economic outlets. The common denominator of both periods was that Jewish residential rights and occupational opportunities were linked to the assumption that the Jews did indeed dispose of the capital required to promote economic activity.

The increasing operational functions of liquid capital correspondingly enhanced the prestige of those who disposed of it. The keener the appreciation of the value of capital, the more favorable became the situation of the Jews—provided, of course, that they lived up to their reputations of possessing or controlling money. Not all Jews had such funds available. Everywhere there was a stratum of poor and even destitute Jews. In contrast to this, however, within the general picture of the Jewish community— and the outside saw only this generality—there were Jews of substantial means who could undertake functions, the decisive importance of which society was beginning to realize. For this reason, this period witnessed a rise in the actual social status of the Jew in society as well as a higher evaluation of his role.

The source of the liquid assets disposed by Jews in this period was a legacy of the Middle Ages. Even at that time, loan transactions required ready capital. Notwithstanding the expulsions and the ever-recurring confiscations and impositions, a fund of capital remained and was handed down from generation to generation. Capital did not necessarily remain within a single family. The rise and decline of families formed a sort of cycle, in which capital changed hands within the confines of Jewish society. Within that society, and especially within its constituent communities, there were men of substance. Capital was transmitted, if not from father to son, at least from one generation to the next.

Possession of liquid funds, however, constituted only one aspect of the Jewish economic potentiality. The Jews' cardinal economic virtue lay in the fact that they made their very existence dependent upon the active employment of these funds, and, as a result, developed into a dynamic factor an activity which often had no parallel in Christian society. This constant application of capital, of course, precluded investment in immovable property. The law did not permit the Jew to acquire land, and this is usually adduced as the reason for the non-acquisition of land by Jews. In fact, the Jew, for his part, made no effort to secure such permission as he did to obtain such privileges as farming taxes or operating the mint and the like. The aversion of the Jew to landed investments was strongly influenced by his constant awareness of his precarious status as a barely tolerated resident. Landed property attracted the ordinary burgher who attained wealth because of the feeling of stability and economic security it gave him and the social prestige involved. But in his peculiar situation, the Jew would set no great store by either. He could not hope to perpetuate his wealth in that locality, nor did he seek a niche in the dominant social and economic hierarchy. The economic nexus linking the Jew with his environment was purely instrumental. Basically, all he sought was the opportunity to exist. The fact that he regarded the environment in which he lived as no more than a field from which he must wrest his livelihood prompted him to seek outlets for his capital, promising a calculable return in the foreseeable future. Thus, he turned to immediately profitable undertakings such as trade and commerce, leasing, minting, and mining. This quality was absent in real estate. Other considerations, such as security or social prestige, which weighed so heavily with the non-Jew, counted little for the Jew.

This employment of liquid assets entailed the use of funds not only of the investor personally but also those of others. The wisdom of purchasing arable land or vineyards with borrowed money was dubious to say the least. To acquire an economic concession or monopoly, on the other hand, was sound business policy—provided the income was sufficient to compensate not only the active investor but also the other subscribers. Transactions of this kind provided the impetus for the creation of credit, the supply of loan capital from which a fund for commercial investment could be developed. The promotion of credit was not, of course, a particularly Jewish invention. It is a basic feature of economic enterprise of the time. However, its wider promotion, application, and practice was undoubtedly characteristic of Jewish economic activity in this period. Jews borrowed from both their co-religionists and from non-Jews, creating an artificial instrument of credit, the *Mamrami,* the internal Jewish bill of exchange, which we shall discuss at greater length later, in order to mobilize the capital necessary to finance their operations. Providing credit became profitable now, since it promised increased returns not only through loans, but also in trade, the leasing of estates, and the development of productive enterprise. Old style money lending by Jews declined sharply from medieval times both relatively and absolutely.

It is obvious, therefore, that the capitalistic character of Jewish society cannot be denied—if this implies that this society was sustained by the employment of capital in enterprises and transactions in which the manual labor involved was performed by members of the surrounding population. This does not warrant the inference, however, that the entire Jewish community subsisted directly on the employment of such capital. First, there existed a class not possessing any visible or regular source of income—the destitute, the mendicants, and the non-earning scholars who fostered the conventional values of Jewish society. The latter accepted the responsibility of supporting the other two indigent categories. Second, another class was engaged in rendering internal services: teachers, rabbis, beadles, preachers, each of which we shall meet in our analysis of communal institutions. Third was a working class of laborers, servants, and skilled artisans who engaged in production, transport, and the management of enterprises financed by Jewish capitalists. Moreover, there were independent craftsmen not directly employed in these capitalist projects.

Such was the physiognomy of Jewish society in this period of increasing social and occupational diversification. We shall deal more fully with this latter aspect in our analysis of the stratification of society. In relation to the economic foundations of Jewish life, however, this process represented no radical change. With the exception of the craftsmen who retained the means for their independence, all other classes and callings were wholly dependent on the operations of the capitalists. In effect, even the craftsmen were sometimes subject to their manipulations, since it was the capitalists who bought up their products for marketing at distant points; this was true irrespective of whether the artisans provided their own raw materials or whether these were supplied by the enterpreneur on credit. Moreover, the right of residence enjoyed by the craftsmen hinged upon the existence and operations of the Jewish capitalist class. Nowhere were the Jewish craftsmen granted such a privilege in their own right. Even later, in their struggle for rights of domicile and work, they were successful only thanks to the Jewish capitalists. It was the latter's usefulness to the authorities which encouraged the tolerance of the presence of Jewish artisans as well.

VII *Jewish Economic Activity*

$\mathcal{W}$E USED THE WORD "CAPITALISTIC" IN THE previous chapter to denote the employment of capital to produce profits. This meaning does not express the sociological significance of capitalism nor does it furnish more than an elementary understanding of the connection between capitalism and Jewish society. A more thorough treatment will distinguish between various types of capitalism with relation to the profitability of the invested capital. The factors which facilitated the accumulation of wealth varied with the terms of the investment and depended on the social structure, as distinct from economic activity in itself. Capitalism may be divided into three types: state capitalism, protected capitalism, and capitalism of the free market.

[51]

In state capitalism, in the full sense of the term, the prospects of investment are based on the use of part of the receipts which governmental institutions collect from the citizens. The outstanding example of this was the farming of taxes and customs. The owner of the capital simply advanced the anticipated receipts to the ruler, his fee being the difference between what he paid out and what he was able to collect. This collection was executed with the aid of the coercive powers of the government by whose authority it was carried out.

Diametrically opposed to state capitalism was free market capitalism, in which the capitalist did not rely on political coercion of any kind; his calculations were based solely on an evaluation of the profits that would accrue from the difference between the total investment and the income anticipated from the sale of the product in the free market. Such investment therefore more strongly required a rational basis of calculating the data than was called for under state capitalism. The sociological condition for free market capitalism was the non-interference of the institutions of government in economic activity. This has perhaps never been fully realized anywhere, but it was in the period of liberalism that the most serious effort to achieve it was made.

Between these two types of capitalism stood protected capitalism, a mixture of both: economic activity was directed at a buyer's market as in free capitalism, but it was restricted by the government, which determined which goods were to be sold, who was authorised to sell them, and the like. The legal system instituted by the authorities imposed restrictions on economic activity and favored particular categories of persons or even individuals. In exchange for these concessions, the government took a share of the income of the concessionaire either directly—by imposing special levies on them—or indirectly—by the increase in the wealth realized by the state from capitalist activity.

Whereas free capitalism has exercised practically absolute

control over the social order only in the modern period, state capitalism is an almost universal phenomenon. It is found wherever economic life reaches the stage of using money as a means of exchange and government is concentrated in the hands of a distinct political institution. The need for state capitalism disappears only with the development of an administrative staff which collects the receipts due to the state against a regular salary. In absolute terms, state capitalism makes its exit only with the transfer of the financial activities of the state to the state's own institutions.

The assistance of state capitalism was required by governments in the period when political power first crystallized in the countries of Europe between the sixteenth and the eighteenth centuries. The farming of taxes and customs was a customary Jewish occupation—particularly in Eastern Europe—until a specialized administrative organization emerged and consolidated itself in Western Europe from the seventeenth century onwards. But the state continued to require the assistance of capitalists for the financing of its extraordinary activities. The advancing of monies for wars by court Jews, an innovation of state capitalism, was essentially no different from the tax farming of the petty capitalist on a Moravian estate. In Poland, the leasing of estates from the nobles constituted another instance of state capitalism. The nobles were entitled to a share of the products raised by the peasants, and this right was often transferred to Jewish capitalists in exchange for a consideration. The expansion of the market and the acceleration of economic production took place in a period in which serfdom still existed, and these developments prepared the ground for the activity of state capitalism.

A similar political background also determined the field of action of protected capitalism. By virtue of their political power, the rulers were entitled to decide who might engage in the production or distribution of goods. The authorities thus granted concessions for these economic activities in exchange for a payment by the concessionaire. Admittedly, the capitalist might expect to earn a profit through his production or distribution, just as in every other activity of this type, but his prospects of profits were also based on the protection he received from the authorities. Again, the extent of the economic activity made no difference. The tavern keeper who purchased the exclusive right to distill and sell brandy in a given locality was a protected capitalist no less than the owner of a factory who held the franchise for producing and selling textiles over a far-flung area.

We now possess the concepts necessary to facilitate a deeper explanation of the ability and the readiness of the Jews to take an active part in the advancement of state and protected capitalism—the two forms on which the state of the seventeenth and eighteenth centuries was mainly based. The rulers of the state, whether the political unit was small or large, were trying to convert feudal revenues, such as their share of the produce and the personal services due them, into cash income. On the other hand, a rational collection system and machinery developed slowly. Thus, if the rulers found agents interested in exploiting the economic situation, they were only too happy to turn over the revenue to them against a fixed payment.

It was merely a historical coincidence that, in eastern and central Europe—Poland-Lithuania and in the German Empire— the Jews were in the best position to offer the required financial service. The necessary capital and business experience were concentrated mostly in their hands. In eastern Europe, there never had existed any class of citizens capable of ejecting the Jews from capitalist activity; whereas in Germany, such a class had existed but had become impoverished and had practically disappeared during the Thirty Years War and its aftermath. In France, the classic example of both absolutism and state capitalism, the very same system existed without the participation of Jewish capitalists.

But when the task did fall to the Jews, it was accomplished in a manner typical of Jewish society and its position. Since the Jewish society boasted close ties with widely separated countries, it was capable of serving as a channel for the transfer of goods and as a basis for the creation of credit which transcended national boundaries. The Jews of different lands not only traded with one another; they also loaned money to each other out of mutual confidence.

A further impetus to Jewish economic activity was provided by their position within the state. Since Jewish society was segregated religiously and socially from the other classes, its attitude toward them was likely to be almost purely instrumental. We have noted in previous chapters what the price of this attitude was from the viewpoint of Jewish society itself. But from the standpoint of the intensity of economic activity, it represented an incomparable stimulus. The members of this society had no social ambitions with regard to the outside world; they regarded it simply as affording scope for their economic activity. We have before us the classic example of a social minority whose very segregation and isolation ideally conditioned it for economic activity—and for that alone. Economic acumen was considered as a specific Jewish characteristic, and this alone was likely to give the Jew a certain advantage over his Christian competitors.

However, in the framework of the economic activity under discussion, the Jew enjoyed a greater advantage than this. Under state and protected capitalism, where political positions were exploited for economic advantage, the most satisfactory partner was a person who lacked political rights and ambitions. The non-Jew had no fear that the Jew would take a partisan stand in the struggle between the rulers and the ruled, who bore the economic yoke of the political privileges enjoyed by the rulers. Similarly, they had little fear that the Jew would be a party to the political struggle after he achieved economic power of his own. The political impotence of the Jew, and the fact that he restricted himself to economic activity alone, forged him into an ideal instrument under state and protected capitalism to be used by those who exercised political power.

These considerations explain the readiness of the rulers to form connections with the Jewish capitalist. As for the Jews, an alliance with the ruling power was essential for their very existence. Their residential rights, no less than their personal safety and the unfettered conduct of their business, depended on those in power. This state of affairs had evolved as far back as the Middle Ages wherever the Jews' right of domicile had ceased to be taken for granted. This situation threw the Jew at the mercy of the government. The more the existence of the ruling power was based on revenue-producing enterprises in which the state participated directly or indirectly, the greater were the opportunities opened to the Jew to become a partner—again, directly or indirectly—in these enterprises. In the nature of things, the Jew regarded the strengthening of his connection with the government as the consolidation of his position and his security.

The court Jew, of course, represents the high-water mark of close association achieved between individual Jews and rulers, and of dependence of the former on the latter—particularly in Western Europe—during the period under discussion. The court Jews served the kings and princes who were converting their feudal domains into absolute states. Monetary income constituted for these rulers a basic prerequisite for the attainment of the political goal: the independence of the central government of the contributions and services of the feudal lords. Under these circumstances, the Jews who were associated with the rulers acquired breadth, variety, and dynamism in the sphere of economic activity.

In essence, however, the function of the court Jews was no different from that of a large portion of the members of the Jewish society who operated on a more modest scale but under similar conditions. For even where the concentration of political power had not yet been achieved, the same cash profit motive existed, shared by all types of petty rulers, princelings, and nobles. It was they who maintained Jews on their estates and used them for converting their own produce and that of their serfs into cash by marketing it locally, elsewhere in the country, or even abroad. The Jewish lessee who rented the tavern on the lord's estate or who produced the potash or processed the hides and other locally available raw materials, or even the Jew who merely bought up the surplus of these products and sold them elsewhere, was something of a court Jew in miniature. Here, too, the Jew's prospects of profits depended on a franchise from the ruler. It was the exclusive right to deal in the production or distribution of goods that ensured the Jew his prospects of profit. The ruler's motive in granting the concession was the Jew's ownership of the capital needed for investment and his desire and ability to put this principal to work to produce profits of which the ruler would receive a certain percentage.

The basis of the alliance between the Jew and the ruler was not altered by the power, the area of the political unit, nor by the amount of capital invested. The principal characteristic of the partnership lay in the link between profitability and the extension of political protection. Indeed, in Jewish society of this period, the petty capitalists in alliance with the petty rulers played quite as important a role as did the large capitalists who operated under the protection of the central authorities. Both served as an expression of the new economic conditions in which the Jew was accorded the position of middleman—not away from the mainstream as with moneylending, but closely integrated in the process of exchange or even directly concerned in production.

It would seem that the types of economic activity which we have described constituted the mainstay of existence of Jewish society in this period. But secondary methods of activity were developed as well. Some achieved *post facto* recognition; while others remained forbidden occupations which were either concealed from the authorities or tacitly ignored by them. When the Jews settled in a place, and particularly if their number came to exceed that originally fixed or estimated, they required additional sources of livelihood, and they exploited every economic avenue.

The most illuminating example is the emergence of artisans in Poland and Bohemia in the seventeenth century. Their rise may be attributed solely to the pressure of economic circumstances. Manual labor was not a living tradition in Jewish society and did not represent a vocational ideal, its tradition of biblical and talmudic times being neutralized by the intervening Middle Ages. The authorities acquiesced in the activity of the artisans only after the event. Nowhere do we find that artisans were invited, or even accepted, as the first Jewish settlers in a place. In fact, they were only a social appendage to the body of merchants, lessees, and moneylenders, tolerated willingly or unwillingly by virtue of their existence by the main body of society.

A similar situation prevailed with regard to certain commercial activities. In practice, the Jew did not limit himself to those commercial pursuits that he had been invited to promote. He took advantage of every economic opportunity that presented itself. In exchange for the surplus of local products he would bring in goods from outside—not always in the form and quantity desired by the authorities. Trade between towns and countries was not always recognized as a blessing from the political standpoint. Some actually condemned it as a factor which disturbed the economy of the country.

The same was true of loans at interest. Although moneylending was not, as a rule, forbidden to Jews, it was not for this purpose that they were granted residential rights during this period, as they were during the Middle Ages (or even during this period in other countries, such as Italy). Illicit economic activities such as smuggling and the exchange and melting down of currency were also rife. The part played by Jews in these irregularities cannot be ascertained. Their opponents presumed a priori that the

Jews were guilty of these crimes. Since these deviations constituted the marginal phenomena of the Jews' legal occupations, the
temptation for them was greater than for the rest of the population. The institutions of Jewish society themselves attempted to
prevent their numbers from violating the laws of the land, but
illegal activities such as smuggling and the melting down of coins
were widespread throughout Europe. Again, the lowest class in
Jewish society was engaged in a struggle for its very physical existence. The chances of preventing this depressed group from resorting to such means of livelihood were slim, despite the deterrent effects of internal and external sanctions.

We may attribute to the members of the Jewish society a
tendency to exploit economic opportunities to the maximum, even
where the path was strewn with difficulties; certainly they were
not restrained by accepted custom in the economic area itself—in
the methods of production and distribution. If the Jew discovered
a new way of increasing profits, he would not be deterred by its
novelty. But the methods of multiplying profits as they were discovered by the generations which developed the capitalist system
of production and distribution, were unknown to the Jews no less
than to the rest of the citizens. They played practically no part in
the rationalization of production methods because their contact
with manufacturing processes was most limited. The idea that
economic life should be divorced from governmental control,
which afterwards became an important principle of economic liberalism, was even less likely to occur to the Jew than to anyone
else, since his reliance on the power of the government taught
him to regard it as the basis of his existence.

The question which preoccupied Jewish society was how to
regulate the tapping of sources of profits so that Jews would not
engage in unbridled competition with one another for contracts
with the authorities. The sources of halakhic law, which had been
handed down by previous generations when different conditions
prevailed, included contradictory traditions on the legal correct-

ness of exercising a monopoly generally based on the principle of "first come first served." Although at the beginning of the era, the halakhic authorities had not yet ruled on this question, with the consolidation of the power of the *kehillot* and super-*kehillot* at the end of the sixteenth century, the tendency to limit competition grew. Henceforth, regulations were promulgated forbidding competitors from entering into negotiations with the non-Jewish lessor so long as the contract of the first lessee was still in force, or even for a certain time thereafter.

The same was true of *hezkat ha-yishuv,* that is, the right of the members of the *kehilla* to forbid strangers from settling in the locality without their permission. Here, too, the halakhic authorities had not decided on the principle involved, but the regulations of the *kehillot* treated it as a self-evident matter. The restriction on strangers' coming and trading in the place had its source in talmudic law, and in this period, there was a tendency to extend this restriction and to observe it strictly. The restriction was justified by the fact that residents paid the local authorities for their right to trade and that outsiders were not entitled to enjoy the prospects of profits gratuitously. The concept of free competition did not, therefore, prevail, either in theory or practice, between the members of the Jewish community. No one advocated the removal of the restrictions. Any struggle between them over the sources of livelihood was conducted within the framework of existing restrictions. Thus, the principle of established rights was not disputed; only those who were entitled to them enjoyed them.

To the extent that free competition did exist, it was limited to the dealings of the Jews with their economic rivals in the surrounding society. Jewish organizations had no control over the larger community, and there was no place for an arrangement that would be binding on both sides. The over-all problems of the country's or the district's economy certainly did not figure in the Jew's calculations. Religious law, too, in its decisions on these matters did not concern itself with the larger issues of the general welfare.

Here we encounter the most decisive expression of the absolute political subjugation of the Jewish society from its negative aspect. Inasmuch as, at the very most, Jews were masters only over their own sphere of economic activity, they were capable of regarding economic issues only from their own special point of view. As far as they were concerned, the non-Jewish society and economy constituted a fixed, unchanging reality with which they had to reach a *modus vivendi*—an arrangement which would both satisfy the rulers and the general population and guarantee the maximum protection to the Jewish society itself. It never occurred to them to make an attempt to bring about any change or exert any influence in the direction of the common interest. Jewish organizations restricted their members' competition, even with non-Jews, wherever resentment, envy, or harm to an individual or the Jewish community might have ensued. On the other hand, many of the regulations were designed to defend the economic interests of the Jewish society against outside competition. This explains the tendency to maintain monopolies among the members of the Jewish society itself. Unrestricted competition over the sources of livelihood that depended on the members of the non-Jewish society would, in the first place, have benefited non-Jews. In order "not to lose the money of Israel" it was necessary for the Jews themselves to bridle their competition with one another.

Thus, the competition of the members of the Jewish society with their non-Jewish economic rivals does not imply that they inwardly advocated the principle of economic liberty and that, in the course of time, they succeeded in having it accepted by non-Jewish society—as Sombart would have it. Admittedly, Jews played a considerable part in promoting the supremacy of free capitalism after it had been discovered by the initiative of others. When capital began to be invested in production for the free market and this was found to be a possible source of earnings, the Jews, too, seized the opportunity and, at times, were among its active promoters. But the intensity with which this new economic activity was undertaken should not be traced to any innate kinship with the "spirit" of capitalism but, first and foremost, to the position of Jews in society. We have already noted how the Jew's position in the state led him to adopt a strictly utilitarian attitude towards business dealings. This attitude predisposed him to evaluate every transaction on the basis of his prospects of profits within a calculable period. Since free capitalism constituted a considerable source of profit, the Jew had no inhibitions about substituting the new method of investment for the prevailing one.

An additional factor in the rapid transition of the Jews to the new income-producing ventures was the social tension prevailing in Jewish society itself. For alongside those who controlled the official Jewish sources of livelihood was always a large class which subsisted on the crumbs which fell from their tables or who eked out a living by various types of occupations of questionable legality. But, as we shall see from an analysis of the structure of Jewish society, these have-nots could find no occupational alternative; they constituted the ever-present candidates for the positions occupied by the monopolizers of the livelihoods which represented their only chance of bettering themselves. Whenever new economic opportunities presented themselves in the surrounding society, persons waiting to exploit them were always to be found, even if those who controlled the sources of livelihood of the society at this time evinced no interest in political and economic innovations. This factor is responsible for the impression that Jewish society was interested in preserving the status quo. If political changes or fluctuations took place in the conditions of production or distribution, those engaged in the old occupations hastened to adapt themselves to the new situation. The change was usually seized upon by the depressed elements in Jewish society hoping to realize their ambition to rise in the economic and social scale. Conservatism and the pursuit of innovation merely constituted symptoms of the political situation in which Jewish society found itself, and the competitive tension which constantly prevailed within it.

VIII

Religion and Economic Activities

THE ANALYSIS OF THE ECONOMIC ROLE PLAYED by the Jews in Europe during the sixteenth to eighteenth centuries has not yet revealed any specifically Jewish trait, innate or acquired, which qualified them to fulfill the tasks that fell to their lot. Such objective data as their political position, their disposal of large financial resources, and their unity amidst geographical dispersion, would seem to provide sufficient motivation for the nature and scope of Jewish economic activity.

The question that remains to be answered is whether the Jewish religion, mentality, and outlook were also directly responsible for the character of Jewish economic activity. Religion might affect economic life through four other components: the practical performance of religious acts; the social doctrine of religion; its psycho-educational influence; and ethical and religious inspiration.

The Jewish community in this period was confronted with new opportunities for earning a livelihood. Some doubt arose as to whether several of these newly introduced activities did not violate Jewish religious prescription. We dealt with one example of this in Chapter III with respect to the trading in gentile wine. This, however, was not the only case in point. The progressive integration of the Jews into the general economy led them to trade, directly or indirectly, in commodities which had not been sanctioned by religious law. Jewish merchants traded in non-kosher meat; Jewish estate managers provided their non-Jewish workers with forbidden foods. When engaged in the adminstration of villages and townships, they were often indirectly concerned with hog breeding. All these activities were forbidden according to the plain meaning of Jewish tradition. The complete and unqualified Sabbath rest specified in the religious codes often presented difficulties for those engaged in farming taxes, managing estates, particularly in retailing liquor, and certainly for transport agents. The same applied to those who leased flour mills, fish ponds, distilleries, potash producers, and the like. Many serious doubts arose concerning the permissibility of benefits accruing to Jews from leavened food stuff during the Passover week.

The conflicts between economic realities and religious prescription usually could be solved. This was due to two factors: the character of Jewish economic activity and the elasticity of halakhic casuistry. The first mitigating circumstance was the fact that a non-Jew could substitute for a Jew on holy days on which the latter was forbidden to work. However, the fact that the Jew did not actually engage in work on a religious day of rest did not satisfy the requirements of the Jewish code, since, from the halakhic point of view, a Jew was not allowed to benefit from work done by the non-Jew for him or in his interest or on commission or in an enterprise bearing his name. As this difficulty was mainly formal, it was removed by a formal solution, such as legal fictions in the contracts of partnerships with non-Jews. The main objective of the Jewish entrepreneur and the chief concern of the rabbinical authorities was to stay away from his place of business on a holy day.

The Jew intuitively shrank from actual engagement in normal weekday business on the Sabbath, even though he might have to act in some capacity. It thus became the practice in wide circles to attend to customers on the Sabbath, to sell them drinks, etc., but not to touch money. Rabbinical authority looked askance at such flimsy compliance with the letter of the law; yet in some cases, they would permit the Jew to be inconspicuously present on the Sabbath in order to keep an eye on the non-Jewish worker, provided that the business was not formally connected with him on this day. Thus he might be permitted to supervise collection of tolls from travellers, so that no advantage was taken of his absence. All these dispensations, whether of popular practice or of rabbinical authority, were based on the assumption that, by and large, the Jew would observe the Sabbath day to keep it holy, would refrain from any actual work, and would spend most of the day in a Sabbath atmosphere. A definite limit was set to the elasticity of the law where it was clear from the start that the basic character of the Sabbath rest would have constantly to be violated. This applied to the employment of Jewish carriers in hauling merchandise over long distances and the like.

By distinguishing between direct, personal contact and impersonal, economic operations, rabbinic authority succeeded in working out a *modus operandi* permitting trading in food commodities that the Jew himself is ritually forbidden to eat. The objection to trading in non-kasher meat sprang from the feeling of revulsion aroused by the idea of dealing in "forbidden" food, or, in the more rationalistic formulation of the religious codes, to safeguard the dealer against eventually consuming it himself.

Such a motivation was valid only when personal contact with forbidden food was involved. The feeling of revulsion abated in cases where Jews managed large estates on commission or administered large-scale enterprises and derived commercial benefit from these forbidden items without personal contact with them. We may see in this development an expression of the progressive rationalization of the economic process in which the traded goods lose their specific character and are considered merely as an object for profitable enterprise.

Inhibitions were most intense with respect to the enjoyment of the profits from pig-breeding, a traditionally accursed occupation shunned by Jews from time immemorial. Those authorities who remained adamant in forbidding any connection with pig-raising injected into their rulings a strong emotional appeal to the Jewish religious conscience. There are attested instances of Jews' endeavoring to remove the offending animals from the tenant farms during their period of management. However, in the farming districts of Volhynia and Galicia, Jewish leaseholders and contractors tolerated pig-breeding on the lands under their administration during the first part of the seventeenth century. Finally this practice found its halakhic advocate in Rabbi David ha-Levi of Ostrog, author of a gloss to the *Shulchan Arukh* (entitled *Torei Zahav*), who reasoned that pig-breeding was just one of the many branches of agricultural enterprises on the farm, "which did not bear the name of its Jewish administrator, nor does the Jew come into personal contact with this branch. . . ."

The most obvious challenge to existing religious norms was posed by the problem of interest. The problem as such was not new. During the Middle Ages, the usual situation was that of a Jew lending at interest to a non-Jew. Some cases also involved the payment of interest between one Jew and another and required halakhic regulation. Various subterfuges were, indeed, evolved to circumvent the prohibition of usury which applied to both creditor and debtor alike, violation of which was viewed in a very serious light. Aside from the relative infrequency of such cases during the Middle Ages, certain extenuating circumstances facilitated the finding of a solution to the interest problem. Among these were the personal contact between creditor and debtor who made the loan effective by signing contracts or exchanging objects of security. The personal contact between the parties concerned made it feasible for the religious authorities to work out a legally acceptable procedure for the formulation of the contract. The loan contract was required to bear the character of a partnership in the enterprise financed by the loan that would promise the creditor-partner profits without any risks to his capital.

The novel aspect of this problem during the period in point is not the ways of circumventing the injunction against interest, but the emergence of conditions which militated against compliance with the formal regulations evolved by religious law in the past. It was no longer a question of merely advancing money in terms of a loan to be repaid with profit. It had become a practice to finance commercial projects, to make capital investments, to advance goods on credit, and to engage in all other forms of capitalist economy. It would appear that these economic activities favored the halakhic requirements by turning the legal fiction of the Middle Ages—i.e., the formulation of interest as partnership profits—into economic reality. The reality of what had been a legal fiction gave rise to new halakhic problems. The direct creditor-debtor relationship of the Middle Ages was replaced by credit activities through the medium of negotiable notes payable to an unknown bearer. The negotiability of these notes complicated the halakhic problems related to the interest derived from these transactions. Ultimately, only experts could handle such deals in compliance with the halakhic requirements; whereas the ordinary businessman, who was conversant with the elementary concepts of usury, only became confused and developed a cynical attitude towards the whole gamut of religious regulations governing this field.

This situation, which developed at the latest towards the close of the sixteenth century, caused religious authorities much concern. They tackled the problem in two ways: from the educational and administrative aspect and from that of legalistic reform. The former aspect is connected with the name of Rabbi Joshua Falk-Kohen, who held a prominent position in the meetings of the "Council of the Four Lands." He has recorded for us the resolutions, formulated by him, of the Council meeting, which convened in Lublin at the time of the Gramenitz Fair in 1607, with the rectors of the various yeshivot participating. In substance, these resolutions imposed controls upon the members of the Jewish communities that required them to execute transactions involving interest under the guidance of halakhic experts versed in the regulations and formulae governing the circumvention of the prohibition of usury. These expert counsellors were charged with the educational task of explaining "the reasons underlying the procedures adopted, in order to preclude ridicule of this and other matters." For the instruction of these counsellors, but also for the benefit of the ordinary businessman, Rabbi J. Falk composed a booklet setting forth the resolutions and regulations. This booklet contains two versions, one presenting the rules in the form of a manual and the other a learned treatise tracing the sources and outlining the train of thought that led to his rulings.

These enactments had no prospect of being realized in practice. Their authors doubted whether any businessman would be ready to divulge the nature of his transactions to the expert counsellors of his own community. They finally provided for an arrangement by which a counsellor could be appointed from each family, so that the businessman could at least consult his own kin. Obviously such an arrangement could not provide a permanent solution.

The second type of solution was directed, as we have described, at "legalistic reform," a term indicative of its inner character, though not of its self-declared purpose. In contradistinction to the educational, administrative type of solution propounded by the supreme forum of the Jewish communities in 1607, the legalistic formulae won immediate acceptance. Such formulae were already current even at the time when the Council issued the resolutions proposed by Rabbi Joshua Falk, and they were employed after the latter published his booklet, though they did not exactly conform with the procedures outlined therein. The dispensatory formulae propounded were based on varying halakhic grounds. Their common denominator was that they did not involve a detailed account of the proposed transaction and obviated the necessity of calling in expert religious advice in each and every case.

The Maharam formula, which transformed any gain by interest into partnership profit (*Hettar Isqa*), enjoyed the widest currency. Rabbi Menachem Mendel Avigdoris of Cracow issued a formulation which appeared in print even before the rectors of the yeshivot convened at the Council meeting in 1607. In the beginning, copies of these formulations were circulated and used in transactions. After they had become commonly accepted and known, the notes and agreements merely bore a standard clause stipulating that the transaction was to be valid in compliance with the instructions issued by Maharam, i.e. Rabbi Mendel of Cracow. These developments marked the lifting of the last halakhic reservations against the dynamic forces of the contemporary economic scene.

The evolution of the *Hettar Isqa* is but one of the most obvious examples of the process of adjustment called for by the rapidly growing business association among members of the Jewish community. The emergence of internal Jewish credit and its dynamism constituted the main changes that had to be contended with. The financial instrument of this credit was the so-called *memrami*, a promissory note payable to whomever presented it. The name *memrami*, and perhaps its legal content, were already known in the thirteenth century. It was, however, only from the sixteenth

century onwards that the *memrami* evolved into the most characteristic instrument of the Jewish merchant in the internal, Jewish
market. The employment of *memrami* definitely ran counter to
talmudic precedent. According to this tradition, a promissory note
was a personal obligation payable only to the party designated,
and its negotiability was subject to a most complicated formal
procedure. The dynamic economic conditions of the period called
for a much more elastic approach to this problem. Again, the
revocation of the talmudic tradition in this matter occurred almost unnoticed, and the completely new approach governing the
negotiability of bills was adopted without a stir. Talmudic law
proved itself remarkably adaptable to the changing needs of the
times.

Since Jewish religious and legal tradition did not militate
against the emergence of a capitalist economy, it may be asked
whether it actually promoted and encouraged such development.

As far as social doctrines were concerned, contemporary
Jewish thinking unhesitatingly approved the acquisition of wealth
as a means to an end. Moralistic teachings did not ignore the
dangers inherent in wealth; they considered both the temptation
to employ improper means for its acquisition and the moral pit-
falls that were its inevitable concomitants. The moralists reacted
by redoubling their warnings against the temptations involved,
admonishing their charges to be "honest in their business dealings." Their main concern was directed against unscrupulousness
in business. They advised that profits be put to proper use and
that the needy be given their due share. One should refrain from
exploiting one's acts of generosity and consider the recipient's
feelings.

The relationship between worldly success and virtue was undoubtedly the subject of differing evaluations. Some regarded
success as a sign of Divine favor, a testimonial from "Him who
dispenseth wealth." Ancient texts could easily be adduced in
support of such an approach. Others refuted this connection

between success and virtue, being prompted by their own personal antipathy to such preaching or by their own experience and social status. Religious tradition provided no clear clue either way. In any event, even those who doubted that wealth was a sign of virtue found no fault with the possession of worldly goods, nothing morally reprehensible in aspiring to worldly success and maintaining it. Poverty was considered a Divine tribulation which man had to suffer and bear. Even the most radical moralists never held up poverty as a virtue in itself for which man should strive. Ancient warrant for the ideal of poverty was not lacking. But supporting texts were either ignored or explained away by dialectic or homiletic argument.

The entire Jewish community depended for its everyday subsistence on profit-earning capital. This fact made it impossible for Jewish moralist doctrine to withhold its approval of such a situation. Far from having his acquisitive instinct checked, anyone growing up in the Jewish community of the sixteenth to eighteenth centuries was bound to absorb views which, after laying down due qualifications and controls, encouraged and promoted this tendency. We may, therefore, conclude that the social doctrine of Judaism during this period definitely favored the economic activities undertaken by the community.

It would be equally justified to regard Judaism—or rather its specific way of life—as affording a psychological and "rational" training for that type of economic activity. By "rational" is meant activity solely dictated by considerations of efficiency. Judaism inculcated purposeful living, demanded the planned utilization of one's time, and disapproved of uncontrolled emotional reactions. In other words, it trained the Jew to lead a carefully planned, rational life. The remarkable commercial talent of Jews may plausibly be traced to their religious upbringing, as has been maintained by some scholars. It should be borne in mind, however, that their religious background did no more than psychologically predispose them in this direction. Sociological research teaches us not to seek the key to an understanding of relationship between religion and economic activity in the socio-logical doctrines of any religion or in the formal psychological preparation it provides. We must also be careful not to overrate the psychological effect of rationalistic conduct in one sphere on that in another. The main impact of religion upon the social realm derives, as Max Weber has shown, from the very core of its beliefs and notion of personal salvation, matters which, at first sight, would seem to have little bearing upon anything outside the purely religious sphere.

This calls, therefore, for an investigation into the purely re-ligious content of Judaism, the function it assigns to man in crea-tion, and the way of life it directs him to follow on the road toward personal salvation. It would then be seen whether it pre-disposes men to engage in the kind of economic activity on which the Jewish community was based. In other words, did Judaism ascribe a positive role to economic activity in the struggle for salvation in the eyes of God, or, psychologically speaking, in man's own eyes as well? In our case, this central question— which Max Weber posed regarding Protestantism of that very same period—has to be answered, unlike Weber's reply in the case of Protestantism, in the absolute negative. Admittedly the acquisition of wealth was permitted, sometimes even commended, but worldly success was never served as the basic criterion of virtue in the sight of God and man. This could only be achieved by the practical performance of the precepts of Judaism and the cherishing of its ideals traditionally summed up in the threefold phrase: "Torah, worship, and good works." Money facilitated the achievement of religious ideals, but it was not an essential pre-condition. The study of Torah, the observance of the command-ments, and, primarily, the performance of good works demanded some financial means. Torah study was furthered by removal of financial worry. The extent of good works and charity was de-termined by the financial means at one's disposal. This harnessing of wealth to religious purposes meant that it occupied only a sub-ordinate role in the hierarchy of Jewish values. The accumulation and disposal of wealth could never become ends in themselves nor act as substitutes for virtue gained through authentic religious media. Economic success could, at best, be regarded as affording corroborative evidence of a person's merit. The crucial testimo-nial must derive from the purely religious sphere, based on strictly law-abiding and conscientious religious observance and the proper use of the worldly goods entrusted to man. Religion is bound to minimize the value of religious works if it wishes actively to promote chrematistic activities. Judaism never reached this stage. It developed an attitude of tolerance towards worldly occupations—but only as a last resort, according them *post facto* recognition, and then only in the form of special dispensations. Activities outside the purely religious sphere were never con-secrated as ends in themselves.

It was theoretically possible for the faithful to discharge the sum total of religious observances demanded of them, in which religious practices reigned supreme, and still devote the remain-ing time to business as a sacred pursuit of secondary importance. But this was precluded by the existence of one precept, the duty to study the Torah, which monopolized by Divine prescription any time left after one's personal needs, livelihood, and other religious observances had been attended to. The study of Torah is obligatory at all times, whenever one is not engaged in an essen-tial occupation. This obligation was, however, fully honored only by a small minority of scholars who dedicated their time without stint to the study of Torah. The majority studied Torah only in their leisure time. The average Jew found ample time to spare for business, and he energetically applied himself to it. Such ap-plication was, however, only condoned as a tolerated practice that required justification in the light of the principle that one should devote the maximum of one's time to Torah study. This obliga-tion devolved on every Jew, layman, and scholar alike. The moralistic literature repeatedly stressed that even one who was incapable of profound study should gain from his text whatever his understanding allowed.

Anyone who devoted more time to the pursuit of worldly gain than was warranted to eke out his livelihood was guilty of idling his time away, a transgression tantamount to the neglect of Torah studies.

Profane occupations were justified in many ways. It was impossible to define clearly what came under the category of "essential occupations." Moreover, ways were found to vicariously engage in the prescribed religious studies by delegating them. He who contributed to the upkeep of Torah students, and, even more so, he who fully supported them, was regarded as a partner in their meritorious occupation. The heavenly reward was shared equally between them, as in all partnerships, since the precept could only be performed by the joint effort of student and patron.

Though the obligation of Torah study did not, in practice, militate against devotion to business and other occupations, it prevented their recognition as ends in themselves. Vocational occupations could not be gainsaid, but they remained workaday in character. Nothing short of a complete inversion of Jewish values could have won direct religious sanction for economic activities.

PART TWO

Structure and Institutions

IX *The Kehilla Organization*

*T*HE LEGAL SEGREGATION OF THE JEWS AND
their religious and cultural isolation meant that Jewish individual
or communal needs could only be supplied internally through
Jewish co-operation and mutual assistance. Jewish institutions
that banded individuals together in competent associations covering the various spheres of social activities were thus essential. The
basic and most customary framework was the local *kehilla*, which
bound together all Jews who were permanent local residents.
Social cohesion was promoted by common needs. The actual
association was implemented on the basis of talmudic law. The
latter derived its validity tacitly or explicitly from the attachment of the members of the community to a common Jewish tradition.

Talmudic law in its later stages of development determined the normative pattern of Jewish society, in all phases of life capable of legal regulation. The problem of how far the community was authorized to force its will on the individual constantly recurred in different circumstances. It was solved on the basis of earlier precedents cited in halakhic literature. Usually the individual was obliged to contribute to communal expenditure from which he, personally, would never derive even indirect benefit. Jewish religious authorities, however, never arrived at comprehensive formula that determined the obligation and responsibility of the individual member towards the community.

In actual fact, communal self-government was not regulated exclusively in accordance with Torah law in its narrow sense. There existed, besides the Talmud, another source of *kehilla* law—that is, *minhag* which means local usage or custom. This had two aspects. First, there was the body of usage and custom common to all sections of Ashkenazi Jewry; it was largely incorporated in the religious codes, and carried hardly less weight than talmudic rulings proper. Second, *minhag* included anything even verbally attested as customary in a certain community. Such local custom did not, as a rule, conflict with the over-all Ashkenazi *minhag;* rather, they were in the nature of local variations resorted to particularly where no general tradition existed. The period under discussion is distinguished by the committing of the local *minhag* to written formulation. Every *kehilla* of standing boasted its own register of by-laws (*takanot*) governing all phases of communal life. It may be safely assumed that these records represented the sum total of resolutions adopted at *kehilla* committee meetings in the past. By the end of the sixteenth century at the latest, we find committees specially appointed by the *kehilla* to draw up communal by-laws, which, after having been endorsed by local rabbinic authority (where this was customary), became binding upon both the leaders of the community and the rank and file.

We are confronted here, therefore, with a combination of rational and traditional factors in the conduct of public affairs. The respect of the local law-makers for established usage indicates a traditional approach. The very procedure of committing them to writing, reveals a rational course of action. These regulations represented a fixed set of rules that were binding on membership and administration alike. The endorsement of communal by-laws by religious authority gave them the sanction of religious law which the Jewish public accepted as a matter of principle.

Halakha, i.e. Jewish religious law in its widest sense, embraced generally accepted usages and local custom. Moreover, no regulations formulated by the *kehilla* would be validated if they conflicted with halakhic standards of justice and fairness. This dependence upon a traditional source for judicial review protected the individual and the community against arbitrary legislation. The supremacy of halakha was also upheld—in theory if not in practice—by the vesting of the rabbinic authorities with the exclusive power of arbitrating any doubts or disputes arising out of the interpretation of the *kehilla* by-laws.

The Polish-Ashkenazi community of the sixteenth to eighteenth centuries cannot be compared to the uniformly knit structure of its medieval counterpart, where affairs were in the hands of learned notables who governed by mutual consent. The first distinction was in respect of size. The *kehilla* in our period numbered from a hundred to a thousand souls, and towards the end of the period, there were communities with ten thousand persons and more. As we shall see later, the *kehillot* were no longer uniform in their property or their occupational and cultural stratifications. Such large *kehillot* required well-recognized institutions of self-government where the power of decision was vested in the hands of the few. A hierarchical social structure and the occasional recourse to disciplinary measures distinguished the community which had outgrown the stage of a primary group in which an intimate and immediate relationship existed between the governing officials and the governed. The social differentiation of the large-scale communities, which arose out of necessity, spread also to the small community. There, the situation in most cases did not warrant a change from the pattern of government by the community as a whole or a single scholar, a pattern which was characteristic of German Jewry in the medieval period.

The primary indication of hierarchical structure lay in the concentration of communal leadership in the hands of a limited group of from four to ten *parnassim* (wardens). Next in the hierarchy of offices come the *tovim* (notables), and the *gabbaim* and *memunim* (overseers). Each of these officers had his own specific field of activity. The notables assisted and advised the *parnass*. The *gabbai* or charity officer administered *heqdesh*— sacred funds (almshouses) or synagogue affairs. The overseers supervised prices as well as weights and measures in the markets and *kashrut*. All these officers served by appointment and as a public service. Though the procurement of such a post may have been due to the pressure of ulterior interests and motives; they were primarily honorary, unpaid positions, a fact which lent them a political-governmental character.

The highest ranking *parnass* was the one whose "month" it was. This office changed hands, on a monthly rotation system, between the different wardens. Its holder was appropriately enough designated *parnass-hahodesh*, "the warden of the month." But the significance of this rotation varied with each *kehilla* management. In one type that was prevalent in the German, Moravian, and western Hungarian communities, the system implied that the warden-for-the-month was chairman of the council of wardens, which he alone was authorized to convene. He filled, too, various other clearly defined functions. Nevertheless, in practice, authority was vested in the council of wardens and even the warden-for-the-month acted with its approval. In the second type, prevalent in Poland and Lithuania, the warden-for-the-month was sole arbiter during his month, taking the initiative, being responsible for decisions, and directing the whole of the executive apparatus. His fellow wardens degenerated into mere assistants, helping him as the one to whom authority had been exclusively entrusted.

The appointed officers acted, as mentioned earlier, within the framework of accepted rules which were based upon *minhag*, and written *taqanot* (written laws). This set of authoritative rules did not, however, exempt those charged with applying them from the need to make decisions. They had to decide whether its rules applied to a particular case, and when and how to implement them. In the absence of any public controlling body, these officers were responsible only to themselves. The only guarantee that they would honorably discharge their office lay in their identification with the values cherished by the community, values of which they were the foremost standard bearers. The *kehilla* by-laws that regulated their official duties and functions took this fact into account. Sometimes these by-laws devised means of mutual control by demanding a quorum of various officers for certain decisions or for the rendering of accounts such as financial reports. In a few instances, fines were levied on delinquent officers. The fine evidently acted more as an incentive to loyal and efficient service than as a penalty. Ultimately, the by-laws relied on the officers' attachment to the values of society. They served to remind the officer of his duty to discharge his public service faithfully and warned him that any infraction of regulations would be tantamount to incurring the *herem* (ban). Where particularly heavy responsibilities were involved, officials were sometimes required to take an oath of loyalty. These included members of the appointments committee, tax assessors, or even *parnassim*. The oath was taken when office was assumed or in the event that the officials had to clear themselves of the suspicion of bringing gentile pressure to bear in favor of their appointment. The *herem* and the oath of office point to the religious character of their responsibilities. Religious fear actually constituted the only guarantee of faithful service; no human deterrent existed. This religious fear ranged from the primitive dread of the magic power vested in an oath and curse to the inspiring *imitatio dei*.

The *kehilla* officers were assisted in their duties by salaried subordinates. The number of such communal servants varied with the size of the community. In some instances, one person combined in himself all the several functions; in other cases, they were discharged by different persons. In large communities, there was a large staff of such servants: scribes, court messengers, watchmen, overseers, street cleaners, etc. All these were salaried positions, paid only partly out of the *kehilla* budget. The rest came from the individuals to whom the service was rendered. The functionary would collect from the party to whom the service was performed regardless of whether this service was or was not to his advantage. The applicant for a legal document or a writ naturally paid for the service. The victim of excommunication or imprisonment by order of the *parnassim* had likewise to bear the expenses the *kehilla* had incurred in implementing them. We may note here that the *kehilla* attained a degree of rationalization in the division of labor that was not achieved in the realm of financing its operations.

This rationalization manifested itself in the scale of fees fixed for every service rendered. The fees were usually listed in the *kehilla* by-laws. It is almost certain that many of these functionaries were only part-time community servants and had other sources of income. The differentiation between the community's governing, administrative body and its staff of executive functionaries typifies the classes of partners sharing communal government. However, this distinction was not always absolutely clear. The servants were not always merely instruments of execution who worked according to assignment. Often they did not carry out merely technical operations, but were called upon to use their initiative. *Kehilla* by-laws ruled that in certain cases its servant was to excommunicate a person on account of his conduct—even without being explicitly instructed by the officers. It was occasionally left to his discretion to confiscate or collect payments without special order of the court.

These instances seem to indicate the community's wish to separate the executive from the legislative branch of the community administration. In fact, it resulted in vesting the authority for making decisions in the executive staff. We should bear in mind, however, that the responsibility and accountability of the two branches were quite different from each other. The honorary office-holder was ultimately solely responsible to his own judgment about whether his decisions were consonant with the values of society; whereas, the community servant was under the threat of real penalties involving the "forfeiture of service," a term which continually recurs in conjunction with the engagement of public servants.

A complete exception to all these rules regarding public servants was one functionary of the large *kehillot* or super-*kehilla* organizations, the *shtadlan*. His assignment demanded that he devote all his time to cultivating his connection with the outside, non-Jewish world, or, at any rate, that he always be ready to make these contacts. Often this would take him away from home. The *shtadlan* of the *kehilla* and certainly of a whole province was called upon to deal with the non-Jewish authorities, who in many cases were located at some distance away. The office of *shtadlan* called for special qualifications not prevalent among other members of the *kehilla:* a command of the vernacular, a familiarity with the political and legal set-up, versatility, resourcefulness, and diplomacy. These qualifications were only rarely united in one person, and could hardly be acquired by study and training either in Jewish or non-Jewish institutions of education. That the office was well-filled was mostly due to personal effort and adaptation that was confined to a few families. Because they were scarce, the *shtadlanim* were granted generous financial conditions which the *kehilla* and super-*kehilla* organizations were ready to accept as a worthy investment.

The Jewish public regarded the contact with the non-Jewish world as the special preserve of their representative bodies at the highest levels. The individual Jew had to delegate some of his business to the wardens and leaders of the *kehilla*. Usually, however, the trouble and expertise involved made it necessary for them to put the *shtadlan* in charge of these contacts.

The *shtadlanim* would, in any case, act as the community representatives even when dealing with the affairs of an individual. For this very reason, it was advisable that the relationship between the *shtadlan* and the individual dependent on him should not be that of an agent to his personal employer. Indeed, in Cracow, the logical step was taken of prohibiting the *shtadlan* from accepting any favors from the person on whose behalf he was negotiating. In other places, he was allowed to collect a fee, but on no account was he to make his assistance conditional on its receipt. These special circumstances produced a type of community servant corresponding closely to our modern, rational notion of a public official who serves the entire community without any personal dependence on those requiring him and who is paid out of public funds.

The inability of the *kehilla* and super-*kehilla* organizations in the eighteenth century to pay their *shtadlan* a fixed stipend symptomized their decline. Before this time, the *shtadlan* took his cut of the current income of the *kehilla* and usually collected, without any limitations, a fee for services rendered directly from the individuals whose interests he furthered.

Any description of those who shared in the self-governing institutions of the *kehilla* would be incomplete without the inclusion of the rabbi, although the governing aspect represented only one side of his functions. Later we shall consider his activities as the competent authority on ritual matters, as a religious judge administering Torah law, as the head of the local yeshiva responsible for spreading religious knowledge, and as a preacher and shepherd of his flock. The discharging of these functions did not necessarily attach the rabbi to a *kehilla*. A disciple who was ordained by his teacher or any other scholar of renown was authorized to practice. The tendency during this period was not to allow private enterprise to reign in the field of rabbinic functions; rather, his duties were concentrated in the hands of persons who had been formally charged with them through their appointment as rabbi of the *kehilla*.

A rabbi was usually appointed from a number of candidates at a meeting of householders or by a representative body of electors. The first condition was, of course, that he be ordained in the manner outlined previously. However, he derived his authority over the *kehilla* from his appointment. This was given official expression by its listing in the *kehilla* ledger and by the delivery to him of the *ktav rabbanut* (the writ of appointment), which outlined the conditions of service.

The rabbi was appointed for a limited period—usually three years. A basic salary was fixed with additional emoluments; in addition, he received gratuities for rendering services to individuals in connection with marriage, divorce and judicial functions. The titles of honor by which he was to be addressed as well as a statement of when he was entitled to be called up to the Torah were also laid down. Where the rabbi was destined to become head of the yeshiva, this appointment was stipulated in the contract, and, in return, the *kehilla* undertook to support a certain number of students from other places. The rabbi was formally inducted at an official ceremony at which his congregation accepted the religious authority vested in his person. Henceforth, he was designated *mara de'atra*, "Master of the Parish," the exclusive exerciser of the rabbinic functions. Henceforth, no other person was authorized to adjudicate in civil and ritual matters or to preach and lecture without his permission or tacit agreement. Admittedly, some auxiliary rabbinic functions in some *kehillot* were entrusted to assistant preachers and rulers on ritual matters, but they were strictly subordinate to the rabbi. Any overriding of his decisions and any slight to him constituted a breach of discipline that the *kehilla* institutions were called upon to combat with all the means of coercion at their disposal.

The emergence of the *kehilla* rabbinate is linked to the strengthening of the Jewish communal organization characteristic of our period. The ability of a *kehilla* to guarantee the major part of a rabbi's livelihood at a fixed salary depended on the existence of a permanent system of tax collection with appropriate coercive powers. Such a situation was far removed from that of epochs previous to the first half of the sixteenth century, a time when the rabbi supported himself entirely from the fees he collected for services he rendered. Again, the emergence of a body with coercive powers enabled rabbinic functions to be entrusted exclusively to one individual. This power also contrasted with the preceding era, when competition to exercise rabbinic functions was rife.

The organizational dependence of the rabbinate also had its negative aspect. In many cases, particularly in Poland and Lithuania, rabbinic livings were purchased. The rabbi or members of his family paid the *kehilla* or the electoral board a single payment in lieu of the office. The social implications of this phenomenon will be examined later. Here we shall merely observe, by way of illustration, that the purchaser of a rabbinic living regarded it as his private preserve for the period stipulated. Had the *kehilla* not been able to guarantee the "buyer" the return of his investment, the "sale" could not have been put into effect.

But the relationship of dependence existing between the *kehilla* and rabbinate was mutual. This fact returns us to the starting point of our analysis: that the *kehilla* government was backed by the sanctity of tradition in its various forms. The Jewish consciousness of that era identified the existence of the *kehilla* with that of Judaism itself. The *kehilla* was intimately bound up with the whole corpus of Jewish teaching, with the Torah and with all its emotive associations. No wonder then, that this feeling demanded an institutional outlet in the appointment of someone to head the *kehilla* as the official bearer of tradition. We have already observed that the rabbi was usually called upon to approve the *kehilla* by-laws—even where he was no party to their formulation. In some places, he was vested with the function of supervising the implementation of such constitutional rulings as those relating to the election of officers. The *kehilla* leaders were certainly forced to resort to the rabbi's authority to provide a religious backing for the *kehilla* constitution, for the penalty for violations, and for approval of sanctions of especial severity. The rabbi was naturally called upon to represent the *kehilla* in its relations with outside bodies by virtue of his religious and halakhic standing. He was, for example, called upon to combat rival rabbinic authorities who presumed to impose their rulings and anathemas on members of the *kehilla* or its leadership.

The two types of leadership—that of the *parnassim* and that of the rabbi—were interdependent; neither side could operate without the help of the other. This mutual dependence, however, could and did lead to quarrels over authority, the division of functions, and prestige. The balance of forces varied with each community. Light on the various types of partnerships between these two expressions of *kehilla* leadership can be gleaned from monographs written on particular communities or districts. Generally, the *kehilla* rabbinate gradually gained a secure niche in Jewish communal life, and a well-defined type of rabbi emerged. Changes of position became less frequent. Appointments were for a minimum of three years, and in some cases, the initial contract was for a longer period. The incumbent was chiefly occupied with his rabbinic functions, though rabbis who engaged in business and money lending were occasionally still to be found.

The more dependable the rabbinate became as a source of regular livelihood and prestige, the more it became the sole occupation of the incumbent. The marks of honor accorded the rabbi symptomize the social acclimatization of his office. The synagogue service began only on his arrival; the reader recited the *amida* only after the rabbi had finished his devotions. It seems that much of the prestige accorded in the early part of our period, particularly in Poland, to the *rosh yeshiva* who sometimes officiated as a rabbi was now transferred to the town rabbi, and did not depend upon his function as *rosh yeshiva*.

The raising of the prestige of the rabbinate led, of course, to increased demands on its incumbent and a greater emphasis on his responsibility towards his *kehilla*. He was, on occasion, blamed for imperfections in Jewish society, and he was held responsible for the integrity of public life. No wonder, then, that the crisis which overtook traditional society at the end of the period manifested itself principally as the crisis of the rabbinate.

X   *The Kehilla's Range of Activity*

*T*HE FUNCTION OF THE *kehilla's* EXECUTIVE body was to assume responsibility for the maintenance of the communal institutions. No department of community life fell outside its purview. Its control was evident in economic activities, in relations with non-Jews, in family and social life, and in matters of religion and education. It did not, of course, wield the same degree of power in each province.

One of its foremost tasks was to represent the *kehilla* in its external relations—that is, to maintain contact with the non-Jewish authorities. Indeed, the appointment of *kehilla* officers sometimes involved the ratification of the authorities or an oath or declaration of allegiance to them. Even in places where their election was ostensibly the internal affair of the community, it was clear to both its members and the authorities that these officials had been appointed to serve as the contact between the two. The leaders were responsible to the authorities for the community's financial obligations such as the payment of taxes and the sending of gifts. The heads of the community were also called upon to meet special demands such as the raising of extra contributions in times of emergency. To no small degree they were responsible to the authorities for the actions of individuals, and they were asked, on occasion, to punish individual violators of the law, or even to surrender them to the authorities for trial.

In return for these services, the heads of the Jewish community enjoyed the sanction and backing of the government insofar as their authority had to be imposed by compulsion. The internal unity of the community did not preclude deviations by individuals in matters that the entire community believed were essential for the preservation of the community. Since the physical means of compulsion were concentrated in the hands of the non-Jewish government, the Jewish community could exercise compulsion only to the degree permitted by the state authorities. The grant of domicile to a Jewish community included the authority to use compulsion, and it sometimes stipulated the methods by which the authorities would assist in implementing this compulsion. For example, it might be stated that a certain percentage of every fine imposed by the leaders of the Jewish community be set aside for the government treasury. The delegation of a limited amount of enforcement power to the *kehilla* was the basis for the much-publicized Jewish autonomy.

First, the community leadership required authority and enforcement powers in the distribution of taxes, the bulk of which were designed to cover the amount due to the government. The method of collecting taxes was based on accepted custom, a mixture of traditionalism and semi-rationalism. Property taxes were calculated on the basis of a sworn statement or on the estimate of assessors who swore to issue a fair appraisal. The assessment did not fix the actual amount the individual was required to pay during a given period; it represented the percentage of communal budget to be paid by each householder. Owing to the considerable fluctuation in the *kehilla*'s expenses and the lack of a system of accounting, the *kehilla*'s executive body was unable to determine in advance the actual amount each taxpayer would have to pay.

Many questions arose about the types of property which should be subject to taxation. Typically, capital loaned out or invested in business was treated as ordinary property. Land and buildings, investments that did not yield full income, were exempted as early as the Middle Ages from the payment of full taxes. With the increasing incidence of credit transactions, disputes arose over businesses operated with other people's money and those based on partnerships with persons who lived in other cities. Because of the obscure nature of capital based on credit, the assessors, and perhaps even the owners of the capital themselves, had difficulty in determining the value of the property subject to taxation.

Another source of revenue was purchase taxes levied on meat, salt, wine, and other products. Certain items, such as the support of the poor and the maintenance of the synagogue, were, as a rule, covered by contributions or fines paid by violators of communal by-laws. A third method of covering specific expenditures was the levying of a poll tax. According to the original *halakha*, this was the system to be used to pay for protection against danger to life and limb that affected rich and poor alike.

Legal precedents and principles were unable to provide for an equitable distribution of the tax burden among different groups and classes without disputes and clashes. The *kehilla* executive body had to combat the pressure exerted by various interested parties by use of concepts of the general and local tradition. The experts in religious law represented the principles of tradition, and they sometimes issued decisions on specific points of dispute.

But, in general, these were matters in which they had difficulty in basing their decisions on Jewish law. Instead of issuing binding judgments, they would propose a compromise or explicitly refer a decision to the *kehilla* leaders. The decision was reached as a result of the operation of pressure groups, and it was executed through the coercive powers vested in the communal leaders.

The other departments of the *kehilla*'s activity we have mentioned—economics, family life, education, etc.—will be treated individually. Here we may note that in matters of this sort the *kehilla*'s executive body functioned in a supervisory and controlling capacity rather than in a directory and executive role. For that reason, it did not require a great degree of coercive power. This was true except for the economic sphere—at least at those times and places where the *kehilla* leadership did not content itself with supervising the activities of individuals, but acted as an outright economic institution. This occurred mainly in Poland and Lithuania in the seventeenth and eighteenth centuries, where the *kehilla* often obtained the concession for various revenue-producing activities such as the distilling of brandy and the collection of taxes and customs.

From the structure of the *kehilla*'s organization, it is clear that in the absence of a cadre of professional administrators, the *kehilla* leadership could not undertake the direct operation of these enterprises. What actually happened was that it farmed out concessions obtained from the authorities to Jewish sub-concessionaires. In this manner, the *kehilla*, owing to its numerous obligations, sometimes became a financial institution that borrowed and loaned and incurred profit and loss on these business deals.

The function of the halakhic authorities in the *kehilla* was not one of shaping and implementing; it was rather, one of supervising and guaranteeing that nothing would be done to destroy the fabric of tradition. This was also true of the judicial functions of the halakhic authorities. Not every legal question was brought before a rabbinic court. The leaders of the *kehilla* themselves served, to some extent, as judges (*dayanim*)—especially in near criminal matters involving defamation, quarrels, and assaults. Even if the lay leaders co-opted the community rabbi when they sat in judgment, they did this only to put their authority on a firmer basis. They were not, on this account, placed outside the category of a disciplinary court. They ruled in accordance with precedents and the provisions of the *kehilla's* by-laws; they did not decide on the basis of halakhic rulings, both with regard to penalties and fines or rules of legal procedure. The same was true in civil cases.

Householders of the *kehilla* were appointed judges just as they might be named to any other task. This was not an honorary position, but an opportunity to render service. The litigants would pay the judges a fee in proportion to the magnitude of the case. Needless to say, the judges appointed were not always scholars. It is also obvious that they did not rule in accordance with Jewish law; not only did the original talmudic law not serve as a basis for the decisions, but there was not even dependence of halakhic sources in the broad sense. They ruled according to their own judgment, and probably on the basis of precedents culled from the province of their own limited, local experience.

Their acceptance of a fee constituted no reason for disqualifying the judges—any more than it did in the case of rabbinical courts, which had long since been accustomed to charge a fee for their services. The ideal of early talmudic times, "just as I [Moses] act gratuitously, so shall you act gratuitously," had long since been thrust aside by social reality. The acceptance of a fee from the litigants (in accordance with the importance of the matter with both sides equally sharing the payment) was an advanced stage in rationalization that went beyond the sanction in the Talmud for indemnifying the judge for his loss of time from his regular work. The idea of reimbursing the judges from public funds in order to free them from any financial dependence on the litigants had been propounded some time before. But the suggestion was not adopted except for the rabbis of the large *kehillot* whose partial salary was regarded as indemnification for their loss of time.

Although these laymen's judgments found formal justification in the halakha, the very existence of this institution was a thorn in the side of the halakhic authorities, as may well be imagined. For this justification relied on the rule that where no scholars were to be found who were capable of serving as judges, it was preferable to resort to Jewish laymen than to non-Jewish courts. This rule fitted the situation in Poland, Lithuania, and even many places in the German states until the second half of the sixteenth century. In any event, the large-scale reference of civil cases to laymen involved a limitation on the authority of halakhic tradition fostered by the scholars. For this reason, in the seventeenth and eighteenth centuries, when study of the Torah flourished and scholars were on the increase and every *kehilla* appointed a rabbi-cum-judge, the demand arose that jurisdiction over civil cases be restored to the halakha and to its exponents.

This explains the sharp criticism of the administration of justice by laymen which was expressed by rabbis and scholars. In many instances, the latter succeeded in guaranteeing for themselves special judicial prerogatives whether through the establishment of a rabbinical court parallel with that of the lay one, or by the co-opting of a rabbi or scholar to that court. However, they were unable to abolish the lay court entirely. The struggle between scholars and lay judges continued. As late as the second half of the eighteenth century, Rabbi Exekiel Landau complained in Prague that petty cases were referred to the scholars, whereas important cases were reserved for lay judges.

The advantage of lay judgments apparently lay in the speed in which decisions were given and executed. The by-laws stipulated a maximum time limit for the duration of such cases. On the other hand, proceedings under rabbinic auspices could drag on and on because of the need of proof and evidence and sometimes even because of a written appeal to a rabbinical authority in another city—a custom which was quite prevalent in the Middle Ages and which persisted down to this period.

Where the litigants both belonged to the same *kehilla,* both types of courts possessed the advantage of being in a position to compel the parties to accept the authority of the court and obey its judgment. The enforcement officers of the *kehilla,* who were not at all powerless, would use all the means at their disposal to ensure compliance with the court's decisions.

The jurisdiction of the Jewish courts was limited by the privileges granted to them by the state authorities. Some types of legal proceedings, like the transfer of property, generally came under the jurisdiction of the non-Jewish courts. In some places, the individual had the option between a Jewish and non-Jewish court —and a public battle was waged by the community to dissuade individuals from exercising this right. The very resort to gentile justice was regarded as sinful, and the Hebrew term for the non-Jewish judiciary, *arka'ot,* acquired a negative emotional connotation, almost as if it were an institution of some heathen cult. At no time was there complete renunciation of the gentile courts, but the community and its representatives reserved the right to decide in which cases the prohibition might be lifted and the individual permitted to resort to a non-Jewish court.

The extent of public control over individual action in the matter of court jurisdiction depended on the power of the *kehilla* organization. Non-Jewish courts were resorted to even by the *kehilla* itself or by individuals who defied the *kehilla's* laws and against whom the *kehilla* was powerless. In such cases, explicit sanction was given to the opponents of these defiant individuals to apply to the gentile courts. However, precisely because the ban was lifted in special cases, it was difficult to prevent other litigants from arguing that their opponents had failed to appear before the Jewish court or refused to heed its judgment—a situation found particularly in cases involving members of two *kehillot.*

In order to protect the *kehillot* against persons who disregarded the law, incorrigible criminals and informers to the non-Jewish authorities who jeopardized the existence of the community or individual life and property, the "informer's trial," which had been prevalent among Spanish Jewry was revived. Though in a few instances, sentences were handed down in criminal cases by the heads of Ashkenazi *kehillot* in the Middle Ages, halakhic literature reflected practically nothing of this. But the similarity of the social-economic conditions drew the attention of the Polish scholars in this matter, too, to the Spanish sources, which dealt with actual cases. Indeed, sentences were handed down in Poland by the community leaders that decreed the death penalty or corporal punishment; these were either secret or made with the knowledge of the authorities. The halakhic authorities were asked for their opinion, and they ruled that the *kehilla* had the right to punish the informer and criminal, to maim him, and even to take his life. We have in our possession incontestable evidence of the execution of such sentences with the consent of renowned rabbinic authorities. There are also indications that some of them recoiled from this despicable job and sought ways of having it done by the gentile courts.

In any event, in no country did a judicial procedure for criminal cases develop. It should be mentioned that, by their very nature, the procedure used in trying informers was not that of an ordinary court. The trial was a secret one; the accused was not present; and none of the manifold safeguards against judicial error instituted in ancient rabbinic legal theory for capital cases was used. The fact that such trials took place in Jewish society clearly reflects how its very life depended on a clear-cut separation from the outside world and a stringent discipline from within.

Thus, it is apparent that the Jewish community did not hesitate to resort to coercion in order to maintain its authority. The term "compulsive powers," in the sociological sense, represents powers broader than the means the courts employ to ensure compliance with their judgments. At the court's disposal were the usual disciplinary measures: the seizure of property, monetary fines, corporal punishment, imprisonment, and, in exceptional cases, the death penalty. But, in addition to these, two other means of coercion were available, the use of which was conditioned on the existence of Jewish society as a traditional-religious one circumscribed by a non-Jewish setting. We refer to the *herem* (ban) and the surrender of a Jew to the gentile authorities.

Excommunication in its formal halakhic sense implied excluding a person from the community—that is, preventing him from joining the other members of the community in both their secular and religious occupations. In the Mishnaic period, excommunication served as a means of internal discipline among groups of scholars. When hegemony passed to the scholars, it became a means of chastisement used by them against the community. At the time of the rise of the *kehilla* organization, it served as an instrument for imposing the *kehilla*'s will on recalcitrant members.

Exclusion of a person from taking part in communal life was one of the chief disciplinary measures employed by the *kehillot* between the sixteenth and eighteenth centuries. The degree of exclusion depended on the seriousness of the offense. Punishment sometimes consisted only of the deprival of some privilege in the field of leadership or of religion: a temporary disqualification from receiving an appointment or from fulfilling a function in the religious ritual, such as acting as reader, being called up to the Torah, or being included in the quorum of worshippers. The proclamation of the formal *herem* included all of these and added to them the avoidance of social contact with the person excommunicated and the members of his family as well: his children would not be circumcised; the marriage ceremony would not be performed for them; and they would not be given a Jewish burial. The intimidating power of excommunication lay not only in its threat to physical existence; its influence derived no less from the fact that it prevented the satisfaction of religious needs, primary for anyone brought up in the Jewish religion. Moreover, since the main social contact of the Jew was restricted to his own society, his isolation from that society constituted his complete withdrawal from any human or social ties. The person excommunicated lost, in his own consciousness, the world in which he had existed—this world as well as the next. This explains the tremendous emotional impact embodied in the very concept of the *herem,* an impact intensified by the external effects which accompanied its proclamation—the opening of the Ark containing the Scrolls of the Law in the synagogue, the sounding of the *Shofar,* and the kindling of black candles.

Obviously excommunication derived its potency from the traditional-religious nature of society. The very pronouncement of the ban had its own special effect. In this connection, attention may be drawn to the magic power of words in general, and of sacred words in particular, in this society, in order to understand that the proclamation of a particular formula was likely to bring about incisive social results. The effectiveness of such a ban may be explained as a magic influence on the object or activity to which it referred. The concept of *herem* clung to prohibitions accepted from time immemorial. *Hezkat ha-yishuv* (right of domicile) was also called *herem ha-yishuv* (the ban of domicile), implying the community's right to exclude newcomers by authority of the ban, and the term *herem* was likewise applied to a whole series of prohibitions pertaining to marital and social relations. New prohibitions were also proclaimed by the *kehilla* and super-*kehilla* institutions to be subject to the rules of the *herem:* tax-farming in Poland at one period, the purchase of rabbinical office, etc. But it is clear that in such instances, where the ban came up against decisive personal interests, it could not serve as an absolute safeguard. There were constant complaints that bans were being violated. For this reason, some looked askance on the use of the *herem.* They felt that whatever practical benefit was derived was offset by the sin committed by those who ignored it. But there was no question about the magic-religious power of the *herem.* It may be assumed that even those individuals who ignored it did not deny its validity nor make light of it in principle. They probably simply found some way of excusing their conduct and proving that the ban did not really apply to their particular action.

The matter of the ban is a further illustration of what has been said previously—that even in places where public leadership was in lay hands, the basic instruments of government relied on concepts deriving validity from their connection with religion. The question of the right to impose the ban was the subject of constant dispute between lay and rabbinic leaders. Yet even in places where this was clearly a lay prerogative, the execution of the ban and especially supervision over its implementation were entrusted to the religious experts, the halakhic scholars. The latter were consulted on whether a particular ban applied to a given matter or activity. It was they who determined the scope of the non-rational ban by the rationalist means of thought at their disposal.

The surrender of criminals to the non-Jewish authorities was typical of Jewish society from another aspect: it was independent only to the extent permitted by the surrounding society. Inasmuch as individual Jews also played a role—particularly in the economic sphere—in the non-Jewish world, the laws and rules of conduct accepted in that society also applied to them. Anyone who violated these laws would fall into the hands of the non-Jewish authorities. He could not escape to the internal Jewish society, and his co-religionists had no right of appeal against the punishment meted out to him.

On the other hand, a Jew was liable to fall into the clutches of the authorities through the arbitrary action of the rulers or false charges by the public. In such cases, the Jewish society felt itself in duty bound to do all in its power to rescue the individual.

This situation securely bound the individual Jew to his society. When the Jewish society withdrew its protection, he was utterly abandoned to his fate. Indeed, in warnings to the public about fair play in dealings with the gentiles, the threat that the Jewish community would not intercede in such cases was occasionally expressed. Such a warning was apparently much more effective than any number of threats of punishment by the Jewish courts themselves. In more serious cases, not only did the society reserve the right not to defend the individual, but to surrender the criminal to the authorities, even where this was certain to result in the imposition of the death penalty. This was a final and extreme disciplinary measure, and the same moral problem applied here as it did elsewhere with relation to the use of physical force in the service of the state: the paradox that the use of force by individuals is prevented by the community through the use of force as an unavoidable measure in time of necessity. The same was true of Jewish society in resorting to this extreme measure. It maintained the prohibition against appealing to the gentile authorities and their courts and it defended its members from arbitrary action on their part. But it succeeded in this only by reserving for itself the right to make use of the forbidden instrument.

Be that as it may, the sanction for surrendering an individual to the non-Jewish authorities when this proved necessary was defended by the recognized halakhic scholars and was even employed by them on occasion. This sanction served as a final instrument of intimidation and compulsion in the hands of the *kehillot* precisely in restraining the conduct of individual Jews in non-Jewish society where it was liable to have grave results for the entire community.

XI

The Composition of the Kehilla

*T*HE AVERAGE *kehilla* WAS COMPOSED OF THE permanent residents of the locality, and one of its prerogatives was the granting of the right of domicile to newcomers. At any rate, every *kehilla* aspired to win this prerogative from the authorities on whom its political and legal autonomy depended. The liberality with which the *kehilla* granted residential rights depended, first, on the terms it had received from the state. The non-Jewish authorities usually limited the number of Jews entitled to residence. The *kehilla* also considered the economic aspect: would a greater population lead to excessive competition or would it act as a spur to business prosperity? In most places during this period, the former view prevailed. To be sure, much depended on

[103]

the nature of the individual applicant. The *kehilla* was interested
in attracting men of wealth who would help it meet its obligations.
The poor were sometimes persuaded, or pressured, to relinquish
their residential rights. Outstanding scholars were not bound by
the laws governing residential rights, and, in theory, they might
settle wherever they wished.

When an individual lived in a place as a temporary resident,
he was regarded as a stranger (*nochri*) so long as the *kehilla* did
not grant him the privilege of permanent residence (*hezkat ha-
yishuv*). Such a stranger did not enjoy the "political" rights of
the members of the *kehilla;* he was not included among the participants in its government, either as an elector or candidate for
office. Even the "civil" rights accorded to temporary residents—
the freedom to trade and religious privileges such as being called
up to the Torah on certain occasions (*hiyuvim*)—were not identical with those enjoyed by full-fledged residents. On the other
hand, the stranger did not share the public financial burden, at
least not on the same basis as residents but through special agreement with the *kehilla* leaders. A stranger would achieve the status
of householder by the formal inclusion of his name in the *kehilla*
register; moreover, this often came about haphazardly, particularly in the new *kehilla*'s early stages of existence. Upon achieving
his new status, the householder would undertake to bear his share
of the *kehilla*'s expenses and, in most cases, would even pay an
initial sum, as a kind of advance payment.

The right of domicile was a personal one retained by the
householder so long as he maintained his residence in the place.
But even if he moved to another town, he might continue to re-
tain his right to domicile in the old *kehilla* and to bear part of that
community's expenses to the extent required by custom or by special agreement. Leaving a place unconditionally resulted in the
cancellation of residential rights after a year or more, depending
on local custom. Inasmuch as *hezkat ha-yishuv* involved obligations as well as privileges, it was sometimes in the interest of the

individual leaving the *kehilla* to hasten the severance of his ties in order to advance the date of his release from payment of taxes. Against such cases, the rule was adopted that a person moving out of a town must continue to share the *kehilla*'s expenses for a certain period—a year or two. Occasionally, the right to leave was made conditional on guarantees that the person concerned would continue to honor his obligations from abroad. In other places, this future obligation could be discharged by payment of a fixed sum that the person was required to pay before leaving the town. Under the law, a person might not be prevented from leaving his *kehilla*, but we know of attempts to bind individuals to the place by means of an oath that they would not abandon the members of the *kehilla*. For occasionally the existence of the *kehilla*, particularly in small communities, was dependent on the continued residence of a few wealthy men—sometimes even of one.

An individual's right of residence extended, as a matter of course, to the members of his family and to domestic servants insofar as their maintenance was not restricted by regulations applying to all members of the community. But the concept "members of the family" required some sort of limitation. For, as we shall see in our discussion of the family structure, relatives of varying degrees of closeness occasionally joined the basic nucleus of the family during this period. The *kehilla* was compelled to protect itself against the illegal penetration of individuals through the aegis of their relatives residing there. In any case, there was never any doubt that immediate relatives were included in a person's residential rights. Sons and daughters, step-children or parents of husband or wife—in short, all relatives for whose support Jewish law required one to provide—were entitled to join the household even though they had never lived in the place before. The inclusion of members of the family in the privilege of residence simply meant that they had the right to join the domicile of the holder of the privilege.

The transfer of the privilege was quite a different matter. The right to reside in a place could be transferred only to one's sons and daughters, and even here, it was not absolute or unconditional. However, the rule did exist that children of householders were entitled to demand the right of residence for themselves even if they had formerly dwelt elsewhere, on condition that they did not delay the exercise of their right beyond the period accepted by custom or stipulated in the regulations—generally two or three years after marriage. But at times, the *kehilla* restricted even the rights of a householder to have all his children marry and settle down in the place. The right depended on the size of the dowry the father was able to bestow on his children.

We now turn to the question of the renewal of appointments, that is, the changes and reshuffles which took place in the *kehilla* leadership—a process of fluctuation experienced by every social structure.

The outstanding feature of the *kehilla* institutions was that no position, high or low, was granted for life and none, certainly, was hereditary. The rabbi and *shtadlan* (interceder with the gentile authorities) were appointed for fixed terms. It is true that these periods could be renewed, there being no requirement that the incumbent resign after his term expired, but the decision was left to the persons charged with filling these appointments. Sextons, scribes, and other minor office-holders were sometimes appointed for an unlimited period, but in any case, they were essentially subordinates. Their appointments could be voided as a punishment for malfeasance or for disobeying the orders of their superiors. The higher officials, however, could not be dismissed during their term of office, since no disciplinary measures applied to them. But their attachment to the positions was limited in that their appointments terminated after a specific period.

The sociological aim of these arrangements is obvious: the periodic replacement of office-holders served as a barrier against an individual's monopolizing office either as a source of livelihood or power. Limiting the period of service or of the retention of the appointment militated to a certain extent against abuse. In the absence of any effective bodies for the control of the activities of the leaders, the change of officials every few years was of primary public importance. By-laws were most strict about the prompt holding of the annual (biennial or triennial in the super-*kehilla*) elections. This regular election timetable was strictly adhered to even in places where the circle of candidates was limited. But public interest in the replacement of office-holders did not derive merely from the aspirations of their prospective successors. It was a matter of concern to the entire community. The changeover in itself guaranteed that the office-holders would take public opinion into account, and it symbolized in the eyes of the community the fact that the governing authorities derived their mandate from the people.

The qualifications demanded for public office were various. For clerks and other minor officials, we find no explicit restrictions. Selection was left to the discretion of those making the appointment. The requirements for the rabbi included the endorsement of his own teacher, or other sages, or of the state rabbis; in addition, the decision depended on personal qualities showing him to be able to serve as head of the yeshiva, judge, and general spiritual leader. In many places, one restriction applied to the choice of a rabbi that had nothing to do with his personal qualifications, namely that he not be related to any of the local householders. This restriction was not universal. It was adopted to the degree that the rabbi attained a central position in the life of the *kehilla* as a judicial and interpreting authority. In such cases, it was imperative that the rabbi stand above the conflicts between different cliques of householders competing for leadership.

A person's eligibility for office in general and for the rabbinate in particular, as well as for posts in the super-*kehilla*, depended, first of all, on his age. This was generally calculated from the time of marriage rather than from the date of birth; such a system was made possible by the custom of early marriage. The minimum age rose with the importance of the position, and regulations were promulgated particularly with regard to raising the minimum age for rabbis and officials in the super-*kehilla*. But even where no explicit regulations existed, it is quite certain that public posts were entrusted only to mature persons. The traditional character of the society made it imperative that public positions be given only to persons who had already absorbed the tradition and could represent it before the new generation.

Indeed, there were places where advancement to the higher positions was made conditional on previous service on lower levels. This slow rise not only ensured the gradual acquisition of experience in dealing with public affairs but facilitated selective promotion. The successful performance of one's duties was evidence of ability to handle a more responsible post.

These two restrictions—age and previous experience—did not, however, operate as absolute barriers to a person's rise. Opposed to these were two other principles of exclusion that possessed far-reaching social significance: the restrictions based on property and on scholarship. Every person who enjoyed residential rights was regarded as a householder. But this right did not automatically include electoral privileges. For these, one had to be a tax-payer, that is, a property owner who was issued an assessment at the fixed time and who participated in all the *kehilla*'s expenditures in proportion to the amount of his property. But rate-paying in itself was not enough to open the door to appointments of every rank; the amount of the tax paid was also a consideration. In many places, taxpayers were divided into categories, generally three, each one of which was entitled to clearly-defined privileges. Appointments of the highest level, such as *parnassim* (the *kehilla*'s executive officers) were open only to persons in the upper tax bracket. The connection between privilege and wealth was not questioned during this period, although persons of limited means tried to weaken the link between the two, while the wealthy strove to strengthen it.

However, the "plutocratic" nature of these regulations was attenuated somewhat by the practice of treating a certain level of scholarship as a substitute for wealth—albeit not an absolute one. As we shall see, persons learned in the Torah acquired the titles of *haver* and *moreinu*. Possession of these titles served, to a certain extent, as the equivalent of the property qualifications required in some appointments. This custom, of course, was of immense social significance, and we shall devote some attention to it in Chapter XIX on the hierarchical pattern of society.

In no place were there direct elections where an electorate chose from those eligible for office. Appointments were invariably made by a five or seven-man selection committee (*m'vor'rim*) who, by majority vote, chose the candidate they considered most suitable for the position. Electoral rights were exercised in taking part in the establishment of this selection committee, itself elected directly by all eligible voters or indirectly by an electoral committee picked by the electorate. Where householders were divided into categories according to the amount of taxes they paid, the higher classes were given preference by the inclusion of a larger number of persons from those classed among the list of eligible candidates.

Two principles governed election procedure: that of chance in the establishment of the selection committee; and that of individual evaluation in the direct selection of the officials. The system was thus rational in part. Chance operated in that the members of the selection committee were chosen by lot, and "heavenly" determination was relied upon. But in the appointments made by the selection committee, it was the good judgment of the selectors that was relied upon. The committee members generally were required to swear that they would be answerable to heaven, would be impartial, and would choose only qualified persons. In this way, a relatively large circle of persons was given

a sense of participation in the elections, while the possibility of
being elected was limited to those who, in the general estimation
of the public, were worthy of the office. Be that as it may, this
system was able to fulfill the sociological function of instilling in
the members of the *kehilla* the feeling that it was they who determined who would lead them. Despite the tenuous connection
between the act of the voters and the results of the elections, it
was enough to maintain the consciousness of participation in determining the composition of the *kehilla*'s management. Although
the number of persons qualified to hold office was limited, the
elections were regarded as events of the utmost importance. A
struggle for the support of the voters was carried on in most of
the *kehillot*, and the suspense over the results of the elections
persisted till the last moment. Even though office-holders were
elected time and again from among the same limited circle, the
competition between them stimulated public vigilance.

The *kehilla*'s leadership was likely to become completely rigid
if a closed clique of persons bound by primary ties retained the
offices in their hands for a considerable length of time. The close
family ties that were maintained even between distant relatives
in Jewish society were the chief danger of the formation of such
rigid social cells. This explains the care taken by the *kehillot* to
prevent the election of members of one family to positions which
involved dealings with one another. Indeed, rules designed to keep
a distance between members of one family were included in the
by-laws of all *kehillot* and other public organizations, and the differences between the cliques sometimes revolved around this very
question: should the rules designed to keep members of one
family from monopolizing public offices be tightened or relaxed.
Leadership was also likely to become permanently concentrated
in the hands of individuals if they were appointed not by the community itself but by the external authorities. Opposition to the
acceptance of appointments by the ruling power, with which we
dealt in a previous chapter, must also be attributed to the ap-

prehension that there would be no time limit to the term of office of an executive who had achieved his office in this way.

The same danger faced the political independence of the community in which the leader gained his position as a result of his economic advantage when most of the community was economically dependent on one wealthy man. These dangers materialized particularly when they were augmented by the fact that the personage who enjoyed influence with the gentile authorities was also the richest man in the community. This applied especially towards the end of the period of the political independence of the *kehillot*, as we shall see in the last stage of our study.

XII   *Inter-Kehilla Relations*

*I*N THE PREVIOUS CHAPTERS WE DESCRIBED THE
kehilla as the organizational and self-governing unit of the Jewish
community within the confines of a single city. To fill in the
picture we should add that direct membership in the *kehilla* of
the city was not the only expression of the individual's attachment to the *kehilla*. Many *kehillot* included individuals who
lived in near-by villages. The individual living in an isolated
village was anxious to link himself to the community and its
institutions, and the same was true of the group too small to
enable it to maintain communal institutions of its own. Owing to
their distance from the *kehilla* center, such persons were not in
a position to take an active part in the work of the *kehilla* institu-

tions, nor did they enjoy all the benefits that would have accrued to them had they lived in town. But the most essential services were made available to them despite their geographical distance from the main body of the *kehilla*. All measures the *kehilla* could take to defend its members against slander and persecution were extended to the village dwellers as well. Religious needs—public worship, religious education for the children, the arrangement of marriage and divorce, kosher food—were supplied to the villagers despite the difficulties involved. The wish to have a Jewish burial was, in itself, likely to impel the individual to preserve his ties with the *kehilla*, which was in a position to ensure him those rites.

The *kehilla* and its representatives also had good reasons for wanting outsiders to join their organization. The village residents undertook to bear their share of the public financial load, and their contribution helped in the establishment of the *kehilla* institutions. Paid or subsidized functionaries of the *kehilla*—the rabbi, the preacher, and the head of the yeshiva—benefited from an increase in potential patrons. Even when they had no expectation of personal benefit, communal leaders were interested in any enlargement of their *kehilla* that would redound to its glory.

The aspirations of both the *kehilla* leadership and the residents of adjoining villages developed along the same lines until the villagers became so numerous that they began to think about establishing communal institutions of their own. When matters reached this stage, a clash of interests was likely to arise, wherein the *kehilla* leadership would invoke the status quo and the villagers would claim that their distance from the *kehilla* institutions deprived them of their full share of the benefits due them. Controversies of this sort were even likely to be brought before rabbinic scholars for a ruling. The same was true when two *kehillot* quarreled over the jurisdiction of villages located between them. But since there was no clear legal basis for decisions in such cases, such struggles were essentially political. The function of the court was, therefore, to reach a compromise rather than to enforce its own judgment. An exception was the super-*kehilla* court, the authority of which both parties were obligated to accept.

Another expression of individual attachment to an organization was the regional union of village dwellers in a "state" (*medina*). This link possessed only some characteristics of the *kehilla*. *Medinot* were prevalent in the German principalities, where the bulk of the Jewish population was dispersed in villages and small towns and where there was no large central *kehilla*. In the nature of things, these organizations were in a position to look after the administrative side of *kehilla* life only: the allocation and collection of taxes and the maintenance of a state rabbi in the largest *kehilla*. The state rabbi would act as judge, arrange marriages and divorces, and supervise the ritual slaughterers, but in all matters pertaining to everyday life in the *kehillot* he could act only on a most limited scale.

It is precisely the curtailed activity of these organizations that testifies to the almost absolute attachment of the individual to the *kehilla* institutions. Even if individuals were unable to meet all their needs in these institutions, they still found it worthwhile to maintain them for those services which were supplied. The desire of the rulers to bind all their Jewish citizens together into one unit and collect the taxes due from them in a centralized manner, facilitated the establishment and perpetuation of the organizations. But even this desire shows that the Jewish community, scattered and divided as it was, still constituted a single public entity, the members of which were unable to form any association except with one another.

Having described the various types of *kehilla* units or organizations, let us examine their inter-relation. Every *kehilla*, of the city as well as the state, constituted an autonomous unit of organization. No obligatory ties existed between one community and another. The members of the *kehilla* came under the jurisdiction of the community's executive both when they were within the *kehilla* area and outside of it; whereas with strangers, the *kehilla*'s authority applied only when they were within its confines. Decisions of one *kehilla* were not binding on those who happened to be members of another. But this was purely a legal distinction. Certainly not all the needs of the community could be met within the framework of the local *kehilla*. In the economic, family, and educational spheres, the members of one *kehilla* were dependent on those in others. Even the *kehilla* organizations themselves found co-operation with one another necessary where considerations of collective security prevailed. Pressure and exploitation by the authorities in libels and pogroms were not, as a rule, localized in a single *kehilla*. In such cases, it was vitally necessary to join forces. Indeed, representatives of different communities consulted each other and called emergency conferences though no regular organizational instruments had been formed between the various *kehillot*.

Kehillot were likewise called upon to assist one another in the event of natural disasters—of which fire was the most usual—and to cover the costs of ransoming prisoners. All this was demanded and granted out of a feeling of national unity, as well as on the basis of the common destiny that welded together all the scattered sections of the nation. This reciprocity was of a spontaneous nature. The obligation to extend aid was made legally binding when it might be reasonably supposed that the danger facing one community was likely to strike directly at others as well. In any event, this legal obligation, which was first promulgated by Rabbi Joseph Colon in the second half of the fifteenth century, was generally accepted and enforced.

Reciprocal relations between *kehillot* were also maintained in the sphere of internal defense against religious deviators. The outstanding example of this was the war against the Sabbatian sect in the period after their leader's apostasy (1666). The battle was carried on mainly by the leaders of the communities—rabbis and laymen alike. They collected evidence, penned the proclamations, pronounced the ban, and imposed punishment on transgressors. These proclamations were not addressed to the members of one *kehilla* alone, but to Jewish public opinion in general. This was based on the simple assumption that, where violations of the principles of Judaism were concerned, there was no geographical limit to the authority of the individual community. This same feeling of unity resounded in the last decades of the eighteenth century in the proclamations of the opponents of Hasidism which, for the most part, were also issued by the heads of the *kehillot*.

An actual expression of the feeling of super-*kehilla* unity was evident not only where the public was battling against a deviationist minority, but also where a controversy broke out among the leaders of the communities, particularly between rabbis who issued religious rulings, and where one side accused the other of an erroneous decision. Such controversies were likely to break out between the rabbis of a single town so long as no clear hierarchy existed and one rabbi was not obligated to accept the opinions of the other. Once a controversy did break out, it generally spread beyond the limits of the *kehilla*, for almost invariably one or both parties would take the case to halakhic authorities in other places. In the nature of things, there was slight chance of obtaining a uniform opinion from all the scholars consulted, for the controversy generally turned on questions where the halakhic sources left room for doubt. An authoritative decision could be handed down only by an institution or personality whose superiority was clearly recognized.

However, no such over-all rabbinic institution was established, and no one halakhic scholar was recognized as the supreme authority of his generation—except metaphorically speaking in laudatory addresses. On the contrary, the multiplicity of organizations characteristic of our period was paralleled by the galaxy of rabbinic scholars who functioned side by side, none of them succeeding in imposing his authority on the others. This explains the large number of controversies stemming from differences in rulings on religious law overlaid with the casuistry found necessary to justify them. This situation precluded an unequivocal decision in all cases of doubt.

Occasionally, of course, a personal element was added to the theoretical dispute, almost precluding any possibility of compromise. Essentially, however, this legal controversy should be regarded as the expression of the paradoxical situation of a society whose component parts were connected with one another by a bond of law and justice but had no binding organic expression of unity.

In the absence of an institution authorized to rule in every case of uncertainty, only moral force stood behind the appeals against questioning rulings issued by the court of another city. A good example is the edict of Rabbenu Tam (twelfth century), which, on pain of excommunication, stipulated that the legality of a bill of divorce which had already gone into effect should not be questioned. This edict was proclaimed with the explicit intention of ensuring the indestructible validity of an act completed by the authority of a court. But, despite the dread of the *herem* and the great reverence for the sage who first proclaimed it, there was no end to the appeals and controversies which turned on the legality of a bill of divorce already delivered. This was sometimes the reason for disputes between the scholars of one *kehilla* when the authority of one central court was not established and several rabbis exercised the function of issuing divorces.

In inter-*kehilla* relations, this breach between rabbinic and court authority was never closed. In the first place, the competitive factor operated even where the courts of different *kehillot* were concerned. The competition was for economic reasons or for prestige, since the issuing of divorces constituted an important source of income for the rabbis. However, even if the rabbis were completely free of selfish motives and of any desire to surpass their colleagues in halakhic learning, controversies were still liable to arise. The prohibition against appealing the decision of a court which had already been implemented was counter-balanced by the obligation to avoid the pitfall of permitting something actually forbidden and thereby being responsible for children's illegitimacy in case a woman remarried on the strength of an invalid bill of divorce. Here we arrive at the heart of the matter.

The right (and duty) of a rabbi in one city to contest the action of a colleague somewhere else was based on two assumptions. The first had to do with the legal nature of the *halakha* which, as revealed religious law, was subject only to clarification and not to change. The task of the rabbi was to discover the law which applied to the case before him. If he erred in the law, his ruling was null and void, regardless of his formal authority or his position as rabbi of the community. If, therefore, it appeared to his colleague that he really had erred, it was his duty to contest it and thus prevent a miscarriage of justice and its repercussions. This obligation to demur, which in theory had no geographical or organizational limitation, was the second assumption.

The mutual responsibility for maintaining the Torah was not subject to any geographical restriction. There was only a gradation of responsibility; those nearest the scene of action were vested with the primary obligation to rectify the error. Indeed, the prevalent view was that, in the first instance, the court closest in proximity had the duty to protest, but after that, it was the duty of authorities anywhere. On the basis of this postulate, the protagonists in halakhic controversies sometimes succeeded in drawing scholars of distant countries into the argument. In any case, until the dissolution of the traditional structure towards the end of the eighteenth century, the scholars of one state never contested the right of their counterparts anywhere to intervene. National unity was maintained in this period without being undermined, at least so far as matters of faith and religion were concerned.

The *kehilla* was apparently entitled to demand absolute autonomy in all that pertained to "money matters," that is, political, economic, and legal rights which were the subject of most of the regulations. Indeed, this autonomy found its expression in the privileges granted to the local residents over "strangers" who lived in the place or happened to be staying there. It never entered anyone's mind to demand equal economic rights for every Jew who happened to be staying in a particular city. In any case, this autonomy did not mean that the *kehilla* might deal as it pleased with members of other *kehillot*. The legal tradition that empowered the *kehilla* to promulgate regulations for the benefit of the local residents also set forth minimum rights and protection for persons from other places.

Developments in the Jewish legal tradition of the Middle Ages were not calculated to undermine the all-embracing national basis of the original talmudic law. The social structure during the sixteenth to the eighteenth centuries, particularly in Poland, was quite similar to that of talmudic times. Once again we find dense Jewish settlements, relatively differentiated occupationally, maintaining close social and economic ties between their various parts, and, to a large extent, basing their income on that fact. Mere mention of the increasing mobility of the basic classes in this society is sufficient: the tradesmen who met at fairs; the young men who wandered from one yeshiva to another; the itinerant preachers; and the beggars, who were considered a veritable plague on the populace. The sense of unity inspiring the different parts of the nation, which was not impaired even in the Middle Ages, now found support in economic and social realities.

In the legal realm, these realities found expression in the multiplicity of claims and counter-claims between members of different *kehillot*. Which court had jurisdiction over such cases,

the court in the plaintiff's city or that in the defendant's? Did
the litigants have the right to take the case before a neutral
court, and, if so, what should be the nature of such a court?
These questions were not adequately thrashed out and remained
unanswered in the legal tradition of the period even in theory.
In the absence of a common framework of enforcement for the
two cities involved in a particular case, the difficulty in achieving
satisfaction from a lawsuit was even greater. For this reason,
they used to resort, even in the Middle Ages, to the doubtful measure of sequestering the property of the defendant—deposits or
loans which were in the hands of others—in order to compel
him to stand trial in the plaintiff's city or in the place where the
property was located.

In a period of interlocking economic ties, when the business
of capitalists was based on the transfer of merchandise from
place to place and on the acceptance of obligations with regard
to the anonymous market, this legal uncertainty represented
an unbearable impediment. It is thus no wonder that people
looked to super-*kehilla* bodies, which were in a position to ensure stable legal arrangements between parties who had constant
economic dealings with one another. Always available, of course,
was the external government and its courts of law, to which the
members of the outlying *kehillot* might address their petitions.
But since this solution came up against the unquestioned
national-religious inhibition, it was essential that the deciding
body be found within the Jewish society itself.

Talmudic tradition itself supplied the concepts necessary for
a solution. This tradition included the notions of *bet din gadol*
(high court) and *bet va'ad* (house of assembly) to which,
under certain conditions, individuals who refused to accept the
decision of the local court might appeal. The source of these
concepts lay in the political organization that obtained in Palestine and Babylonia, where the *bet va'ad* and the *bet din gadol*
were judicial institutions enjoying real power of enforcement.

The need to ensure the fulfilment of agreements, on which a credit-based economy depends, led to efforts to establish permanent institutions within a broader framework. These efforts were, in fact, successful in every place where the non-Jewish authorities did not deliberately set up obstacles to the formation of fixed judicial institutions. This was the case in Germany, for example, where the attempt of the Frankfurt Assembly of 1603 to lay the foundations for such a judicial organization came to naught as a result of the spread of false rumors about its intentions. But this precise incident proves that, in places where super-*kehilla* organizations were set up, the impetus for them could not be given by the ruling powers even where they made use of the organizations for their own purposes and sometimes even directly facilitated their establishment. Even where that was their deliberate intention, the authorities were incapable of creating something out of nothing. The organizations were founded on the basis of Jewish legal concepts and the Jewish public consciousness. The outside rulers could help or hinder, but that was all. The emergence of super-*kehilla* organizations may be traced to the need for organizational unity evinced by a society which, on the one hand, avoided resort to the state institutions, and, on the other, maintained increasingly closer contact between its own component parts.

XIII

Super-Kehilla Organizations

$\mathcal{B}$EGINNING WITH THE SIXTEENTH CENTURY, super-*kehilla* organizations began to emerge in the different countries of central Europe, in some parts of the German Empire, and in the Polish-Lithuanian state. They continued to function until the second half of the eighteenth century. Every organization underwent a metamorphosis of its own, and each, in itself, could serve as a fruitful subject of inquiry. But outside individual variations, we find features common to all of them, springing from the similarity in the factors leading to their formation. The conditions of existence, the functional pattern, the institutional structure, and the system of operation were similar. We are, therefore, justified in trying to abstract

[122]

the essential historical social nature of the *medina* (literally, "state," the term applied to this super-*kehilla* organization) and to trace its development—to the extent that this was not the result of special circumstances but of a relation of fixed forces which operated along the same lines in every case.

By way of summary, let us list the principal facts which call for analysis. Super-*kehilla* organizations functioned from the second half of the sixteenth century to the first half of the eighteenth in Poland, Lithuania, Moravia, and western Hungary. The area covered by these organizations was called a *galil* (district) or *medina,* and these names were also applied to the organization itself. The organizational structure differed from place to place. In some places, the representatives of the communities which comprised a super-*kehilla* chose a committee to function in the name of the whole. This was the practice in Poland and Moravia.

In Lithuania, all the *kehillot* within a given district were subject to the leadership of the principal *kehilla* in all matters pertaining to the central management of the district; they did participate in the establishment of its operative institutions. In practice, the leadership of the principal *kehilla* and that of the district were identical.

In any event, the unity of the *kehillot* found both actual and symbolical expression in the personality of the *rav ha-medina* (the rabbi of the super-*kehilla*) or the *av bet din* (the chief rabbi of the principal *kehilla*), to whom all the *kehillot* were subject, in principle at least. The merging of the *kehillot* into a district unit constituted the first stage in overcoming their tendency to split up. But where a number of such districts existed within the area of a single kingdom, the *kehillot* united among themselves and thus arrived at a broader unit or organization— the *medina.*

In Moravia, the *medina* consisted of three districts; in Lithuania, of three to five; and in Poland, from four to ten.

The increase in the number of districts in the period in question is an indication of the rise in population and the consolidation of new centers in the super-*kehilla*. The operative institutions of these organizations were always bodies elected by representatives of the organizational units which they included.

Since both the *gelilot* and the *medinot* were internal Jewish units of self-government, their formation and existence were conditioned by factors on which we dwelt in our description of the *kehilla*. In the first place, the super-*kehilla* organizations existed only by the grace of the ruling authorities. The European state of the sixteenth century was based on the existence of estates, each one of which appeared, and occasionally was even represented vis-a-vis the central government, as a political and social unit in itself. Thus, the recognition of the Jewish social unit as organized in the super-*kehilla* did not involve any unique concession. On the contrary, it represented a degree of rationalization which the leadership of the state achieved in this period, wherein the respective estates were responsible for the conduct of their internal affairs.

The state demanded merely the specific participation of each class in the political burden. The particular Jewish contribution lay in the payment of taxes in cash. These taxes were not paid by individuals but by the collective representation of the community. Where only the local organization of the *kehilla* existed, it was that body which bore responsibility for the payment of taxes to the authorities. But where the *kehillot* were united under a common roof, it was convenient even for the state to have direct contact with the central body. In return for accepting the responsibility for payment of the Jewish taxes *en bloc*, this organization was accorded a degree of political power which otherwise would have been vested only in the local *kehilla*.

In the relations between the state and the super-*kehilla* organization, the determination of reciprocal rights and obligations required constant attention. Subjects of recurrent negotiation between them were the amount of taxes, the acceptance of special obligations, and the answering for the actions of individuals or groups in the Jewish community; also discussed were the protests from Jews in defence of granted rights, in protest against arbitrary action by government officials, and efforts to prevent encroachments by the authorities on the organization's autonomy.

Having listed the conditions that governed the formation of these organizations, let us turn to a description of their internal structure. Formally, the structure of the *medina* was evidently similar to that of the *kehilla*. The super-*kehilla* was headed by lay leaders or wardens (*parnassim*) chosen by representatives of the committees or the districts in the same way that wardens were elected in the *kehilla* by the local householders. Elections to committees of the *medina* were no different from those of the *kehilla*. In some places, the selection committee which chose the *kehilla* officials also appointed persons to represent the *kehilla* in the over-all organization; all such representatives together formed the executive body of the super-*kehilla*. In other places, the *kehilla* representatives nominated leaders from among their own number who would serve as heads of the *medina*. The former procedure was widespread in Lithuania and Poland—in the districts and the Council of the Four Lands; the latter was practiced in Moravia. Appointments to the super-*kehilla*, like those in the *kehilla*, were honorary posts with no financial recompense. Accordingly, personal wealth was an important factor in determining a candidate's eligibility. In principle, office holders were not entitled to derive material advantage from their positions, though they were reimbursed for their expenses from organizational funds.

In addition to the lay leadership, at the head of every organization was the *rav ha-medina* or *av bet din*, who exercised religious-halakhic authority. In the Council of the Four Lands and the Lithuanian *medina*, the rabbinical leadership was composed of a committee of rabbis each of whom enjoyed equal authority. The division of power between the lay leadership and the rabbis was likewise very similar to that obtaining in the *kehillot*. The executive committee of the super-*kehilla* decided on the internal and external political measures to be taken. It was they who distributed the tax burden and special levies, again through assessment committees as in the *kehillot*. The regulations adopted by the committee assemblies were occasionally the work of persons especially appointed for the purpose. In any case, the regulations were formulated with the consent of the lay leaders. The same was true of the regulations which dealt with such religious questions as prohibited foods, Sabbath observance, and the prohibition of usury. Regulations of this sort could be formulated only by outstanding scholars and, in general, they are attributable to the rabbi or rabbis of the super-*kehilla*. But even these regulations were proclaimed in the name of the leaders of the super-*kehilla* who, like the lay leaders of the *kehillot*, recognized their obligation to champion the principles of religious law. Indeed, there was no clear-cut dichotomy between the lay and rabbinical authorities: the wardens assisted in ensuring the dominance of religion in public life; and they were assisted by the rabbis, the paramount representatives of religion, in maintaining the regulations in other spheres.

Differences sometimes did occur between rabbinic and lay leaders who governed the super-*kehilla*. Even outright protests by the rabbis against actions of the wardens were not unknown. However, the mutual dependence of the two authorities, and the fact that the occupants of the positions in both cases belonged to the same social class, were sufficient to keep such conflicts to a minimum. In their public proclamations, the lay leaders and rabbis appeared practically as a single entity. The rabbis did not hesitate to sign regulations pertaining to economic or political matters. But even where they did not sign, so long as they made no protest, the lay leaders were entitled to assume that their deeds had the approval of religious authority.

The lay leaders had a purpose in employing religious concepts in making their proclamations, and occasionally they even made use of the ban—an instrument of religious authority— without enlisting the active participation of its official representatives.

The rabbis enjoyed an independent position in the structure of the *medina*—as they did in the *kehilla*—to the extent that they served as judges who issued halakhic rulings in the broad sense which we discussed in Chapter X. The fact that the rabbis were bound by the halakhic sources served as a guarantee of their ability to rise above vested interests, including those of the *kehillot* where they functioned as rabbis throughout the year. Theirs was the court of last resort in all inter-*kehilla* and inter-district disputes. The very existence of a central court of this kind epitomized the unification of the *kehillot* into one over-all body.

Our discussion of the similarity of the structures of the *kehilla* and the super-*kehilla*, however, should not overshadow the great differences in their operative methods. If we consider the limited number of paid officials in the super-*kehilla* in proportion to the scope of the field for which, in principle, it was responsible, we shall begin to understand the difference between the two organizations. The super-*kehilla* maintained a permanent staff only to the extent that this was necessary to keep in contact with the external authorities, to collect taxes, to do the bookkeeping, etc. The judicial function which constituted an important foundation in the life of the *medinot* was exercised only periodically— whenever there was a fair or conference. Only in Moravia do we find indications of constant judicial activity by the heads of the *medina*, either in conjunction with rabbinic leaders or without them.

To perform its functions, the *medina* employed, first of all, the *shtadlan*, who acted as deputy of the *parnassim* in dealings with the authorities. Others were the *ne'eman* (trustee), the *sofer* (scribe), and the *shamash* (attendant). The first two worked as bookkeepers and clerks, and handled the records of the committee. To the extent that the activities were seasonal, even the scribes and the attendants were employed only during the committee sessions and during fairs.

The size of this staff was infinitesimal in comparison with the scope and nature of the decisions issued by the *medinot*. As a matter of fact, we find that most of the *medina*'s decisions were not imposed on its own institutions but on those of the *kehillot*. It should be borne in mind that for most of the year, the *medina* was hardly more than a theoretical concept. After the committee adjourned, the *medina* leaders dispersed to their respective communities. Though they bore such high-sounding titles as *rosh medina* ("head of state"), *rosh galil* ("head of district"), *manhig va'ad arba aratzot* ("leader of the Council of the Four Lands") and that they had to report to the next session of the committee on the implementation of its decisions, their report would turn principally on what had been done or left undone by the *kehillot* and not on the state of affairs of the executive committee of the *medina*. The task of the super-*kehilla* leaders, insofar as most decisions were concerned, involved control and supervision rather than direct implementation. The execution of the decisions was the task of the *kehilla* leaders, with the help of the paid officials at their disposal. The *medina* leaders only spurred *kehilla* leaders or, if necessary, reported their recalcitrance.

In the final analysis, we thus conclude that the super-*kehilla* was utterly different in nature from the *kehilla*. Whereas the *kehilla* was a self-governing unit, the super-*kehilla* was merely a federation of autonomous entities which joined together from a recognition of their unity of interests. The units which constituted the federation restricted their own freedom of action in theory, but they did not delegate to the central organization the instruments of power which would have made this self-limitation permanent and irrevocable.

The distinction between the sociological nature of the *kehilla* and the super-*kehilla* is revealed in the means of compulsion each exercised. The *kehilla*, as we have seen, made use of practically all means of punishment—from monetary fines to curtailment of freedom of movement and corporal punishment. The super-*kehilla*, it is true, also proclaimed sanctions against persons who violated its regulations. But the significance of its decisions on fines, dismissal from a post, etc., always lay in the fact that the *kehilla* institutions were required to impose, within their area of jurisdiction, the punishments decreed by the *medina* committee. It can practically be said that the power of the super-*kehilla* was verbal alone.

However, we should not underestimate, particularly in the period with which we are dealing, the power of the edicts of a recognized institution, exalted by the halo of religious authority which surrounded it. Among these edicts was the *herem*. It is true that most of the bans proclaimed by the *medinot* were not directed against specific individuals but against some anonymous transgressor. The power of such a ban was limited, serving, for the most part, as a means of intimidation rather than of punishment. When necessary, however, the leaders of the *medina* even proclaimed a ban against specific violators, either individuals or entire communities. The ban, unlike other means of compulsion, was well-adapted to the super-*kehilla*'s organizational structure. The authority proclaiming the ban did not have to carry it out; the general public was enjoined to refrain from contact with the excommunicated person or was even urged to cause him harm. The social significance of the ban lay in the fact that the person excommunicated was deprived of the protection of the institutions of government and justice.

This sanction was typical of a loose government organization which lacked its own instruments for executing punishments. Even the Council of the Four Lands, the largest super-*kehilla* organization of the period, had no means of imposing its authority directly on a recalcitrant community—if it did not wish to invoke the assistance of the government. But the very threat of removing its protection from unfair action by the authorities served as an effective means of coercion. Even more effective was the removal of the legal protection afforded the community in question in its relations with the other communities; this involved releasing debtors to that *kehilla* from payment of their debts, for example, or permitting the seizure of members' goods on the roads. No *kehilla* was capable of withstanding such measures for any period of time.

What matters could be better promoted by the *medina* than by the *kehilla?* It is worth recalling the entire complex of problems which arose, as we have seen in the previous chapter, from the fact that the Jews who were dispersed over wide areas constituted a single society—both economically and socially. An institutional solution to the problems was thus a sorely-felt need. The *medina* represented an attempt to arrive at a partial solution, at least with regard to the *kehillot* located within the territory of a single kingdom.

In the first place, the ability of the Jewish community to withstand external threats was strengthened by the existence of the national organization. A threat or a false accusation directed at an individual or a local community was ordinarily referred to the central organization. For obvious reasons, the words of *medina* representatives carried greater weight than those of local functionaries. The *medina*, in any case, enlisted the participation of all its members in rescue activity. The principle of mutual aid, which, as we have seen in the previous chapter, developed as an abstract legal principle, here received a stable organizational expression. Among the members of the *medina*, there was no need for a legal discussion to determine whether the obligation to participate applied to them. Membership in a *medina* determined the mutual responsibility in a fixed, institutional manner.

Moreover, the accumulation of power in the hands of the super-*kehilla* converted the quantitative force into a qualitative one as well. The *medina* was in a better position than the *kehillot* to muster the ablest leadership. The *medina* even succeeded easily in referring the consideration of accusations to higher authorities. The Council of the Four Lands sent an emissary to the Pope requesting a statement against blood libels—a tactic always considered desirable in combatting such false accusations.

In the legal sphere, the *medinot* enjoyed a direct advantage by virtue of the fact that they were super-*kehilla* organizations. The question of which authority should decide controversies between members of different *kehillot* and between the different *kehilla* organizations was resolved by the establishment of a central court to which both sides were subject. The central court of the *galil* or the *medina* enjoyed jurisdiction over all Jews living within its confines. The degree of actual power enjoyed by the organization depended on whether the means of compulsion at its disposal were sufficient to enforce attendance at court and obedience to its decisions. Be that as it may, the legal vacuum which had characterized the period preceding the establishment of the super-*kehilla* was eliminated. Formerly, it had been difficult for anyone with a claim outside the *kehilla* to obtain legal redress. Binding legal frameworks were created with extensive jurisdiction. They served as a guarantee for the continued close economic contact between members of different communities.

We may cite several other examples where the super-*kehilla* had the advantage over the local community, although the implementation of the regulations remained the task of the latter. The practical value of decisions issued by the super-*kehilla* sometimes lay in the very fact that they were handed down at a central place and were binding on all the *kehillot* concerned. A ruling that a particular tractate of the Talmud be taught during a given period in all the yeshivot of Poland and Moravia

served as a means of aiding the publishing houses to find a wide
market for a volume fresh from the press. But it also involved
technical aid in the central supply of educational materials, as
well as an educational policy facilitating the transfer of pupils
from one *yeshiva* to another. It is unlikely that any considerable
opposition arose to rules of this sort, the benefits of which were
obvious, but in any case, the rules could not have been issued
except by a central organization.

Other decisions pertained to the distribution of financial
responsibilities among different bodies, e.g., whether villages
which boasted no *yeshiva* should be charged with the maintenance of *yeshiva* students during vacation periods or whether
communities were obliged to accept students from other *kehillot*
or orphans from other *medinot*. Although the implementation
was the task of the very bodies who were financially affected,
the authority of the source of the decision was probably great
enough to ensure that it would be obeyed. Had it not been for
such decisions, matters of this sort would have been left to
chance—to the detriment of the students and orphans.

In other cases where implementation was the task of the
local bodies, the decision of the central organization served to
strengthen the hand of the general public against individual
arbitrariness. Even though the imposition of the prohibition
on customs farming in Poland or the control of customs tariffs
in Moravia were only in the nature of instructions to be implemented by others, they probably were not without effect. The
position of the community vis-a-vis individual upstarts was thus
strengthened, and at least a partial protection was found against
their domination.

Bolstering the authority of the *kehilla* leaders in activities
which could presumably be accomplished entirely on their own
initiative constituted a very important basis of the central
leadership of the committees. The collection of the *memremeh*,
without the legal procedure of the endorsement of the docu-

ment that the *medina* of Moravia decided on, was performed by local functionaries. The execution of these decisions called for force and occasionally even inhumanity, going as far as the quick foreclosure of the defendant's home and property. This and similar rules governing bankruptcy, which have been mentioned earlier, were issued with the aim of ensuring confidence in the economic field. However, though these economic severities were recognized as important public necessities, their actual execution was likely to encounter snags, particularly within the small community, where primary ties existed between the members and where everyone knew everyone else. The central decision that backed the continued application of these extreme measures probably served to dispel doubts and to bolster the law.

Similarly, we find decisions designed to combat individual feelings of pity where they clashed with the public welfare. The wandering of the poor from place to place was a virtual plague in the *kehillot* of Europe—in fact, in the entire European society. With the aim of limiting the movement of the poor to their own localities, the Lithuanian Council called on the *kehilla* leaders to refrain from assisting wandering mendicants and from permitting them to extend their visits. From the wording of the decision, it is clear that those who formulated it regarded Jewish compassion as the main factor inhibiting the implementation of their decisions.

We have before us a clear sociological phenomenon: within the framework of the many-faceted society there was an increasing tendency to institute principles governing internal social regulation without regard to their effect on the individual. The small society of the *kehilla* in the Middle Ages had not been capable of developing abstract principles of this sort, but neither had it required them. Now problems of this kind found their solution on the basis of a direct relationship to the cases in point. The incorporation of the isolated *kehilla* into a society possessing wide reciprocity forced the leadership to chart its course by an over-all, abstract system. Henceforth, each problem was considered as it affected the existence and welfare of the society as a whole. The fate of the individual seems to have disappeared from the view of those who formulated and executed the laws. Indeed, this was both the strength and the price of the over-all federal type of communal organization.

XIV   *The Family*

*T*HE JEWISH FAMILY IN THE PERIOD UNDER
discussion was a small one. It was composed of the marriage
nucleus of husband and wife and the children born into it or
introduced into it from a previous marriage of one or both
parties. All the members lived in one household, and the property which served as the basis for the family's existence belonged
to the father—whether considerable wealth was involved or only
the bare means of subsistence. The mother had certain rights in
the use of this property. She was entitled to make the ordinary
expenditures involved in housekeeping and to meet religious
and moral obligations such as giving the customary amount to
charity. To the extent that she shared her husband's business

activities, her word was as binding as his. In fact, there were instances where the task of providing for the family lay entirely or primarily with the wife, the husband devoting all his time to the study of Torah. The children were regarded as dependent on the will of the parents, particularly that of the father. They did not enjoy economic, legal, or political independence.

This inner family nucleus was frequently supplemented by living partners of secondary connection: the father or mother of the husband or wife or other relatives without homes of their own. The right of the parents to be supported by their children was guaranteed by custom and law. Other relatives, and occasionally even an orphan who was not related at all, were taken to live with the family as an act of charity and mercy. An intermediate position was occupied by sons- and daughters-in-law who lived with their parents-in-law for the first few years after their marriage. Though their relationship was definitely a primary one, their joining the household was based on a contract which ensured the young couple their maintenance for a predetermined number of years. A contractual relationship without any family status bound the menservants and maidservants, the cook and the wet-nurse, as well as the teacher, who was something of a private tutor. The latter was generally found in the rich homes.

We have before us a monogamous, patriarchal family structure as this developed in the urban culture of Europe. In any event, close examination reveals typically Jewish traits, both in the mode of life and in the consciousness which accompanied it. The purpose of this study is not comparative, however. We are not interested in discovering the differences between the Jewish and non-Jewish family, but in thoroughly understanding the Jewish family—its structure, functions, atmosphere, and, if we may so express it, the spirit or the ideology which gave it life.

The specific character of any given family structure is reflected in the way in which the family evolves. The Jewish family

of the period was founded by an agreement between those regarded as the natural representatives of the couple—the parents
—or, if they were no longer alive, their relatives or public guardians. No formal bond (that is, a matrimonial tie which would be
severed only by divorce) was created except by the personal act
of the couple themselves—by the man's act of betrothal and the
woman's voluntary acceptance. This tie took effect at the *huppah*
when the marriage ceremony actually occurred, in contradistinction to medieval practice, when it was still customary to make
the betrothal precede the marriage ceremony by several months
or even years. But betrothal was always preceded by the writing
of the "betrothal terms," which was an agreement in which the
parties plighted their troth and which stipulated the amount of
the dowry, the wedding date, and the place where the couple
would live. As a rule, the couple themselves had no voice whatsoever in formulating the terms of the agreement. Only in a second marriage, where the parties were independent in a domestic
sense, or, in exceptional cases, where the marriage was post-
poned until soci-economic independence was achieved, were the
betrothal terms fixed by the couple themselves. But even in such
cases, the formal signing was delegated, as a matter of courtesy,
to the parents or other representatives.

As we have said, the signing of the betrothal document did
not create matrimonial ties nor did its cancellation require a
divorce. But, in practice, the document contained guarantees of
sufficient substance to warrant regarding the future of the couple
as entirely settled upon its being signed, no less than upon their
entering into actual betrothal. In the first place, each party undertook to pay a heavy forfeit for violating the agreement—generally half the amount of the dowry. Second and more important,
the undertaking involved the acceptance of a ban regarded as "a
ban of the *kehillot*," i.e., as a decree of the Early Sages, on anyone who violated the betrothal terms and injured the good name
of the other family. The seriousness of the bond forged by the

betrothal document was supported by public opinion, which frowned on its cancellation. The writing of the document was executed at a public ceremony in the presence not only of the members of the family, but also of prominent personalities, the rabbi or preacher, a scribe, and witnesses. Anyone who violated the agreement without receiving the dispensation of a competent court not only had to suffer the consequences by paying the forfeit, but he would be held in contempt and his chances of again making a favorable match would be diminished.

The parents were given the power to make the match because the parties themselves were young, inexperienced in life, and did not know their own minds. Indeed, the tendency to arrange a marriage as early as possible was typical of the period. This tendency sprang first from the parents' desire to settle their children's future while they were still alive. But perhaps even more important than the personal, material concern was the influence of the accepted code of religion and sexual morality. All sexual contact and erotic satisfaction outside of monogamous marriage was prohibited. The ideal of sexual purity applied equally to men and women. Moreover, sinful thoughts in a man were regarded as more reprehensible than in a woman, for they might lead to nocturnal emissions and masturbation, offences for which there was practically no atonement other than difficult and bitter self-mortification. This view of sexual morality was derived from talmudic literature, and it became even more entrenched through the ethical literature of the period, which was saturated with the ideas of the Zohar and other cabalist works which are most strict on this subject.

On the other hand, that literature itself, from the Talmud and the *Midrashim* to the *musar* works, appreciated the intensity of the ordeal of sexual temptation. Talmudic Judaism is far removed both from the optimism of Catholic sexual morality, which believes in man's ability to overcome his desires, and from the glossing over of the problem and the minimizing of its importance of the liberal view. Jewish law and ethics emphasize, in no uncertain terms, that a celibate has practically no hope of withstanding the temptations of the flesh. A Jew who was bred on this outlook was left with no alternative but to arrange as early a marriage as possible both for himself or for his sons, as the case might be.

There were thus many incentives for carrying out the ideal of early marriage, and anyone who could do so fulfilled this ideal. Sixteen was considered the proper age for a girl and eighteen, at the very latest, for a boy. Parents who arranged a match—or even married off—their daughters of thirteen or fourteen or their sons of fifteen or sixteen were considered praiseworthy and were certainly not criticized. However, it would be a mistake to suppose that such early marriages were the general rule among the society as a whole. Admittedly, of course, the subjective restraints which sometimes delay the finding of a mate, where marriage is conditioned on personal attraction were absent. The great majority of matches were arranged through the agency of others, and every eligible person was open to marriage proposals, particularly from professional matchmakers.

The matchmakers' beats extended far beyond the local parish, and they often matched couples living in different countries. It is safe to say that no one with the necessary qualifications for establishing a family would find any difficulty in arranging to meet a suitable mate. The hindrances to marriage at the desirable age, or to marriage altogether, derived from these "necessary qualifications," which were more difficult to come by at times than we are likely to imagine.

The establishment of a family was regarded as the establishment of a new economic unit. Although it was customary for the newly married couple to eat at the parents' table for two years or more, this time was devoted either to further study (at home, at a *yeshiva* or at a *bet hamidrash*) or to acquiring one's first experience in business. When the specified period elapsed, the new couple left the house, or at least started to manage their own affairs while continuing to live with the parents. In order to make such economic independence possible, a sum of property was brought into the marriage by one or both parties. If the couple themselves or their parents did not have the wherewithal for this sum, they had to fall back on other sources: the generosity of relatives or wealthy donors, the funds of charitable societies which were sometimes especially earmarked for this purpose, or even the funds of the *kehilla* and super-*kehilla* organizations.

The readiness of individuals and public bodies to help in the marrying off of poor girls is evidence, in the first place, of the religious importance attached to early marriage. But this readiness is also an expression of the assumption, self-evident in this period, that entering into marriage required the ownership of means which would serve not only as the basis for establishing a home, but also as an instrument for furthering independent economic activity. The first condition for a marriage was thus the existence of an adequate endowment of property. The larger the endowment, the greater the prospects of achieving a suitably balanced match.

The marriage payment was not the only consideration in the match. The new couple had to acquire the right of domicile in one *kehilla* or another. If one of them was heir to such a right and it also passed to the spouse, this was sometimes a consideration of the first order. For the *kehilla* was often responsible for the postponement of marriages in its wish to limit the number of breadwinners in the locality, and it imposed a marriage ban for a specific period, limited the number of marriages, or made them conditional on the couple's possession of a certain amount of property. In other places, it was necessary to purchase the right of domicile from the local prefect. An undertaking to do this on the part of one of the parents constituted one of the preliminaries to the marriage agreement.

Some weight—although very limited—was placed on a good

lineage, i.e., descent from prominent scholars or other famous personages. In contrast, an apostasy or sexual irregularity in the family constituted a stain which had to be compensated for by other considerations. Finally, there were also personal considerations—the prospective groom's learning or the bride-to-be's efficiency; where a woman had had previous domestic experience or had helped, for instance, in her first husband's business, her value was increased. Some weight was attached to good looks, too, although not to as great an extent as in a society where the system of free choice in marriage prevails.

A person's eligibility could be determined both in terms of the age at which he would marry and the match he would make. Sons and daughters of the rich and scholarly ruling class might expect to find mates from the same class and at an early age, just as the ideal prescribed. The great mobility of this class is indicated by the fact that the prospective bride and groom were brought together from distant places and at times even from another country, the only limit being the social and cultural frontiers of the Jewish center concerned. The chances were slimmer that a young man or woman of the lower classes would find a mate of first rank or marry at an early age. The geographical area from which a match would be proposed to such persons was also more restricted. Their marriages were almost always with persons from the immediate locality and took place at a later age than most marriages.

But social considerations, as has been indicated, were not the only concerns. Negative or positive personal traits might decrease or increase the prospects for making a good match. Even a rich and well-educated widow or widower, a status quite common in those days of early mortality, would be content with a mate from a lower class, particularly if the widowed person was left with a number of children. This was even truer in the case of a person with a physical deformity or in whose family there was a stain of one kind or another, even through no fault of his

own. Conversely, an individual endowed with some personal
mark of distinction in scholarship, looks, or business standing
could expect to rise in the social scale through marriage. But it
was precisely such gifted individuals who were likely to defer
marriage until they had a chance to show their mettle, the tal-
ented scholar until he distinguished himself in his studies and
the commercial adventurer until he made a name for himself in
the business world. As a matter of fact, only the members of the
upper class who were outstanding in both wealth and learning
could afford the luxury of an early match without lessening their
prospects. They were ensured of a "good match" by their very
position. Members of the lower classes, however, would carefully
appraise their present and future prospects before making a decision.

Even the weight attached to the religious ideal of an early
marriage varied from family to family, depending on the intensity of its loyalty to religious values. The *musar* works reflect
this problem when they warn against postponing marriage in the
hope of making a better match later on. This problem was one
which faced the middle class in particular. The lower class, in
this respect, was dependent on factors beyond their control, such
as the generosity of others, finding a domestic position which did
not interfere with setting up a family, and obtaining a permit to
settle in a particular locality. The ideal of early marriage, in their
case, operated more through its influence on public agencies
facilitating matrimony than by any personal effort in that direction on their own part.

The outstanding feature in the attitude of members of society
towards arranging a marriage was the cold, calculated approach
with which they weighed the pros and cons. Personal compati-
bility, not to speak of romantic attachment, was not taken into
account at all. This does not imply that there were no instances
of love affairs between young people. We shall see that, in many
places, there were even opportunities for contacts of an erotic

nature, such as dances and excursions on the occasion of celebrations or holidays. Nevertheless, the erotic ideology did not support the right to choose one's mate on the basis of falling in love, even after a person had already been caught in "the web of desire." Certainly, the erotic ideology did not regard falling in love as a necessary preliminary to a matrimonial proposal. Even if it happened that the matrimonial choice, in a particular case, was made on a personal basis, a matchmaker would be employed for appearance's sake, and, in any event, the negotiations and the formulation of the betrothal document were entrusted to the parents or their substitutes. Every effort was made to give the impression that the match had been arranged in the customary way.

If a boy or girl who had fallen in love encountered parental opposition, they would give up their choice almost as a matter of course. But even if they attempted to circumvent their parents' will, they did not easily achieve their object. Situations of this kind were often echoed in the questions regarding "clandestine betrothals" which were the subject of considerable discussion in the responsa literature of the period. It was usually a case of a youth who had betrothed the girl in the presence of witnesses, without any previous official matrimonial negotiations. Public opinion censured this as an attempt by irresponsible elements to usurp the parental privilege to choose their children's marriage partner. Moreover, such surprise marriages were condemned as violations of social etiquette. In this manner, a person from the lower classes could illicitly achieve a match beyond his station.

This last consideration will help us to understand one of the reasons for the opposition to marriages based on free choice. We have before us a society based on a strict class division but which lacked adequate barriers between one class and another. Precisely because Judaism ruled that "all families are presumed to be fit" and might intermarry with one another—and in exceptional cases did so—society could not permit the choice of a spouse on the basis of a chance encounter. As life was organized in the isolated *kehilla*, members of the different classes were bound to come together in casual meetings. Members of the same class, on the other hand, who, on the basis of objective considerations, could be suitably matched, were often geographically separated and would meet only if an interview was deliberately arranged.

However, the likelihood of such meetings was certainly not the only reason for the society's concern. The objection to marriage by personal choice was bound up with the society's entire conception of the role of love and sex. As we have seen, the temptations of the flesh were clearly recognized and frankly admitted. On the other hand, there was no deliberate cultivation of the erotic life, in which the individual might find an emotional outlet or even room for self-expression. Sexual activity and the accompanying erotic experience were relegated to the marriage institution. Even within marriage, sexual activity was restricted by the religious laws governing the menstrual period, which add about one week each month to the time that physiology rules out sexual intercourse. Within the permitted period, however, there was no ascetic tendency.

In any case, married life was not subjugated to its formal religious purpose of procreation. Permission was given to have intercourse with one's wife even where conception could not possibly result—for example, where the woman was already pregnant or was not capable of having children. Although such sanction seems to run counter to the severe condemnations of masturbation by the *musar* writers, scholars who pointed out the discrepancy managed to resolve it dialectically; in practice, the sanction was never doubted. On the contrary, the severity of the prohibition against all sexual contact or erotic thoughts outside the marriage bond strengthened the need to give the sexual impulse a legitimate outlet.

Religious law and ethics here pay perhaps more attention to

the needs of the woman than to those of the man. If the man tends to asceticism and would like to curtail sexual activity to a minimum, this curtailment is limited by the husband's obligation to satisfy his wife's sexual needs. This reciprocal attachment between man and wife is an erotic one as well. The wife is admonished to attract her husband's attention to the point of completely monopolizing his erotic impulse. The husband is exhorted to show consideration for his wife's feelings, and to refrain from regarding her merely as an instrument for gratifying his lust or for observing the Divine command to procreate. The height of erotic-cum-religious experience was reached in married life where the influence of the cabala had taught the couple to regard their union as symbolic of parallel processes in the Divine sphere, a concept which became widespread in the period through the cabalist *musar* literature, especially the *Sh'lah* of Rabbi Isaiah Horowitz and cognate works.

Though an internal criterion of the success of a marriage existed, wherein some couples derived more satisfaction than others, marriages, as a rule, were not dissolved except after they had obviously and signally failed through the complete absence of sexual satisfaction, infidelity (especially on the part of the woman), childlessness, or social incompatibility such as public and perpetual bickering. Indeterminate dissatisfaction with one's husband or wife or the wish to find happiness in another marriage, were not considered grounds for divorce. The absence of any philosophy promising happiness in marriage, on the one hand, and the many difficulties facing the dissatisfied partners, on the other, served to prevent divorce unless objective circumstances forced it on them. For the husband, the economic aspect of divorce acted as a serious deterrent. The original aim of the *ketuba*, the marriage contract, "that it should not be a light thing in his eyes to send her away," also operated in this period. The amount of money that the husband had to pay the wife upon divorce stipulated in the marriage contract was fixed in accordance with the size of the dowry, and the latter was generally invested in a business which would collapse if the money was withdrawn.

As for the woman, the status of a divorcee was such as to deter her from demanding a divorce from her husband. The chances of a divorced woman's remarrying were slight, particularly if it was she who was at fault, whether through childlessness, suspicion of infidelity, or shrewishness. For a woman to be independent in this society was no advantage from any point of view. Only a widow with children, who might be considered as a substitute for her husband, was likely to maintain the family's economic and social position: an example is Glückel of Hameln. But it was doubtful whether a young divorced woman would be able to fit into economic life, and she certainly could not maintain an independent social position. She had no choice but to seek asylum in the home of others, either with her parents or relatives, or, in the lowest class, as a servant in a rich home.

All these considerations acted as deterrents to hasty divorce as the solution for tension in family life. In fact, in many instances, rabbis were asked to permit a marriage to continue even when, according to law, the husband was required to divorce his wife: e.g., if she had not borne children after ten years of marriage. The secondary economic and social functions imposed on the family carried such weight that they were capable of sustaining a marriage even where it fell short of its primary erotic and biological purpose.

Although public opinion and personal motives alike impelled the individual to get married, it is clear from all that has been said that not every individual was capable of fulfilling this demand. Voluntary bachelorhood was not accepted by society and was certainly far from being an ideal; even a person who lost his mate once or twice through death or divorce would try to remedy the situation by marrying a second and third time. But if voluntary bachelorhood was not to be found, enforced bachelorhood was. It usually stemmed from the various obstacles to matrimony we have already enumerated. It followed, therefore, that from its public aspect, the problem of sex was not always settled. The door was open to what society considered sexual deviation of greater or lesser seriousness. While it is difficult to estimate the extent of such deviations, there is no question that they occurred. The ordinances of important *kehillot* set forth the rules of conduct to be observed towards those guilty of deviation, and the *responsa* literature, in every generation and in every locality, deals with cases in point. As has been indicated, violations of the sexual code may be traced to involuntary bachelorhood: men and women who did not find a mate in good time; domestic servants whose jobs condemned them to long years of bachelorhood; unattached widows and widowers; *agunot* (widows whose husbands were missing) who had given up hope of ever seeing their husbands again; bachelor teachers who had left their homes to follow their calling; travelling salesmen; and itinerant beggars. The very nature of their lives made all these groups suspect. They also served as a constant temptation to possible deviation on the part of others. To be sure, even marriage was no absolute guarantee against the evil inclination. As the Talmud so realistically puts it, "There is no guardian against unchastity."

Even this society, therefore, had to fight against violations of the sexual code. But it may be said that this battle was not one between one part of society and another, but rather a fight in which both the successfully chaste and the defaulters made common cause. Deviations occurred not as part of any conscious free thinking, but as temporary lapses regretted by those who committed them. This fact explains the inquiries regarding ways of doing penance for sexual sins, ranging from masturbation to adultery, in which the responsa literature abounds. The concept of *ba'al tshuva* (a penitent) was applied almost exclusively to persons who had committed a sexual offence; only manslaughter and apostasy (voluntary or compulsory) were dealt with so severely. The tradition of the German Hasidic movement (thirteenth century) bequeathed to this generation a veritable catalogue of penances for each separate sin. The severity of the mortification and self-debasement that these penances involved goes beyond what people today are likely to regard as reasonable or within man's capacity to endure. The fact that the guilty parties themselves asked for severe penances to atone for their sin—and there are cases where the rabbi gave a more severe ruling only in order to pacify the questioner—indicates that although sexual purity did not reign supreme, the ideal itself was firmly entrenched, and that it operated both as a restraining and a corrective force which, even after the deviation, restored the equilibrium.

XV   *Kinship*

$\mathcal{A}$LL THAT HAS BEEN SAID IN THE LAST CHAP-
ter applies only to the "small family," an institution which occupied a well-defined place in the structure of society. But its
members, who actually shared day-to-day living, felt themselves
part of a larger whole which embraced a number of small families. The traditional Jewish family took a broad view of the concept of kin relationship—both from the aspect of the scope of
the circle and from that of the nature of the obligations of relatives to one another. In Jewish religious law, the concept of kinship is defined only in the context of forbidden unions and the
disqualification of witnesses. Marriage is prohibited only within
the inner circle of relatives, between brother and sister or aunt

and nephew (but not between uncle and niece). Disqualification from bearing witness and from acting as a judge applies to great-uncles and cousins as well. In practice, it does not matter whether the relationship is one of consanguinity or marriage; even if it is the women of the family who are related, the disqualification applies to their husbands. This definition of kinship also served as an example for disqualifying a person from taking part in the ruling institutions of the *kehilla* and the super-*kehilla,* as we shall see below. Here, as in the case of the judicial institutions, there was need for a fixed legal definition. But with regard to the feeling of family solidarity, no such restriction was recognized. Anyone who was known to be related came within the terms of the injunction, "Hide not thyself from thine own flesh" (Isaiah 58:7). This text, as interpreted by the Talmud, constituted a proverbial expression denoting a person's obligation to come to the assistance of his less fortunate relatives.

Aid to one's relatives implied, first of all, supporting them in the event of economic setbacks and actual poverty. Ancient religious law obliged the benefactor to give his relatives preference over the poor in general. According to the view prevalent in the period we are studying, a person was expected to help his needy relatives more substantially than he would an ordinary charity case. Particular emphasis was placed on the duty of helping to marry off the daughters of one's poor relatives, particularly if the girl's father was dead. To bring up and eventually marry off the orphan of a poor relative was regarded as an especially meritorious deed, and one which charitable persons took pride in performing.

The obligation to support one's relatives was regarded as an accepted norm in society, although the degree of such support naturally varied from person to person. In this readiness to aid one's relatives, the object of preserving the family honor constituted, at the most, a secondary motive. For even the richest families were not in a position to maintain a uniform socio-economic standard among all their members. The fundamental condition necessary for the purpose was lacking: namely, property of permanent value, such as land. Business methods and conditions led to fluctuations in the social hierarchy. Well-to-do families kept their poor relations in mind; they could perhaps save them from destitution, but they could not sustain their socio-economic position.

The obligation of inter-family assistance constituted a norm which evolved out of the actual functions discharged by ties of kinship under the prevailing social conditions. The chief economic activity of this society was intimately bound up, as we have seen, with its continued unity despite the geographical dispersion of its members. The possibility of constant communication with people living in other countries, with whom there existed a kinship of language and culture, gave an economic advantage to the Jews, who were scattered over many lands.

But even in the competition of the members of this society between one another, the connections of secondary groups, whose members were related and loyal to each other, constituted an advantage over individuals without any outside ties. This advantage was not confined to the economic sphere alone. To the extent that common political interests existed, whether these involved intercession with outside authorities or with the internal organizations, primary ties were regarded as an asset. Connections with persons outside the immediate locality were helpful in every field of activity which was not completely parochial in character. The roving talmudic student, the rabbi who was called to serve another *kehilla,* and even a person who had made a match with someone in a distant city, needed assistance or, at least, information. The family was the only institution or agency to which the individual could turn for assistance in making contact with persons outside his locality.

Moreover, family ties were important within the life of the *kehillot* themselves. In the struggle for power by individuals and groups, and in the attempt to acquire economic or social advantages, the opposing forces occasionally divided along family lines. Here, too, the reason was mainly negative: the lack of groupings on a class or ideological basis. Although these were not entirely absent, they were not yet strong enough to serve as cohesive forces, as we shall see. The struggle, for the most part, was between equals in property, class, and general outlook on life. The conflict was essentially over the question of who would acquire power, honor, and prestige. Under the circumstances, it was natural that the opposing forces should crystallize on the basis of the immediate family connection, and this was a common occurrence in the history of the *kehillot* of the period, with entire families engaged in struggles—sometimes remorseless—against one another.

Now we can return to define the social conditions which particularly favored Jewish family solidarity in this period. Economic, political, and social life had become so diversified that the activities of secondary groups offered substantial advantages to those who belonged to them. This situation paved the way for the formation of groups which filled the need for a secondary cohesion. But, first and foremost, these conditions strengthened the cohesive power which existed "naturally"—the cohesion of the family.

Mutual family responsibility became an uncontested principle. It was observed not only when it was to the individual's advantage, as in the case of the poor man who was assisted by rich relatives or the community leader who owned his authority to the support of the members of his family in the *kehilla;* it was also followed when it meant fulfilling the moral obligation to give financial assistance to one's less prosperous relatives or advancing their interests in the *kehilla* or the super-*kehilla*. But owing to the social conditions we have described, this family attachment did not operate without clashing with other principles. Family interests did not always harmonize with those of the communal institutions. The judiciary, the government, and the economy, by their very natures, transcend the narrow family basis. Their function is to serve members of different families, and they must operate irrespective of family connections.

The problem is clearest with regard to judicial institutions. A court is a public institution which, intentionally and as a matter of principle, has been removed from the family ties which exist between the members of society. Talmudic justice is supra-family justice; it does not recognize any privileges on the basis of a family relationship between the judge and the judged. Contemporary Jewish society relied on a clear tradition which had evolved under conditions similar to its own. For even in the period of the Mishna and the Talmud—excluding the biblical period on a number of counts—law was based on the public principle transcending tribal or family connections. Later, as family ties increased, Jewish law tended to be excessively strict over the barriers to be maintained between relatives by blood or marriage.

In the judicial context, however, there was no clash between the principle of the law and the family tie. Anyone who violated the rules of the law with regard to the composition of the court, or who took family ties into account in judging a case, was regarded both by himself and others as deviating from the principles of Jewish law and ethics.

The governing institutions—the *kehilla* and super-*kehilla*—were regarded as standing above family ties as a matter of principle. Rules were therefore adopted which precluded relatives from participating in the governing institutions, whether local or countrywide. Particular care was exercised in the composition of the assessment committees charged with the function of distributing the tax burden among the members of the *kehilla*. In fixing the degree of family relationship permitted, institutional authorities relied on the accepted tradition governing the judiciary. But no clearly defined tradition directly applied to this sphere. This explains the different usages that prevailed and the clashes that took place over the definition of kinship where public bodies exercising functions of secondary rank were concerned. Were relatives precluded from serving only on the communal board of management or did this apply even to membership in the broader body of the whole community and the committee which chose the leaders?

Such questions arose with respect to the rabbi in relation to the members of the *kehilla*. Many *kehillot* adopted the rule that a rabbi might not be elected if he had relatives among the congregation. Possibly they wished to ensure that the rabbi would be qualified to serve as head of the *bet din* in any dispute that might arise between members of the *kehilla*. But it would also seem that the rabbi's official status as the supreme arbiter of his community impelled the *kehillot* to find a person who would stand above the differences that sometimes crystallized on a family basis.

But even this preventive measure concerning the rabbi was neither general nor consistent. Not every *kehilla* strictly observed this prohibition. Those communities that scrupulously adhered to the principle did so only *ab initio*. If the rabbi formed a marriage connection with a member of his *kehilla*, he did not forfeit his position. The same practice was usually observed with regard to other official appointments on communal bodies. If the families of communal officers intermarried during their term of office, they were not *ipso facto* disqualified. Obviously, communal institutions, unlike judicial bodies, which had explicit halakhic warrant, could not exclude the incidence of kin connections. Certainly they were not so careful about observing the rules forbidding relatives to hold communal appointments as they were about those pertaining to judicial institutions.

While we have attributed a unifying influence to the economic activity of the period, at least within the framework of the greater family, we must point out that it also acted as a disunifying and isolating force. Jewish economic activity of the period, in almost all its stages, was based either on money or on what could be calculated in terms of money. This fact put each small family on an independent economic basis. The son or daughter, unless they entered into an actual business partnership with their family, relinquished all economic connection with it on receipt of the dowry. In that case, however, the bond between the related partners was no different from that existing between ordinary partners. After the settlement of the dowry, the only economic ties existing on the basis of family relationship were those of inheritance and of support in case of need. Financial support was something which ordinarily involved relatives of quite different economic positions. But relatives of the same economic class would help one another only on a business basis—as agents, lenders or borrowers, buyers or sellers. This kin connection, however, in no way removed the barrier which existed between the small family units, each one of which existed on its own economic basis.

The more economic activity came to be conducted along anonymous lines of credit, however, the less personal considerations figured in the calculations of profit and loss. A negotiable promissory note would eventually be presented for collection by someone other than the person to whom the money was originally due. Once the note entered the market, the creditor could not waive reimbursement even if he wished to do so. The individual increasingly found himself facing not parties well-known to him, but the market, which also included his friends and relatives. Inasmuch as every small family constituted an economic unit in itself, economic responsibility was felt mainly with regard to the existence of this unit. Far-reaching concessions to others were likely to destroy the equilibrium of the independent economy. The talmudic dictum, "Your life takes precedence over that of your fellow man" (Baba Metzia 62a), was applied in this context, and this included relatives as well.

In brief, in the economic context, the family factor played the positive roles of bringing people together and providing assistance in time of need. But the fundamental fact which determined the framework of economic activity was the independence of the small family, which forced the individual to stand on his own feet, trusting in his ability and good fortune. In spite of the much-publicized closeness of the Jewish family, in the society with which we are dealing, the responsibility of individuals to one another was quite limited, and this applied even to members of the same family if they did not live together in one household. The unit in the struggle for existence was actually the small family, with the larger kinship circle available in times of necessity.

XVI

Associations and Social Life

$\mathcal{P}$ARTICIPATION IN THE LIFE OF THE FAMILY and the *kehilla* did not exhaust the social activity of the individual. Ample scope for social activity remained beyond the confines of these two institutions, activities in which not all members of the *kehilla* or the family took part. Voluntary social activity and improvised social groupings probably existed even in the smallest *kehillot*. But formally organized associations arose as a consequence of the population increase and social differentiation which took place in the Jewish communities of Germany and Poland between the sixteenth and eighteenth centuries. In the smallest *kehillot*, even where activities not imposed by the *kehilla* took place spontaneously—e.g., Torah study by adults—

they were probably carried out by institutions of the *kehilla*. But in *kehillot* containing hundreds or thousands of families, the over-all organization of the *kehilla* was too broad to serve as the framework for the social-religious activities of its members. Moreover, with the increase in the *kehilla*'s population, the likelihood increased that persons sharing the same interests would join forces to carry out the activities which set them apart from the rest of the *kehilla*.

It appears that the first division sometimes came about because the local synagogue was not large enough to accommodate all the worshippers. Newcomers to the town and young men coming of age led to an increase in the population which left no choice but to establish a new place of worship. The daily meetings of the congregants of each synagogue were likely to create a social differentiation between them and the others. The importance of this fact will become apparent when we consider the social significance of the religious ceremony. As we shall see in the chapter on religious institutions, daily religious worship also created a framework for the public self-identification of the participants. It may be assumed that occasionally changes also took place in the customs of the various synagogues. Even if the changes were only slight variations of no ritual significance such as a change in the melodies or the adding of psalms, they gave the congregants a sense of religious communion.

The association's right to exist depended on its identification with one of the accepted values of society: the study of Torah, the giving of charity, and the pursuing of other philanthropic activities. The religious principle of showing kindness to the dead was the first to inspire the formation of a special social framework—the burial society (*hevra qadisha*). Kindness to the dead was regarded as one of the noblest principles; it constituted the only example of "pure" kindness "the kindness of truth" (Genesis 47:29). The members of the burial society undertook all the tasks connected with burying the dead; occasionally they also supplied the needs of the sick and stood at the bed of the dying.

Although similar societies are mentioned in the Talmud, these societies were not direct continuations of the earlier ones. The small German *kehilla* of the Middle Ages did not need to delegate its functions. The societies were formed as a result of conditions in the large *kehillot*—like Prague and Frankfurt—when the increased population made it impossible for the members of the *kehilla* to attend to each individual. After the societies were founded in the large *kehillot,* they spread to the small ones, which may not really have required them at all. Personal motives played a part in the formation of the burial societies. Each member thereby provided for his own funeral arrangements and ensured that nothing that tradition required would be lacking at the time of his decease. From the broader aspect, the duty of providing every Jew with a Jewish burial was transferred from the congregation to the burial society. All burial matters of the *kehilla* were entrusted to the *hevra qadisha*. The members of the society enjoyed special privileges such as an honored spot for their grave and having the burial ritual observed with special exactitude. The *hevra qadisha* thus remained a closed society, with membership depending, in theory at least, on the moral and religious standing of the candidate. The members of the society formed something of a moral elite in the *kehilla;* they were so considered both by themselves and the general public.

Just as the burial society fulfilled the function of performing the final services for the dead, so other associations furthered one or another of the ends which were valued by society. Study groups were organized for Torah classes on different levels of scholarship; philanthropic associations were formed for customary and special charities, such as raising dowries for poor brides or supplying firewood to indigent scholars. There were associations for the promotion of Torah study which provided for the education of poor children or sometimes of all the children in the *kehilla*. All these tasks were originally imposed on the general organization of the *kehilla*. Where no special associations existed for the purpose, they were, indeed, carried out by the *kehilla*. Associations were formed in order to carry out these religious precepts in a more fitting manner, and they evolved through the spontaneous activity of persons eager to perform good deeds.

This definition may seem inapplicable to the associations of artisans which existed in Moravia, Bohemia, and Poland-Lithuania from the beginning of the seventeenth century. These guilds protected the interests of Jewish artisans in their struggle with their Christian competitors, systematized relations and restricted competition among the Jewish artisans, excluded persons who were not recognized craftsmen, controlled the standards of production, and regulated dealings between artisans and customers. In short, they attempted to ensure the conditions which, from the viewpoint of the times, would guarantee the economic welfare of the class.

Membership in associations of this kind was thus not voluntary. Anyone who practiced a trade was obliged to join the association of his fellow craftsmen. Precisely this exception proved the rule that, under the prevailing view, no association had the right to exist unless it worked for the realization of religious and ethical values, be it only as a secondary interest. For even these craft guilds, both by their own statement of purpose and by their activity, were interested in furthering such values as the conducting of public worship, the maintenance of a rabbi, the holding of Torah classes, the supporting of the needy of their own trade, and even the burial of the dead. The economic purpose which made the organization of these craft guilds necessary was, in itself, insufficient to justify their existence. Only this engaging in good works, which was typical of the other associations as well, constituted the public justification of the craft associations. However, such an approach should not be considered mere rationalization. Artisans' associations were entitled, if they wished, to use the designation "holy society" just as were other associations.

The motives for establishing and maintaining the association were mixed; sometimes the economic preceded the religious and ethical objective; sometimes it was the reverse. The concern with non-economic values not only justified the existence of the guilds, but helped them maintain themselves. For this concern furnished symbols of self-identification to the members of the association and created an atmosphere of mutual dependence. Without this religious motivation, it is doubtful whether the economic aims would have sufficed to maintain their existence.

Although we have defined the aims of the associations as the realization of one of the values hallowed by tradition, we have not exhausted the range of functions which they actually fulfilled. First, no one association devoted itself exclusively to any one value. Once an association was organized for a specific purpose, it would also occupy itself incidentally with the achievement of other ends. Members of a burial society or a philanthropic association would also set a time for group study; while a study group would sometimes also engage in mutual aid.

Moreover, the associations also engaged in activities which originally were devoid of any religious character. Every association brought its members together for celebrations and feasts— on such occasions as when a new Scroll of the Law was acquired by the synagogue, when a study group completed a tractate of the Talmud, and when the "feast of the association" took place on a day commemorating some event in the association's life or in Jewish tradition. Although the content of such celebrations in no way constituted part of the good works which occupied the association, they shared something of the atmosphere of dedication which permeated the deeds of the association as a whole. In this way, they did not arouse the misgivings with which social entertainment was viewed when it had no religious or ethical motivation.

This religious-ethical cover for apparently neutral social activity testifies to one of the typical phenomena in the life of this society. Social activity for its own sake, that is, the coming together of people to enjoy themselves simply by being together, was regarded as a religious and moral hazard. If the group included men and women, the risk was of an erotic nature. As we have already seen in the chapter on family life, a man was enjoined by the prevailing sexual morality to remove every thought of sin from his heart and to avoid anything likely to excite him erotically. Social amusement of the two sexes was thus regarded as a deliberate invitation to sinful thoughts. Even social intercourse between persons of the same sex was viewed with misgivings. It was believed to open the door to such transgressions as gossip, slander, and bickering. Apart from these apprehensions, however, social intercourse for its own sake was thought to be a sheer waste of time.

We have already explained that the ideal of studying Torah demanded the exclusive employment of one's time as a matter of principle: every free moment that remained after fulfilling religious obligations, making a living, and taking care of other essential needs, was to be devoted to the study of Torah. In practice this ideal was, of course, not fulfilled except by those rare persons who devoted themselves wholly to the study of Torah. Yet the demand pervaded the atmosphere of society as one which was not to be contested, and it penetrated the consciousness of the community through works of *Halakha* and *musar*, including popular summaries of these for the general public. The acknowledgment of the demand served, in principle, to discourage all social activity which was designed simply as a way of spending time. Every social amusement, even if it consisted simply of dining with friends or inviting someone to one's home where no *mitzva* was involved, was considered a waste of time that should be devoted to the study of Torah.

As has been said, there was a considerable divergence here

between theory and practice—greater than in most spheres of religion and morals. The reason for this lay mainly in the difference in spiritual stature between those who set the standards and those who attempted to carry them out. The former, who preached these values to the community, were scholars who could very well be called upon to devote their whole time to the study of Torah. But for the general public, with a limited knowledge of Torah, the demand was extravagant. Although the average man might be capable of following a lecture given by someone else, he could not study Torah on his own. The better educated could, perhaps, set aside time for study in their own homes or in the framework of the institutions with whose workings we have already become acquainted. But pre-occupation with activity which bore the hallmark of religious approval still left some leisure time, the amount of which depended on actual conditions and the class to which one belonged.

Indeed, social amusement was not eliminated entirely; it was merely curtailed and, to some extent, banned. Strolls on Sabbaths and festivals, dances on secular holidays, games, cards and chess, were indulged in almost everywhere. The regulations of the *kehillot* restricted given amusements to specific days or events: for example, a woman recuperating after childbirth was permitted to play cards with her neighbors. But amusements and other neutral manifestations of sociability were never entirely eliminated. For the most part, there was no clear and definite wish to do so.

In any event, the needs of social intercourse were satisfied illegitimately only by groups who were ready to deviate from prevailing ethical standards, not by those who strove to practice what was preached. For the latter—and for society at large—the solution was found in the fitting of social amusements into the framework of institutions whose religious and ethical role served as a cover for their neutral activity. It was the family and the associations which served as the basis for social activity. Even

families, however, were not entitled to arrange social gatherings
for their own sake. However, ample legitimate social opportunities were provided within the framework of domestic religious
occasions. The people tended to exploit this sanction to the limit.

A single family event, like a circumcision or a marriage,
would be the occasion for a number of receptions. A whole series
of festivities preceded and followed the marriage feast proper.
The same was true of circumcision, which was marked by special
celebrations on the eve of the ceremony and on the Friday night
preceding and, in some places, by an additional feast on the
third day following. It was also customary, in some localities,
to mark the naming of a girl child and the first appearance of
a mother in the synagogue after giving birth by a celebration.

The Redemption of the First Born (*pidyon ha-ben*), too, involved a party. A *bar mitzva* banquet became a regular custom in
this period. Some would also hold a celebration on the Sabbath
when the boy, even before reaching his majority at thirteen, was
first given the honor of chanting the *haftara* (prophetic reading)
in the synagogue. The building of a new house was the occasion
of a feast of dedication.

The religious codifiers attempted to establish which of these
gatherings came under the category of *se'udat mitzva* (a religious obligatory banquet), which the Talmud not only authorized but even allowed scholars to enjoy. They tended to extend
the concept by including gatherings which the Talmud and the
early authorities did not regard as a *se'udat mitzva* and which
were not covered therein. The community regarded none of these
receptions as ordinary meals or mere social amusement even if
the rabbinic authority found no basis for investing them with
the status of *se'udat mitzva*.

The community leaders were prompted by economic and social considerations to limit social amusement. They wished to
check extravagant spending and avoid exacerbating social competition between individuals and classes. The aim of the *kehilla*'s

regulations was not to eliminate gatherings of this sort, but to restrict their scope by limiting the guests to persons related to the family or by limiting the number of guests altogether. These regulations assumed an austere character only at times of great public mourning. Thus, after the pogroms of 1648–49, the Lithuanian Council prohibited, *inter alia,* the playing of musical instruments "even for the amusement of the bride and groom, except at the marriage ceremony itself and at the ceremony of the covering of the bride's head." But this prohibition was limited a priori to a period of three years. The principle that social amusement was carried on under the aegis of the family was not abrogated.

The same was true with regard to the gatherings of the various associations. Study groups would hold a celebration to mark the completion of a tractate of the Talmud, and this was considered a *se-udat mitzva.* The annual banquets of the other associations, particularly of the burial societies, had no basis in the early sources. Some evidence indicates that the custom of holding a feast and even some details of the accompanying ritual were taken over from the neighboring Christian societies, but the participants in the rites were, in the ordinary way, unaware of their historical origins. The feasts of the burial societies were invested with a specific Jewish character and hallowed by the fact that they were preceded by a day of fasting and by their being linked to a significant date in the Hebrew calendar—the seventh of Adar, the date of Moses' death.

The feast was invariably accompanied by a scholarly discourse, an edificatory address, and the chanting of Psalms and hymns. Attempts to base the customary ceremonies on good Jewish homiletical doctrine were made. Those present felt that the feast was divested of an everyday, secular atmosphere. At the same time, it intensified their feelings of fellowship and demonstrated their distinctiveness. With less ritual, but with an approach quite similar to that of the burial societies, the members of the other associations celebrated their own special holidays. The general function of these gatherings was to satisfy the need for good fellowship in conformity with contemporary values and the institutions which embodied them.

Delineating the declared purposes of the associations and noting the secondary objects which they accomplished by no means completes the sociological picture. We may ask what contribution the associations made towards the maintenance of society as a whole and the preservation of its structure and values. In fact, the emergence of the associations was connected with the growth of the *kehilla* and the broadening of its scope. The *kehilla* of hundreds and occasionally even of thousands of families could not transmit the feeling of direct belonging required by the individual. Second, the executive tasks in the central institutions of the *kehilla* were monopolized by a relatively small number of persons, with the great majority of people precluded from taking part in any public activity at all.

These two factors induced individuals to found associations or join them. Admittedly, the associations were established and functioned under the supervision of the central authorities, who sometimes directly appointed some of their officers. But as a rule, elections were held among the members of the associations itself, and they were carried out in accordance with the practice of the institutions of the *kehilla*. The founders and active members of the associations appeared to belong to the middle class, those who were capable of undertaking public activity but who could not hope to attain the central leadership of the community. This "middle-classness" is clearly reflected in the secondary caliber of the spiritual leaders of the associations, who were preachers rather than authoritative scholars. The same was true with regard to the lay members: the rich and well-established were usually attracted to the central leadership; while those in the middle range found satisfaction in running the associations.

Although occasional tension and actual struggle existed between the associations and the *kehilla*, the net result was that the *kehilla* benefited from the existence of the associations. The outlet they afforded for the desire for civic activity relieved the pressure on the primary positions of leadership. In addition, younger men found an opportunity to gain experience in conducting public affairs on a small scale before they reached the stage of shouldering the responsibility of governing the entire community.

The associations, in a way, also formed social foci for mutual control—a role which, with growth, the *kehilla* institutions had difficulty in carrying out. Membership in a restricted association carried prestige, but it also demanded the representation of the values which the association was designed to foster. Occasionally this responsibility was explicitly set forth in the association's constitution. Members were obliged to participate in public worship and in study classes under penalty of a fine. The association's management reserved the right to expel members who violated its code of behavior or that of the society at large. But the principal control was probably carried out informally through the creation of a basis for identification by the members with the values the association represented. By evoking their members' loyalty to its special values, the association also ensured their loyalty to the values of society as a whole.

XVII   *Religious Institutions*

$\mathcal{W}$E HAVE ALREADY ENCOUNTERED THE INFLU-
ence of religious concepts and institutions in our description of
Jewish society in various spheres of life. The very definition of
this society as traditional predicates the concept of religion, for
the tradition on which the society was nurtured was a religious
one. Even traditional forms of minor importance from the halakhic viewpoint, such as the manner of dress and the forms of
speech, were treated as having religious grounding of at least a
secondary degree.

But the all-pervasiveness of religion does not prevent us from
focusing attention on its own specific sphere and institutions.
Even in this society, which was, as it were, an entirely religious

one, there were some institutions where religion played merely a secondary role and others where it was the be-all and end-all. Both the synagogue and the rabbinate were clearly designed to satisfy religious needs—the former for public worship and ceremonies that were primarily of a religious nature, and the latter as a judicial and regulatory instrument deriving its authority from the Halakha.

We shall deal first with the institution of the rabbinate, noting the way in which it performed the religious functions for which it was designed. We use the term "rabbinate" here in a somewhat different sense from that employed previously in our discussion of the *kehilla*. There, an office of recognized standing in the *kehilla* organization was implied. The local rabbi was entrusted with the power to regulate or decide any matter which could be defined as religious. But the rabbinate existed in Jewish society independently of the *kehilla* organization. As a religion of positive precepts (or, at least, as one including positive precepts) Judaism called for the existence of an authorized body to rule on questions which were likely to arise and which the layman was incapable of deciding.

Admittedly, a Jewish education and participation in the life of the community did give the layman a basic knowledge of tradition by which he was guided as long as circumstances remained unchanged and nothing unexpected or unusual occurred. But, in fact, the unexpected and the unusual were a daily occurrence. Questions about the dietary laws, worship, and the prohibition of work on Sabbaths and festivals were always likely to arise. The person who was guided solely by accepted ruling could not know how to act in every instance, even if the more erudite might have no doubts. Questions occasionally arose for which even the learned did not have a ready answer. Such cases called for a decision by qualified persons who were not only thoroughly versed in tradition, but who also regarded themselves as authorized to interpret it and apply the accepted rules to new circumstances.

Scholars who possessed the necessary knowledge and the power to decide religious questions fulfilled the function of the rabbinate in practice, irrespective of whether they were officially appointed by the *kehillot.* In this sense, the existence of the rabbinate did not derive from, nor was it dependent on, the organization of the *kehillot.* It was a natural concomitant of Judaism, dictated by a tradition which was disseminated in two ways. It was imparted, on the one hand, through the institutions of society, the family and the synagogue. On the other hand, it was transmitted through literary media that could only be mastered by deliberate and intense study. It can be said that the extent to which a Jew could act as "his own rabbi" lay in direct proportion to his religious knowledge and ability to adjudicate in matters of tradition. The layman engaged the services of a rabbi insofar as he felt it necessary to refer his religious questions to someone else. The rabbi may have held an official position or have been simply a talmudic scholar qualified to rule on religious matters. During this period, this qualification was not restricted to official rabbinic incumbents.

The title *moreinu* (our teacher) was conferred on anyone who had attained a certain level of Talmudic scholarship. This title authorized him to hand down halakhic decisions irrespective of whether he occupied the position of rabbi at the time. It was not even essential that he held the title *moreinu.* If no rabbi was available, anyone who was versed, or imagined he was versed, in the relevant sources would lay down the law. Only in such highly specialized fields as divorce and *halitza,* where the religious responsibility was great, was it regarded as essential that the person dealing with the matter be ordained, or even that he hold an official rabbinical post.

An unofficial hierarchy of scholars qualified to rule on Jewish law existed. "Spontaneous" public opinion in the *kehilla,* in the super-*kehilla*, or even in the entire Jewish world, determined the place of each scholar in this unofficial hierarchy. Obviously, opinion did not always uniformly appraise the relative qualifications of the different rabbinic authorities. For this reason, the existence of this spontaneous hierarchy gave no assurance of authoritative decisions and certainly not of any higher institutional review of the rulings of lower authorities. Occasionally such rulings were set aside, however, if appeal was made to a recognized higher authority.

Casuistic literature, including summaries like the *Shulkhan Arukh,* apparently simplified the task of issuing religious rulings. But the spread of such works did not render the rabbinate superfluous. Mastery of this literature presupposed prior halakhic preparation, and, although we know that halakhic learning was widespread in this period, authoritative knowledge was confined to the few. No mastery of tradition, however complete, released the scholar from the obligation to consult others occasionally. Rulings were not issued *ex officio*, on the basis of the institutional authority of the person making the decision (as is the case with a Catholic priest). It was the rabbi's knowledge of the halakha and his ability to deduce a new ruling from existing principle or precedent which gave validity to his decision. If the rabbi was unable to make up his mind definitely, he was not capable of handing down a decision. A sense of modesty and reluctance to legislate for fear of making an incorrect decision sometimes kept even leading rabbinic authorities from handing down their own judgments. Many responsa penned by leading authorities conclude with the proviso that their conclusions may be considered valid only if other authorities concur with them.

In addition to interpreting religious law, the rabbinate—in the broader sense in which we have been using it in this chapter—was charged with the task of public exhortation to the observance of the law. The formal justification for such activity was in the commandment, "Thou shalt surely reprove thy neigh-

bor" (Leviticus 19:17). In other words, Jewish mutual responsibility with regard to religious precepts has no limit, either of
geography or of class. In theory, nothing debars any person from
rebuking his fellow man for misconduct. On the contrary, he has
a clear responsibility to do so.

But in practice, there did not develop in Judaism, as there
did among other religious denominations, the "lay preacher,"
who gets up in public and points out the sins of other members
of his fraternity. The reason must be sought, again, in the nature
of the Jewish religion as one of practical deeds and of casuistic
ethics. Ignorance was regarded as at least as great an obstacle
to the fulfillment of religious obligations as perverseness of
heart. And if, with respect to perverseness of heart, the enthusiasm of a lay preacher might be even more effective than the sermon of a scholar, with respect to ignorance, only a person qualified to lay down the law, and not just apt at administering
reproof, could do the job.

Indeed, the task of administering reproof had long since been
considered the special province of the members of the scholarly
class, the graduates of the *bet hamidrash*. The aim of their sermon was as much to teach as it was to admonish and inspire.
Instruction in the sermon ranged from practical rulings on specific questions of religious law to highly abstract halakhic disquisitions. Talmudic casuistry or *pilpul* was then in its final and
most extreme stage of development. Even non-halakhic sermons
included a sprinkling of citations from the Bible, the Midrash,
and the Talmud. This was true even of the popular sermons delivered to the general public by professional and amateur preachers. Since the sermon fulfilled the function of imparting knowledge, the position of preacher was reserved for the expert, the
graduate of the *bet hamidrash* and *Yeshiva*.

In this period, when Torah authority in the life of the community was vested in the office of the rabbi, its incumbent was,
in theory at any rate, charged with the task of preaching as well.

The local rabbi was the official corrector of his congregation. He was expected to deliver a sermon on at least two Sabbaths a year—on the "Great Sabbath" (*Shabbat Hagadol*), the one immediately preceding Passover, and on the "Sabbath of Penitence," which falls between Rosh Hashana and Yom Kippur.

The institution of preaching developed to such an extent in this period that the local rabbi proved unequal to the task. In the larger *kehillot*, preachers were appointed whose principal function was to deliver sermons at fixed times and on special occasions. At the same time, itinerant preachers functioned throughout this period. The latter held no regular position, but wandered from place to place and received a fee from the *kehilla* as well as private contributions. Since the sermon did not contain binding halakhic rulings, the right to preach was not made dependent on the title *moreinu* which was tantamount to rabbinic ordination. Ordination for preaching was never instituted (as it was for ritual slaughterers, for example). Some preachers were, of course, scholarly men, and in the larger *kehillot*, the position was often filled by individuals who were destined to become the halakhic leaders of their time. But scholastic attainments and vocational training never figured decisively in this field. The preacher gained his reputation on the basis of his innate ability to captivate his audience. Public control precluded undesirable individuals from following the vocation of preaching. Such control was regarded as especially necessary in view of the activities of the Sabbatian movement and Hasidism, whose exponents frequently made use of this channel of influence. But the need for control was felt even earlier, particularly with respect to itinerant preachers, who lacked any fixed institutional ties. This control, however, was not exercised systematically. The written recommendation of some neighboring, or even remote, authority, or an interview with the local rabbi or warden, were enough to open the doors of the synagogue to the preacher, unless there was a regulation which limited the right to preach to a rabbinic incumbent.

The existence of the institution of preaching, as we have said, may be explained by its basic religious aim, the need for public exhortation. It served to remind the people of the system of values to which the society adhered, exploiting the religious atmosphere of the synagogue and the inspiration of the Sabbath or festival service. The preacher measured the conduct of his audience by the yardstick of Jewish values or acted as the voice of public opinion in criticizing its institutions and leaders. The congregation and its leaders here allowed themselves to be reproached, but this does not imply that the sermon acted as a powerful reformatory stimulus.

Though preaching was an institution of public criticism and control, it was not revolutionary. It did not promote even absolute consistency in the realization of accepted ideals. There were some preachers whose fervor reached an ecstatic pitch, imparting to the audience a deep religious experience. These men sometimes succeeded in persuading their listeners to lead a changed life, confess their sins, and adopt ascetic practices. But as a rule, preaching played no revolutionary or reformatory role. It acted rather as an emotional safety valve, something in the nature of a public catharsis. Though it may not have aroused many people to a fundamental change, it helped to preserve the customary way of life.

At the height of the homiletical development of the seventeenth and eighteenth centuries, outstanding preachers achieved amazing artistry in the construction of their sermons. The opening theme was designed as the central thread. This might disappear at times, but just as the central theme had disappeared unnoticed, it was destined to reappear suddenly in order to create a feeling of unity in the audience. The sermon finally concluded by returning to its point of departure and offering a solution to the original problem which the preacher had deliberately left open. The listeners who followed these mental gymnastics were not to be denied the aesthetic pleasure produced by the tension built up and then released. Moralists vainly pilloried this method of preaching, arguing that it debased the words of Holy Writ and that it transformed the purely corrective function of the preacher to that of providing entertainment.

Our description of the institution of preaching has already led us to touch upon the second outstanding religious institution besides the rabbinate, the synagogue. No Jewish milieu was complete without it. Here, too, in attempting to understand the functions and structure of the institution, we must concentrate first on extracting the significance of its basic function, the maintenance of public worship. This function was undoubtedly religious. Prayer is likely to become devoid of its content with the undermining of faith and the weakening of the attachment to transcendental values. But so long as prayer exists, it is nourished by the need of man to approach his Maker, to petition his needs, confess his sins, seek communion with God, or even simply to divest himself of the atmosphere of secular things and enter the realm of the sacred.

Private or public prayer, even in the traditional Jewish society, varied depending entirely on the religious convictions inspiring it. But different views concerning the nature and function of prayer did not prevent the worshippers from participating in a common service. Only professional mystics gave external expression to their special view even in prayer, expression such as changes in the liturgical rite or in the pronunciation, and only they set up their own places of worship. But in general, fixed traditional patterns for prayers reigned supreme.

These patterns were a heritage of the Mishnaic and earlier periods, though they possessed a few medieval accretions and some insignificant local variations in custom. A Jew who moved from one place to another might find the practices of the new congregation different from those of the one to which he was

accustomed—in the melodies, liturgical rite, and customs it
employed. But these differences did not involve fundamentals.
Within the territorial confines of one center, such as the German-
Polish one that we are discussing, these changes were nothing
more than slight nuances which did not even serve as a psychological barrier to joining the congregation immediately or after
a short period of adjustment.

Jewish prayer is public prayer, not only with respect to content, but primarily from the aspect of performance. Jewish observance admittedly requires the individual to pray thrice daily,
even when he is on his own. He fulfills his obligation to the letter
by private meditation, even where nothing prevents him from
attending public services. But in this period—in contrast to the
Mishnaic—private prayer was regarded as the exception. The
proper form of worship in communities large enough to maintain a *minyan* (the quorum of ten males of the age of thirteen or
over) was public prayer in the synagogue, in the *bet hamidrash*
or house of study, or even in a private home, where one or two
rooms had been set aside and equipped for the purpose by the
installation of an Ark with a Scroll of the Law. Such improvised
synagogues were the rule in towns with a small Jewish population,
and they were later resorted to also in the large cities, when the
decentralization of the communal framework began. But during
the apogee of the traditional *kehilla,* the small and medium-sized
kehillot had a single synagogue proper, while the large *kehillot*
had several branches in addition. But even these auxiliary synagogues preserved their public character and were subject to the
local customs and community authority.

The advantage of public over private prayer was stressed
even in Talmudic tradition, and the first ten men to arrive at the
synagogue, who thus ensured public worship on that particular
occasion, were deemed especially meritorious. The superiority of
public prayer received tangible expression in the addition of
kaddish and *kedusha,* prayers that are not said unless there are

at least ten men present. Because of their quasi-mystic content and exclusively public character, these selections were accorded particular attention by the commentators and were considered especially important by the worshippers. One who absented himself from public prayer forfeited the reward which religious belief accorded such participation and was deprived of a valuable religious experience.

The congregation, as an organic unit, regarded itself as responsible for the maintenance of public worship. The right granted members of the congregation by the Talmud to enforce communal erection of a synagogue was later extended, with some qualification, to that of maintaining a quorum in the synagogue for daily, and especially Sabbath and festival services. Public prayer was equated with the daily offering in the temple, and its absence was tantamount to the abrogation of the daily offering. The community that had been deprived of shouldering this joint religious duty felt itself guilty, not only as individuals who had failed to fulfil one of the precepts, but also as a community that had defaulted in respect of something that guaranteed its right to existence.

The individual's obligation to participate in public prayer was exploited for disciplinary purposes. The first stage of excommunication was to deprive the offender of the privilege of public worship. Conversely, the victim of injustice could interrupt the service as a means of compelling the congregation to heed his grievance. In the first case, the individual felt himself excluded from the ranks of those privileged to take part in public prayer; in the second case, the entire congregation suffered the religious stain of an interruption in its devotions and regarded itself as standing condemned before God.

The attachment of the individual to the congregation in the sphere of prayer and its attendant ceremonies was subordinate to the general framework of religious manifestations. Obviously, social circumstances conditioned the expression of this attachment in the first place, and subsequently, the attachment had its repercussions on the social milieu as a whole. We may justify the first assertion by recalling that the daily obligation to participate in public prayer, morning and evening, could be met only where Jews lived close together, where the hours of work permitted, and, in general, where the exploitation of the time factor was still not essential for economic success. Synagogue attendance was facilitated where the store or workshop was located on the same premises as the home. When the menfolk were absent—and it was only the men whose attendance was required in the synagogue—the women would substitute for them in the store; in any case, it was not necessary actually to close the store during the hour of prayer. Under these conditions, the entire congregation could very well assemble for public prayer twice a day, and could be expected to implement it.

The concentration of homes in one area made it possible to signal the hour of prayer, and the beadle or *shamash* who summoned the worshippers was characteristic of the life of the Jewish quarter in this period. Synagogue attendance was also easily subject to mutual control, and the admonitions of the rabbis and preachers were thus supplemented by the informal criticism of the congregation itself. In the small *kehillot*, this control was exercised by the *kehilla* leaders themselves; while in the large *kehillot*, this was accomplished through the associations, which obligated their members to attend services.

Nevertheless, it should not be thought that the ideal of synagogue attendance twice daily was ever realized completely. Certain occupations took some individuals away from the Jewish quarter, particularly at the hour of afternoon prayer, during the short winter days. Others, like artisans and domestic servants, were tied to their work at prayer time. Religious authority made allowances for them, insisting only that they attend the synagogue on the days on which the Torah was read or on Sabbaths and festivals alone. The greater the significance of the day, the less need there was to insist on synagogue attendance. There is ample evidence of preaching and moralizing which stressed the importance of participation in public prayer on weekdays. But there is no trace of such sermonizing with regard to Sabbaths and festivals. Attendance was assured by the stronger drawing power of the synagogue on those days, and by the absence of those factors which stood in the way of the would-be worshipper during the rest of the week.

But there was interaction between the religious sphere, to which public prayer naturally belonged, and the social area. Wherever public worship was feasible, it, in turn, had repercussions in other fields. The synagogue was the place where warnings were issued, excommunication pronounced, oaths taken, and which punished individuals by excluding them from it.

The synagogue itself required organization and management. These functions were entrusted to wardens who discharged them in person or through the beadle. The wardens were appointed in the same way as other communal leaders. At times this position served as the stepping stone to advancement because of the experience in leadership it afforded. But the synagogue also served as a place which fulfilled less obvious social functions. As the regular meeting place for the members of the congregation, it furnished the setting for conversation about secular matters as well—including business negotiations. Admittedly, religious law forbade discussion in the synagogue of any matter which did not concern the prayers themselves. But precisely because of the frequency of the synagogue meetings in this period, the rule was no longer observed in practice. Indeed, the leaders themselves took advantage of the congregation's coming together for their own purposes, and the rank and file followed their example. It is unlikely that they had any qualms about discussing business in the synagogue at times when absolute silence was not enjoined.

But the principal social use to which the visit to the synagogue was put was not to use it as a place to arrange business deals but simply as a setting for gossip. Even the formal Halakha laid down a sliding scale in the degree of devotion and silence required for the various prayers and ceremonies. It imposed strict silence only during the main parts of the service. But whether talking was actually forbidden during the rest of the time was a moot point. Strict and thoroughgoing moralists attempted to prohibit all secular talk within the confines of the synagogue. But the frequency of the meetings between members of an amorphous congregation militated against the acceptance of such stringency. This demand could be achieved only in synagogues attended by a select body of persons who spontaneously formed themselves into a separate conventicle.

In addition to fulfilling its central task in the life of the community, the synagogue also gave expression to the social stratification of the community. The seating arrangements themselves served as a means of distinction. Proximity to the Ark, reader, rabbis, or the platform from which the Torah was read were all considered places of honor. The first row near the eastern end (*mizrah*) was invested with a special value of its own. Seats were purchased outright by the members of the congregation and they sometimes passed from father to son.

The synagogue framework offered the well-to-do various methods of displaying their wealth. Rich families would donate Scrolls of the Law, curtains for the Ark, and ritual objects. In a manner typical of the period, such gifts were not incorporated completely into the general property of the synagogue. The donor's name was inscribed on his gift, and he and the members of his family were given the honor of using them on the days designated for the purpose. Occasionally a quarrel broke out over the question of whose gift should be employed on a particular occasion.

Another criterion of a person's social rank was the *aliya* (being called to "ascend" to read a portion of the Law). Here, too, there were gradations, depending on the importance of the day and other considerations. The *aliya* was bought, the purchaser either taking the honor for himself or bestowing it on someone else. It also served as an opportunity to announce contributions to charitable causes and, at the same time, as a means of publicizing one's financial capacities. However, the receipt of the honor of an *aliya* did not depend solely on the financial factor. The regulations of the *kehillot* and the super-*kehillot* reserved some *aliyot* for such personages as the local rabbi, the district rabbi, scholars, and the community leaders. The minuteness with which the rules were set forth, not only in the regulations of the *kehillot* but also of the super-*kehillot*, is evidence of the sensitivity of people with regard to fixing a person's place in the social scale. The synagogue ritual afforded the principal opportunity for demonstrating this publicly.

Apart from the active participation in the synagogue service, the assembly of the community on festivals and holy days offered an opportunity for one to exhibit his wealth through his own external appearance—in clothing and ornaments. Men could adorn themselves by using silver ornamentation on their prayer shawls; here the women found the best opportunity for displaying their wealth and position. The regulations which, for various reasons, attempted to restrict the use of luxuries sometimes made an exception when it came to synagogue attendance. The honor of the Sabbath and festivals required one to be well-dressed, and this could serve as a pretext for the demonstration of social status. Even if the intention of the individual was simply to observe the precept of glorifying the Sabbath or festival, the fact remains that each person's appearance in public, dressed in keeping with his purse, served as a means of social classification.

The phenomena listed above are secondary, social functions which became attached to the religious institution, not always in accordance with its aims and, at times, even in distinct opposition to them. Be that as it may, the chief social function of the synagogue was not in these incidental concomitants. The synagogue served to maintain society precisely where and to the extent that it avoided all social motives. The congregation which assembles for prayer becomes united insofar as it succeeds in forgetting itself and communes, in accordance with its religious consciousness, with its God.

We have already observed that the more the religious ceremony is charged with sentiment, the more the individual is dependent on the congregation in his worship. At the climax of Jewish public devotions, on Rosh Hashana and Yom Kippur, when the likelihood is greatest that the individual will turn his thoughts away from his selfish motives and social ambitions, he is likely to be absorbed almost completely in his society-congregation. This experience of coalescence, though it is temporary, is not likely to go without effect. The internal cohesiveness of the Jewish community was undoubtedly nourished by the depth of the religious experience of the ever-recurring ritual.

Durkheim's judgment on the unity of religion and society is substantiated here, although not in the sense that religion loses its independence and becomes a mere function of society. Only where religion lives on its own independent resources—man facing God—is it unconsciously and paradoxically also transformed into an all-important social preservative.

XVIII *Educational Institutions*

THE FACT THAT THE JEWISH SOCIETY IS A TRA-
ditional one—that is, one based on knowledge and values of the
past—does not exclude the future from the scope of its consideration. Only the importance of the present declines as a result of excessive attachment to the past. As to the future, there
exists the hope that the values of the past will be restored. As
in every other idealistic society forced to compromise with reality, the hope was repeated again and again that the ideal would
be fully realized by the coming generation. The new generation
in the process of growing up is, for the time being, exempt from
the struggle of life and does not have to stoop to the compromises
which reality imposes on the active participants in the society.

For this reason, the institutions of education present the values of society in their purest form in addressing themselves to the rising generation. In the traditional Jewish society, activated by the ideal of perpetuating its religious heritage, the institutions of education fostered and transmitted the traditional values to the new generation.

The education of the new generation, that is, the introduction of the young to the framework of social life—"socialization" is the sociologist's word—was not carried out only by the institutions especially designated for the purpose. Other social institutions participated in this function within their respective spheres. Although they were originally created to cater to the needs of the existing society, they were also charged with the auxiliary task of serving the requirements of the growing generation.

The family, of course, was the foremost of these secondary institutions of education. But the family's educational role did not derive directly from its biological objective. Its educational influence was dependent on the breadth of the social base, on its internal structure, and on its cultural endowment. From all three aspects, the traditional Jewish family must be regarded as an educational factor of the first order. In the framework of family life, the child absorbed the atmosphere of the traditional society as a whole. The structure of the family was similar to that of society. The father stood at the head, representing the traditional values in virtue of which he reigned supreme. The mother was close to him in status, but she was not equal to him in authority. The children and the other members of the family each occupied positions in accordance with their age and qualities. The child who grew up in such a family was trained to know the difference between higher and lower rank and was accustomed to a hierarchical discipline.

The family served as the basis for certain religious ceremonies, beginning with the Sabbath eve meal—or even with the daily meals, to the extent that the family dined together and recited grace before and after meals—and ending with the Passover Seder. The family was thus a repository of religious values. The emotional cords binding the child to his family were thus fused with the religious experience derived from the ceremonial observances. Religious and family attachment alike gained by this co-operation. The family also unconsciously served as an educational instrument when it fulfilled its social functions. Since it provided the principal framework for adult social activity, children, too, took some part in it, whether in accompanying their parents on visits or in receiving guests in their homes.

The foundations for the broad family solidarity were probably laid in these early childhood experiences, when the child was given an opportunity to observe the close relations which existed between the members of the larger family. On all sides, the family was an educational factor, even if we take no account of the actual task of teaching which was imposed on its adult members. Morals and good manners and the elementary customs of religion and tradition, prayers and benedictions, were learned by the children from the older members of the family as a result of a planned effort or of the ever-recurring chance opportunities.

The services at the synagogue occupied second place among the auxiliary educational institutions. From their early childhood, children attended the synagogue accompanied by their parents or, as we shall see, supervised by their teacher. The service was conducted by the adults, while the children, until almost thirteen, played no active part in conducting the ritual. However, they joined in the congregational chant and responses. They learned the customs connected with the service, the text of the prayers, and the accompanying melodies. The child acquired a feeling of belonging to the religious community, experiencing the immediacy of his communion with the divine, from direct participation in the synagogue ritual. In a similar fashion, he was initiated into the traditions pertaining to this field. Through hearing the sermons and discussions in the synagogue, he absorbed at least fragments of what was regarded as formal knowledge that were directly disseminated by the educational institutions.

All the *kehilla* institutions must be regarded, in the broadest sense, as educational instruments for the new generation. Under the cramped conditions of existence, with the activities of the public institutions as intertwined with one another as they were, it was impossible to keep the children from seeing and hearing everything that took place in the community. The life of the community was carried on before the eyes of young and old, as in a public arena, and from their vantage point, the children were in a position to absorb as much as they were intellectually capable of.

A similar situation prevailed with respect to preparation for practical life in the economic field. Here no formal training of any sort existed. At the very most, the learning of Yiddish or Hebrew spelling or the first essentials of arithmetic in the *heder* or elsewhere served as a formal preparation for practical life. The children of the rich also had the opportunity to study the vernacular or the language, often Latin, used by the government officials, under private tutors. A knowledge of the language facilitated the approach to the authorities, and the person qualified in this respect had an advantage in winning the post of *shtadlan* (interceder with the authorities on behalf of the Jewish community) or in exploiting his contacts with government representatives.

The knowledge required for running a business was acquired through practical experience. The first years of marriage, when the couple lived with their parents, offered a good opportunity to gain such experience. The commercial methods in vogue among both Jews and non-Jews made such a method of learning feasible.

The same was true of manual trades. The apprentice helped his master and learned the trade by watching and imitating him.

The preparation for other vocations—rabbis, preachers, teachers and sextons of all types—was even more improvised. In this period, formal training was not customary for any occupation or profession.

This brings us to a definition of the methods and content of the formal educational institutions which functioned in this society: the *heder* and the yeshiva. These institutions dealt only with initiating pupils to the permanent values of society. Their principal function was to transmit Jewish tradition at different teaching levels. The *heder* supplemented the knowledge of tradition which the child absorbed from the direct social channels (the family, the synagogue, the street, etc.) with the basic knowledge accumulated in the religious-national literature. In keeping with its general public task, the *heder* was to be found everywhere in the traditional Jewish society. Even the isolated Jew living in a remote village strove to employ a tutor for his children or to send them to a teacher in a nearby town to receive instruction in the rudiments of Judaism. Poverty did not, as a rule, prevent one from providing his children with a Jewish education, at least of an elementary nature. Under religious law, it was the father's duty to provide his children with an education and to bear the necessary expense. The extremely wealthy sometimes employed a private tutor for their children; the tutor lived with the family and served both as teacher and mentor to the children, with whom he stayed all day long.

However, education was largely furthered in publicly supervised institutions. Though the father was expected to bear the cost, education was regarded as more than an individual obligation. The employment of a teacher constituted one of the duties which Jewish religious law obligated the residents of a town to fulfil, even at the price of mutual compulsion. But in this period, matters usually did not reach such a stage. For the most part, an ample supply of teachers offered their services to parents.

The *kehilla* thus did not bear the expense of instruction, and usually did not even have to organize the educational system. Its task was limited to supervising the teacher and providing for the education of those children whose parents could not afford to pay. In the smaller *kehillot*, these functions were entrusted to the *kehilla* leaders themselves.

But in *kehillot* which had reached the stage of differentiation in the division of functions, special trustees, known as Talmud Torah wardens, were appointed for this task. In other *kehillot*, special associations, known as Talmud Torah associations, were organized, and the officers were responsible both for the supervision of the teachers and the provision of a free education for poor children. The financial resources required for the latter were considerable. Certain sources of income were specially allocated to the Talmud Torah fund. Part of the current synagogue contributions were set aside for this purpose. The Talmud Torah trustees were also permitted to solicit donations on suitable occasions. In some localities, a tax was levied on the members of the *kehilla* to cover the education of needy children. Special teachers were employed and, occasionally, special premises were set aside for this purpose. The private teachers who taught the children of the well-to-do were sometimes required to teach poor children free of charge or at a reduced fee. But the hiring by the community of a single teacher for all the children was customary only in small *kehillot* where individual parents could not afford a private tutor.

Education thus assumed a public character not from the organizational or financial aspect, but from its supervision and control. Supervision did not extend to the selection of qualified teachers through prior examination. Since there was no formal licensing system for teachers, nothing could prevent any local resident from serving as a teacher through a private agreement with parents. Would-be teachers were sometimes required to give evidence of their qualifications, if, for example, it had been decided that only a person who had been awarded the title of *haver* by the local rabbi might serve as a teacher. Even this title, however, proved nothing more than the fact that its holder was a scholar of sorts who had studied a number of years in a yeshiva. Thus, such control as did exist applied, at the very most, only to the teacher's knowledge, while his pedagogical ability could be judged only in the course of actual teaching.

The success of a teacher was measured by the pupil's achievement. It was customary for the pupils to be periodically examined by representatives of the public: the rabbi or someone acting for him, the Talmud Torah trustees, or other persons specifically appointed for the purpose. The supervision was aimed particularly at ensuring the proper conditions necessary for the success of the teacher's work: that he should not accept more pupils than could be satisfactorily taught, reduce the hours of instruction, or employ the children on extraneous tasks.

Public control also extended over salaries, the times of payment, the method of collection, and the prevention of unfair competition where the supply of teachers was greater than the demand. Appropriate bodies exercised another sort of control by seeing to it that parents did not put their children to work, either for themselves or for others, at an age when they should be studying. The minimum age for starting work varied from place to place, but it generally ranged between thirteen and fifteen.

Thus, in essence, *heder* education was entrusted to teachers who were not distinguished either by their knowledge or their formal preparation for the task. Although society placed a high value on the teaching function, the prestige of those who performed the function, the *melamdim*, was not very high. Their low salaries, their dependence on individuals, and their almost complete enslavement to their work turned them into a type hopelessly chained to the job without any prospects of advancement.

It was a religious duty (based on Deuteronomy 6:7) to teach one's child, and communal bodies employed various means of persuasion and pressure to ensure fulfilment. Traditional education, therefore, embraced all members of society with hardly an exception. The subject matter absorbed in the first stages of the *heder* formed the basic layer in the national-religious consciousness of the entire community. This subject matter was the Pentateuch with a translation into the vernacular and, in the second stage, with Rashi's commentary. The peculiar position of the Jews as a chosen people, the inherently mythic distinction between them and the nations, an understanding of the fate of the Jewish people in the Diaspora and their faith in their coming redemption—all of these penetrated the child's consciousness through the popular homiletic light of Rashi's commentary, which was originally written with a didactic purpose in the Middle Ages, a period of outstanding religious tension and awareness. Children thus gathered the fundamentals of the faith incidentally, through the study of the sources, particularly the Pentateuch with Rashi's commentary.

The lack of systematization and comprehensiveness in pedagogical goals was a typical feature of this educational system. Even in the study of the Pentateuch, no attempt was made to follow the continuity of the Biblical narrative. Each week the pupils began to learn the Biblical Portion of the Week, and if they did not finish it by the end of the week, they skipped over the last few chapters.

The subordination of school to synagogue was a hallowed ancient precedent. It was also based on the constant need to prepare the pupils to follow the congregational prayers and the reading of the Law on the Sabbath. Thus, synagogal needs overrode logical curricular considerations.

By any rational criterion, this method of teaching must be considered unsatisfactory. Despite the considerable public attention paid to education, some person remained unable to read, write, or even sign their names. But even those who did absorb the knowledge which the *heder* was in a position to transmit were equipped with formal achievements of an unquestionably fragmentary nature. From the viewpoint of its social function, however, this education fulfilled its purpose. The Jewish child who attended *heder,* if only for a few years, successfully mastered the rudiments of tradition. His knowledge and religious attachment enabled him to join the congregation in prayer and act in accordance with its major prescriptions.

The critics of the *heder* attributed its lack of success in teaching partly to the fact that teachers failed to attune their syllabus to the pupil's age and mental capacity. In the light of these criteria, they should have taken as their goal a thorough knowledge of the Bible and familiarity with the Mishna. Instead, these goals were regarded merely as preparation for the ultimate aim of education: to turn the pupil into a scholar (*talmid hakham*) with a thorough training in Talmud, who eventually mastered its contents and the work of its codifiers.

This goal could be achieved only by studying at a yeshiva, the highest educational institution of traditional society. It was clear that this goal would be achieved only by the minority— those who were capable of benefiting from prolonged study. Though the *heder* was a popular educational institution, it was forced to cater to the aims of the minority. Before the pupils had acquired a fundamental knowledge of the Bible, or even of the Pentateuch, they started to study the Talmud. In this field, in particular, a teacher stood to win appreciation. Clever teachers, whose livelihood depended on their making a good impression on the parents, perfected techniques which led to remarkable accomplishments—though they were illusory and even harmful in the opinion of some of the outstanding critics.

The fact was that the *heder* was simply harnessed to the system of values on which the entire Jewish society was based. A thorough knowledge of and preoccupation with the Talmud, although acquired only by a minority, constituted a value of supreme importance to society as a whole. The educational aims which applied to the entire people—a basic knowledge of Judaism and the observance of its precepts—were considered only by-products of the ultimate goal, the rearing of scholars.

The educational framework for the raising of scholars was the *yeshiva*. The existence of a yeshiva depended, first of all, on the presence of a rabbi, a scholar capable of teaching the Talmud and its commentaries. One had not only to have mastered the subject matter, but also to have the ability to give original interpretations of the sources. Obviously, neither the extent of a rabbi's knowledge nor his originality were subject to any single, universally accepted definition. Even here, the level of the qualifications required varied according to time and place. The head of the yeshiva did not need to be formally licensed for the position, as was the case with a rabbi, nor was he subject to institutional control, as was the *melamed*. The public opinion of the students and scholars alone determined who was worthy of the position.

Unlike the *heder,* which was a local institution that did not cater to children from other towns, the yeshiva provided an education for students from different towns and villages and, occasionally, even from other countries. The difference was based, first, on the age of the pupils in the two institutions. The *melamed* taught pupils up to the age of twelve or thirteen, generally the age at which a boy entered the yeshiva.

Boys of yeshiva age were not only capable of living away from home, but they even looked forward to the parting and to spending their adolescence years among boys of their own age, revering the head of the *yeshiva* as their mentor and instructor. They were not motivated simply by a desire to find a more superior level of teaching. Even boys from large *kehillot,* where there was no dearth of good teachers, would go to study in different towns. By cutting themselves off from home and joining an educational institution, the adolescents could immerse themselves in an atmosphere devoted exclusively to the furthering of traditional values.

The presence of students from other towns gave the yeshiva its special character. Although the local residents who studied at the yeshiva might outnumber those from out-of-town, they formed only the periphery of the yeshiva. This was in contrast to the other *kehilla* institutions, where the local residents invariably constituted the dominant nucleus which absorbed any outsiders. This was caused by the absolute dependence of the students on their rabbi, and this dependence arose from their self-imposed isolation from other institutions. The nucleus of the yeshiva was formed by the students whose right to study there and even their physical existence were dependent on the rabbi's decision. Once this nucleus was created, it was likely to attract local elements— youths of study age, young married scholars living with their fathers-in-law, or simply laymen who came to hear the lectures. But the basis of the yeshiva organization was the group of outside students, for only they fulfilled the condition of complete devotion to studies and unswerving attachment to the rabbi, who represented the values they had deliberately come to absorb.

The existence of the yeshiva depended, too, on the extent to which it catered to the needs of out-of-town students. These needs were loyally met by the local public, reared as it was to appreciate the paramount importance of Torah study. The *kehilla* and super-*kehilla* institutions undertook the responsibility for maintaining the yeshivot. The burden of supporting the yeshiva students was imposed on the *kehilla* members. When a new rabbi was appointed, he would generally specify the number of such students he expected the *kehilla* to support. The direct responsibility for the students' maintenance was delegated to members appointed by the *kehilla*. As was the case with the *heder*, the maintenance costs of the yeshiva were borne by the public on a semi-voluntary basis.

In some places, contributions for this purpose were given spontaneously, and in others, communal bodies set aside special occasions for such donations. The trustees of the yeshiva students' fund were also entitled to call upon the *kehilla* members to provide room and board for students in their own homes. The task of the super-*kehilla* was, first of all, to dissuade the *kehillot* from evading their duty to maintain the yeshivot. Second, they extended help, or at least gave the initial impetus, in places where yeshiva affairs constituted more than a local concern. The yeshiva students were distributed by a central body on the basis of the economic capacity of the *kehillot*. Villages which could not afford to maintain a yeshiva of their own were called upon to contribute toward the one in their district. Small communities were required to designate definite dates when contributions would be solicited and forwarded to the yeshivot. The villages, too, directly supported the students by accommodating them during vacation periods, no small part of the year. In this matter, the super-*kehilla* organizations tried to work out an arrangement dividing the burden fairly and guaranteeing the educational needs of the students away from home.

It may be said that the yeshiva, in the period we are discussing, was an institution which created scholars with the highest intellectual training. The scholarship of yeshiva students reached such a stage of complexity and acuteness that no one who had not devoted several years to intensive study could follow a lecture on their level or a learned discussion between them.

This state of affairs resulted from developments in the study of Halakha which, particularly after the compilation of the *Shulhan Arukh*, split into two branches, practical and theoretical. The practical study of Halakha was generally based on the authority of the classic codifiers (*poskim*) of the preceding age. The study of the original sources served merely as an opportunity for exegesis and familiarization with the Talmudic mode of argument. This resulted in a tendency by scholars to indulge in farfetched argumentation divorced from reality. In its extreme development, beginning with the sixteenth century, this tendency led to the evolution of the famous *hilukim* (dialectical talmudic discourses). The scholars who delivered these discourses set themselves the problem of reconciling contradictions in the Talmud and its commentaries on the basis of logical hypotheses, although they themselves sometimes admitted the far-fetched nature of the questions or the doubtful value of the answers. Teachers offered a pedagogical justification for putting scholarship to a use which led neither to the discovery of truth nor to guidance in practical conduct. They claimed that the *hilukim* sharpened the mind and thus prepared the students for future study in the desired manner.

As a matter of fact, the students were employed upon this exaggerated casuistry (*pilpul*) only during part of the school year. Each semester—in the summer, from the first day of *Iyar* (May) until the fifteenth of *Av* (July), and in the winter from the first day of *Marheshvan* (October) until the fifteenth of *Shevat* (February)—was subdivided into two terms. Only during the first half of each semester—in the summer until the *Shavuot* holiday and in the winter until Hannuka (six and nine weeks respectively)—was the casuistic method used, this reaching a climax in the *hiluk* delivered by the rabbi or by someone on whom he bestowed the honor. The second half of each semester was devoted to the study of the early and later codifiers. Here, the necessity of arriving at a practical conclusion based on the sources limited the student's ability to resort to unbridled casuistry. But the method of precise analysis of the meaning of the early codifiers was also sufficiently complicated so that only several years' study in a yeshiva would equip a person to follow such a course.

In any event, prolonged and constant study was essential if one wished to be recognized as a scholar. The preparation of pupils for this kind of learning was beyond the capacity of *heder* teachers. Even in the yeshiva itself, the students were divided into two categories: the *bahurim*, who could study Talmud on their own, and the *naarim*, who required coaching.

In return for the financial assistance which they received from the yeshiva management, the *bahurim* undertook to coach the *naarim*, i.e., to prepare them for the rabbi's lecture. The preliminary study of the topic itself and, usually, the review of the rabbi's own's interpretations, were conducted in small groups consisting of a "teacher" and two or three students. These groups studied in their own rooms for most of the day and went into the *bet midrash* only to hear the rabbi's lecture.

But even a *bahur* who persisted in his studies at the yeshiva did not attain the level of scholar (*talmid hakham*). Not even the first academic title of *haver* (fellow) was granted when a student quit the yeshiva at the marriageable age of eighteen or so. For this it was necessary to continue one's studies for at least two years after marriage. Such study was carried on either independently or in conjunction with the local yeshiva. At the expiration of this period, the student was awarded the first title, not necessarily by the rabbi under whom he had studied, but just as often by the local rabbi whose yeshiva he attended after marriage. The title *moreinu*, which entitled one to rule on religious questions, was awarded only after a longer period, the minimum apparently being six years after marriage.

The number of years of study required for the award of the titles of *haver* and *moreinu*, as well as the other conditions, were stipulated in the by-laws of the *kehilla* and the super-*kehilla*. This control by the *kehilla* and communal bodies over the granting of titles was no chance arrangement. They were interested parties, since the possession of a title accorded the holder special privileges within the *kehilla*, such as exemption from taxes and eligibility for office. This explains the fact that although these titles were earned on the basis of study in the yeshivot, they were awarded not by these academic institutions but by rabbis officiating in the *kehillot*, occasionally even under the direct supervision of the leaders of the *kehillot* and super-*kehillot*.

The yeshiva, in its historical evolution from the sixteenth to the eighteenth century, was thus distinguished by more than its particular method of learning. The identity of purpose of the rabbi and the yeshiva head, which was customary in this period, was another typical feature. The yeshiva existed, in this period as in all others in its history, because of the value attached to the public teaching of Torah. It was the duty of the Jewish scholar to instruct the people in the Torah and to increase the number of his disciples. Since Torah scholarship was not a matter of mastering certain practical techniques, the rabbi never appeared as a mere transmitter of facts. He represented to his students the incarnation of the traditional values which he was imparting to them through the intellectual contact of the learning process.

Moreover, since the nucleus of the yeshiva consisted of students whose only loyalty was to their rabbinic head, an atmosphere was created conducive to the creation of a close personal link between them. These circumstances facilitated the formation of an educational framework of an unusually intensive nature. However, it is doubtful whether advantage was taken of this opportunity during this period. The combining of the tasks of president of the local rabbinic court and yeshiva head decreased rather than increased the prospects that this would happen. The advancement of the yeshiva was, after all, only one of the rabbi's many tasks. It is true that the yeshiva provided the rabbi with something of a counter-balance to his activities and struggles in public life. In the yeshiva, he lived in a world over which he held almost absolute sway. From here he could expect to gain prestige which would carry over to the other fields of his activity. The rabbi's greatness in learning was expressed in the number of his disciples and the depth of their attachment to him.

The relationship of the *kehilla* to the rabbi, which was not lacking in conflict and tension, was likely, for its part, to have its equilibrium restored through the halo which surrounded the rabbi in the line of his yeshiva duties. The honor accorded the rabbi as head of the yeshiva and as disseminator of learning among the people, values that were universally esteemed, also strengthened his hand as he carried out his function as arbiter of the values of the entire community. The fact remains, however, that the educational function was exercised by someone whose chief field of activity lay elsewhere. The limitation of the academic year to only seven months was adopted not so much because it benefited the students, but because the rabbi was unable to devote more time to the yeshiva, and the community could not maintain the students for a longer period. The long vacations, and the moving of the students from one yeshiva to another, jeopardized the continuity of the contact between the student and the rabbi and prevented the formation of close ties between them at this time.

A striking symptom of the neglect of educational considerations in the yeshivot can be detected from the end of the seventeenth century. Public bodies and moralists found it necessary to warn the yeshiva heads not to turn their institutions into a supplementary source of income by taking fees from the students anxious to gain admission.

Despite the decisive influence of the out-of-town students in shaping the yeshiva, the institution was absorbed into the life of the local *kehilla* which maintained it. It is doubtful whether the yeshiva, in this period, excelled in any unique religious quality. Unlike the periods in which the unifying force of the *kehillot* underwent a decline and the yeshivot took upon themselves the responsibility of becoming the standard bearers of tradition, in this period, the *kehilla* was regarded as responsible for fostering the society's values, while the yeshiva was hardly more than just one of its various institutions.

XIX

Stratification and Mobility

*T*HE ANALYSIS OF A SOCIETY WOULD BE INCOM-
plete without determining its hierarchy of functions. It is likewise essential to trace the fluctuations that take place between
individuals and groups within this context. The nature of these
fluctuations will determine the extent and direction of the society's mobility. Social stratification, as well as constant fluctuations in hierarchical values, were not absent in the traditional
Jewish society either. Admittedly, the Jewish society consisted
merely of one section of the over-all society, thus whittling down
the scope of stratification. Occupational stratification was ruled
out by the lack of a wide vocational diversity. The artisans alone
tended to form a kind of classified vocational group. Their low

rank in the hierarchy was determined by the nature of their occupation. But even this collective grouping never achieved exclusive and hereditary proportions. No inhibitions interfered with the adopting of a new trade. Indeed, we find no ideology to justify the separateness of the artisan group. Manual labor was resorted to only as a matter of necessity, and no barriers were placed in the way of anyone capable of breaking away from it.

Class petrification on the basis of political factors was also precluded both by the dependence of the Jews on the non-Jewish authorities and the performance by Jews of political tasks assigned to them. Admittedly, the Jew's dependence on the authorities had decisive repercussions on his status. If he was granted the right of domicile where such privilege was not acquired through the Jewish community and, to an even greater extent, if he worked for the government in some economic or administrative capacity, his status rose, even within the internal Jewish society.

In some places, a sliding scale of privileges was accorded to Jews by the authorities, some receiving a hereditary right of domicile, others merely being granted it for their own lifetime or an even shorter period. Some were merely tolerated or were dependent on the residential rights of their fellow Jews. The latter conducted themselves as retainers of the Jews who enjoyed protection, but at times they employed their supposed connection as a camouflage for engaging in some business of their own. In any case, a lack of any personal right of domicile impaired their status even in the Jewish society.

The Jew could acquire influence and even real power in non-Jewish society. But owing to the mutual exclusiveness of the two societies in the social and cultural spheres, he was unable to convert his influence and power into a representative position in non-Jewish society. This power could be expressed socially only within the Jewish society itself. The exploitation of this source of power to buttress one's position internally was not considered reprehensible as such. Closeness to the authorities could be interpreted as a form of spontaneous representation of Jewish interests before the authorities for both the individual and public good. If one fulfilled this function as the ideal demanded, he would receive legitimate honor and prestige within Jewish society. Personal influence with the authorities was discredited only when abused; if, for instance, its possessor utilized it to usurp communal office. In such an event, political power lost its social approval, and even if society did not succeed in routing the "influential man" or the "informer," the esteem ordinarily due to him would be converted to contempt.

Where the Jewish population was divided into persons enjoying different rights, it is almost possible to speak of class divisions in the sense of estates. The distinctions operated not only in practice, they were proclaimed and recognized by the authorities and possessed legal validity. From this point of view, class differences in the Jewish society were given bases no different from those of the other classes in a country with estates. But another fact must be noted which weakens this comparison: the additional privileges which the Jew acquired from the authorities were not rights in perpetuity, as were the rights of the indigenous nobles. Even the highest positions of the Jew were "bought" positions that the authorities granted to anyone able to pay the price. These positions, therefore, could not secure for their occupants either external signs of recognition or a philosophy of justification or a lineal attachment. Unlike the internal positions of leadership and scholarship, whose holders bequeathed something of their prestige to their children, political distinction was something linked to the individual alone. These positions of preeminence were, in effect, nothing more than convenient bases of activity, enabling those who filled them to act in various fields with greater ease. They never reached the stage of possessing any intrinsic value.

We shall arrive at similar conclusions if we examine the in-

ternal government of the Jewish community and those who exercised power within it. Those who occupied official positions, as
we have seen in the analysis of the *kehilla* institutions, enjoyed
material advantages and were invested by the people with signs
of honor indicating the importance of their task. Communal
office thus formed the basis of the stratification on which the
social hierarchy was constructed. It is clear, likewise, that the
ascent of this hierarchical ladder was not within reach of every
individual. The exclusion of the poor was given an explicit institutional expression in regulations which limited the electorate
to taxpayers and scholars. At times the various communal offices were monopolized by a limited circle, and new appointments merely implied a reshuffle between its members.

All this does not mean that the office-holders strictly constituted a ruling caste. Although the changes in officials en-
compassed only a small minority of the *kehilla* members, they
did serve to prevent the formation of a vested right to rule in-
definitely. A considerable proportion of the *kehilla* took part in
political activity by voting or influencing public opinion in favor
of one candidate or another. Hereditary appointments, in which
the few would deprive the majority of the possibility of office,
never even entered their minds. The essential fact is that the twin
conditions for joining the electorate of property and learning
could be fulfilled by all.

The individual did not regard himself as permanently and
irrevocably excluded from the positions of leadership by either
lack of property or of learning. He might one day accumulate
the necessary financial means. No miracle was required for a
man entirely without means to rise to the top under the dynamic
economy of the time. The prerequisite of scholarship could be
achieved by one's children if they were gifted in this direction
and, indirectly, by marrying one's daughters to outstanding
scholars.

The openness of the circle of persons who enjoyed special

political privileges—whether these were based on political power outside the *kehilla* or on the holding of an appointment within it—derived, according to our analysis, from the fact that the acquisition of capital was determined on a class basis.

This brings us to the third sphere, the economic one. Here, too, the holders of power and privilege did not succeed in insulating themselves within exclusive class barriers. This was a result of the inability and even the unwillingness of Jews to acquire real estate in the place of residence. This circumscribed even the highest economic achievement within the form of current capital. In the first place, it militated against capital transference from one generation to another. Further, the danger in store for Jewish capital did not derive solely from political insecurity, including the ever-present possibility of unlimited levies or even outright expropriation by the authorities. The very fact that this was current capital put in question its stability over a period of generations. A sudden loss of fortune as a result of unsuccessful business ventures was a common occurrence. Conversely, the swift accumulation of wealth through good luck and business acumen was not unusual.

But from the aspect of class stratification, another outcome of this situation is even more important: that is that even the greatest Jewish capitalist was not in a position to give his economic achievements a qualitative expression, as can the person who invests his commercial profits in real property. Many non-Jews did this during this period, not only investing his property with stability and security, but giving a different qualitative expression to his economic power, placing himself on a basis quite different from that of the owners of current capital. But since this path was closed to the Jew, even the tremendous differences in capital which existed in Jewish society in this period, remained differences in quantity only.

Also almost entirely absent was differentiational lineage in the religious-sacral sphere—the third principle which usually serves as a basis for the class stratification division in human societies. After the collapse of the real basis for the sacral distinction between Priests, Levites, and Israelites—originally based on the performance of actual duties in the temple service—no new stratified basis has evolved similar to it. We do find some claim to special privilege being made on the basis of lineage by the descendants of outstanding religious personalities—pietists, cabalists, or Torah scholars—to whom spiritualist or magical powers were sometimes attributed on the strength of their learning. The claim could easily be put forward that these charismatic traits were hereditary, and the way was thus open for laying a new basis for sacral-lineal stratification.

However, at least until the rise of Hasidism, this new tendency was incapable of creating a new basis for status even for a few generations. Indeed, the essential condition for this was lacking: an attachment of the dynasty to some kind of temple or at least to some stable center of worship. In any case, the conditions of existence in the Diaspora—geographical dispersion, political insecurity, and the absence of a strong bond with the place of residence—undermined the value of lineage as a formative factor.

Existing conditions were far more favorable for the scholarly type, whose religious authority rested on the acquisition of knowledge, which is mobile and independent of time and place. The scholars had inherited the role of the priests after the end of the Second Commonwealth, and they maintained it until the period of the hasidic and *haskala* movements. They were in a position to provide their sons with favorable facilities to continue their tradition by giving them an outstanding education and an atmosphere of learning. But they could not bequeath their learning nor block the rise of the sons of the uneducated. In theory, religious leadership remained accessible to the entire community, and even in practice, there were only varying degrees of obstacles, but no class disqualifications. Those religious functions in Judaism that were not affected by the destruction of the temple, such as ritual slaughtering or serving as Cantor or Reader of the Torah, were likewise dependent on knowledge which, in principle, was accessible to all.

Thus, from all aspects—occupational, political, economic, and religious—traditional Jewish society appears as an open society. But this openness does not, of course, imply equal opportunity for each person to achieve a certain position. There was considerable distance between the top and the bottom in all the scales of stratification. Wealth and poverty, learning and ignorance, key ruling positions and lack of all political power, lineal distinction and complete absence of family ties—all of these were found side by side in their extremes. Admittedly, positions of prominence were not circumscribed by symbols and norms, and the individual was entitled—and in the field of scholarship, even enjoined—to strive to reach the top. Nevertheless, we must be extremely cautious in measuring the extent of the society's mobility. In theory, nothing might stand in the way of one's rising in the social hierarchy, but in practice, something was. The obstacles arose from the combination of the sources of power that tended to become concentrated in the same hands. Possession of wealth and political position, external or internal, were conditioned on one another—in one direction absolutely. Political office went hand in hand with wealth. Even the remaining two bases of stratification—scholarship and family connections—tended to be bound up with the others. The sons of the rich could continue their studies until they attained a high level of scholarship. If they reached that stage, their wealth, family connections, and sometimes even their influence in the courts of kings and princess helped them give their learning an institutional expression and they were appointed rabbis in the *kehillot*. Even the position of *rosh yeshiva* was likely to be more easily attained by the person who was financially independent, and even more easily if he or his family were in a position to help support the needy students as well.

Sometimes the tendency of the sources of power to combine operated in the reverse direction; rabbis here and there managed to accumulate capital from their incomes, and yeshiva rectors were sometimes showered with so many gifts from their admirers that they become wealthy. Scholarship and wealth might also be linked indirectly. If an unlettered person married into a family of scholars, he would bask in the reflection of their glory. Generous financial support to scholars earned one the reputation of "cherishing the Torah," and the merit so acquired was equivalent to that achieved by study itself. The court Jews in Germany in the seventeenth and eighteenth centuries made considerable use of this indirect method. They established trust funds to found houses of study (*batei midrash*) and supported the students. Another way of acquiring reflected glory from Torah study was to assist scholars in publishing their books. Hardly a book was printed in Germany during this period whose title page did not mention the name of the patron whose support made its publication possible.

Concentration of the various sources of power in the same hands gives one the impression that this society maintained a well-defined social classification in its structure at all times. The place of each person in the social concentration manifested itself not in distinguishable lines of demarcation setting class apart from class, but in the verdict of public opinion, which set a value on the position of each individual. This appraisal had some basis in facts that were obvious to all. The extent of one's influence with the authorities was common knowledge, and this was even truer with regard to the holding of a position in the *kehilla*, the super-*kehilla*, or one of the local associations. Scholarship could be ranked by the official titles, and the public discussions between scholars created authoritative public opinion as to their respective merits. Information relating to pedigrees and family ties was known in this society, where, in the upper circles at least, everyone knew everyone else. As to economic power, even if precise information might not be available, one could easily make estimates that would not be far from wrong. The public assessment of taxes, the customs of publicly announcing charitable contributions, and the publicizing of the dowry given to the children, all enabled the rest of society to identify each member's niche in the hierarchical pattern.

At this same time, an exceptional class sensitivity typified the non-Jewish society as well. This sensitivity was expressed in the demand, likely to be based on moral grounds, that each person be given the respect due him according to his value, i.e., the sum total of what he possessed on the various bases for stratification.

In the Jewish society, owing to the restriction of the spheres of existence—the physical, the occupational, and the social—secondary frameworks could develop only in the most rudimentary form. In the *bet midrash*, during a discussion of religious law, a man's wealth or political influence was probably disregarded, and knowledge of Halakha alone determined one's rank. But the other bases of stratification—wealth, official position, and lineage—did not each create a separate milieu for itself. Those who possessed the various values were constantly measured against one another. This found particular expression in the synagogue, which was the common meeting place for the entire community and which provided the opportunity for public demonstrations of social differentiation.

The question of precedence among those to be "called up" to the Torah, which caused no little friction in congregational life, is a good illustration of this. Those who prepared the by-laws made considerable efforts to arrive at acceptable rules of precedence for such occasions. But, of course, such by-laws could lay down only general rules, and could not provide a clear cut solution for every eventuality. This friction of rank was not eliminated. There are grounds for assuming that the multiplicity of synagogues, particularly in the eighteenth century in heavily populated communities, must be attributed in part to the desire of the wealthy to avoid this social friction by building a private synagogue of their own.

Though the absence of clear cut class distinctions aggravated the friction between the bearers of the different values, it facilitated mobility. A rapid social rise was made possible by an excess of values in one field which served to counterbalance a shortage of values in the other. An outstanding expression of this situation was the custom of waiving for scholars the usual restrictions governing the right to vote or to be elected to posts in the *kehilla* and super-*kehilla*. Scholarship, in this instance, served as a substitute for wealth and privilege of domicile.

This system of alternatives also applied to marriage. A person's prospects in making a match were determined by his share of the different bases of stratification. Money or scholarship could compensate for lack of lineage and vice versa. In this way, the paths of mobility were created from below upward. Not all roads were equal in the speed they permitted. The acquisition of wealth was likely to raise a person to astonishing heights within his own lifetime. Scholarship and lineage, on the other hand, were consolidated only in the course of generations—with the son or son-in-law at the earliest.

But, when compared to class societies proper, even these bases of stratification were established easily. It was enough for one generation of a family to excel in wealth, in public affairs, or in learning for the succeeding one to benefit, not only from the advantage of a good start, but even from the reflected glory of the genealogical connection. Indirectly, too, the rise of one "small" family influenced the status of all the members of the clan. This process was reflected not only in the direct assistance afforded to the poor relations, which we have already discussed, but also in the unmeasurable indirect distinction radiated.

Looking at the matter from another aspect, no family succeeded or even strove to shut itself behind a class barrier. Owing to the personal nature of the advantages determining social position, families were unable to guarantee all their members a substantial share of them. Learned men could certainly not make scholars of all their relatives. Even the wealthy could do no more than support their poor relatives; they could not assure them riches or even a comfortable living. The concept of a distinguished family is not the same here as in the aristocratic society, where all the members of such a family share the social distinction deriving from its status. Family distinction, whether in wealth or in learning, simply meant that these qualities were to be found in this family. But alongside the scholars and the wealthy men, there were always relatives lacking these values, who hung on, with greater or lesser success, to the family's more fortunate members.

Just as there was no uniform level of superiority among the families of the elite, so there was no complete segregation from undistinguished families. Some exceptional individuals—such as intellectually gifted persons and newly-rich—always penetrate into the best families. Conversely, children of undistinguished families had to resign themselves to marrying persons with mediocre connections. That is why it often happened that a widower with a number of small children could not aspire to a wealthy girl or one with good lineage, but had to settle for a capable wife from an ordinary family.

Thus, the picture of stratification which emerges is one of a society with a steep structure, with tremendous distances between its peaks and valleys. But the gulf between even the most extreme points in the structure was bridged by the fact that there was no insuperable barrier between them. He who aimed to reach the peak had a long, steep road to climb, but if he had the strength, the ability, and the will, nothing would prevent him from achieving his desire.

PART THREE

Disintegration

XX

The Impact of Historical Events

THE ANALYSIS OF STRATIFICATION AND MOBIL-
ity pointed out the changes which continually recurred in the
appropriation of key positions by individuals and groups. But
this constant reshuffle did not necessarily bring either a structural
change or any addition or diminution in the performance of the
functions. Other factors, however, in addition to the transfer of
office from father to son and fluctuations in the hierarchical pattern, also make for change in societies. Even in the traditional
society with which we are concerned, we encountered transforma-
tions in institutional modes of activity which must be regarded
as marking a change of structure and function. There is some
justification for not applying the concept of evolution to this

[213]

transformation. In spite of the Jewish ideology of traditionalism, which regards the present as no more than an attempt—unsuccessful as a rule—to perpetuate the ideals of the past, in practice, each generation adds a tier of its own to the structure of tradition. This addition is partly the unique creative contribution of each succeeding generation and partly the result of each generation's reactions to current events.

But in any case, the traditional nature of the Jewish society of this period severely limited the extent of possible changes. Even the gravest events were not likely to evoke reactions transcending the framework of traditional modes of thought and action. This is proved by the massacres of 1648–49. The slaughter of tens of thousands, the flight of many more before the sword, the destruction of communities, and the deprival of entire provinces of their means of livelihood) resulted in frayed nerves and a feeling of insecurity that prompted a fundamental all-around stock-taking. But the reaction, both in thought and deed, did not deviate from the traditional pattern. Rescue work remained on a haphazard basis, although the circle of the participants was enlarged and its proportions expanded. This time all the Jews of Europe, including Turkey, took part in the rescue activities, and the *kehillot* went out of their way to cancel the restrictions which had been adopted to keep strangers from seeking their livelihood within their boundaries. However, there is no record of any program of action being instituted to prevent the recurrence of such an event. Although a realistic understanding of the cause was not lacking, no political or social conclusions were drawn from the historical experience. As a matter of fact, the realistic explanations were overshadowed by the traditional view of divine providence, so that the lesson that emerged from the stock-taking was a religious-moral one. The composition of *selihot* (penitential prayers), the proclamation of fasts, the imposition of further restrictions on dress and banqueting, and the voicing of stronger warnings about the observance of the precepts were the sum total of the reaction in the area of social values. This reaction to the events of the time was not different in quality from that of any other generation in the period of traditionalism.

The extent of the contribution made by one generation to the traditional superstructure, or the depth of its reaction to the events of its day, did not alter its essential attachment to tradition. A real break with tradition is implied only when it is re-evaluated and no longer serves as the basis for justifying the changes that take place, but becomes the point of departure for reservations and criticism. In this sense, it can be said that the Jewish society preserved its traditional character until the second half of the eighteenth century.

Admittedly, one momentous event did occur, which, for a brief period, violated traditional patterns; this was the appearance of Sabbatai Zevi (1666). The reader will recall that Sabbatai Zevi presented himself as the Messiah, having the authority as such to abrogate accepted norms and to open a new chapter of law-giving and teaching in Israel. The majority of people at the time deferred to his authority. Although during his brief period of activity, Sabbatai Zevi did not succeed in whittling down many traditional practices, his abrogation of sacrosanct holidays and his institution of new ones pointed to the extreme direction in which he was heading.

Actually, however, the activity of Sabbatai Zevi does not represent a break in the line of tradition. The very appearance of Sabbatai Zevi constituted a spontaneous awakening of forces latent in traditional society at all times—that is, the longing for redemption. The traditional messianic doctrine itself authorized the abrogation of tradition in days to come. The annulment of tradition by the Messiah would represent its fulfillment rather than its repudiation through the abandonment of its basis. At the moment of action, the revelation of the Messiah gave an impetus to the Jews' preparedness for crisis as a single, catastrophic change. What the faithful looked forward to was not a gradual social change but a complete new order of things—in both the material and spiritual sense. When the tension of the crisis relaxed after the great disillusionment, the entire society returned to the state of relative stagnation. A new layer of reactions to the convulsive event and an apprehensiveness of its repetition remained. The authority of tradition as a whole, and even of the messianic idea itself, was not broken, and the hope of redemption was preserved, even for the coming generations, as an irrefutable article of faith.

This return to the *status quo ante* was accepted by all but a small minority. This minority continued to believe in the messianic pretensions of Sabbatai Zevi even after his conversion. The actualization of the Messiah was not diminished by the fact that the messianic objectives were not achieved in their entirety. The messianic period had begun with the appearance of Sabbatai Zevi, and this belief called for certain conclusions with respect to the authority of tradition. But, as we know today, this minority was divided among itself on the question of how far to take these conclusions. Some limited the abrogation of tradition to laws and customs, such as the fast of the Ninth of Av and the recitation of the night prayers for the restoration of Israel (*tiqqun hatzot*), which constituted unequivocal expressions of the belief that the period of exile was still in full force. The removal of these symbols was sufficient, in the view of the moderate Sabbatians, to demonstrate their faith in the beginning of the period of redemption. None of the other components of the tradition, and certainly not the traditional system of thought in its entirety, was discredited.

Opposed to this view were those Sabbatians who drew the logical conclusion that the beginning of redemption implied the total abrogation of tradition and its system of values. As far as they were concerned, the door had been opened to a new historical development on a really revolutionary basis. But in practice, the members of this sect did not exploit this avenue at all. They did not strive for a change in the structure of society, or even for an interchange of classes or a rise in the social status of their members. The sect made no attempt to take its case to the world, except in the case of Jacob Frank (1726–91), and his failure is proof of the impossibility of maintaining a social unit midway between the Jewish and Christian societies. For despite his attempt to maintain his community as a separate denomination— neither Jewish nor Christian—in the end, Frank found it necessary to be converted and to take his followers along with him.

Even the extreme Sabbatians followed the traditional pattern of the Jewish society. Their members were enjoined to conform externally by their own code. They denied the traditional values and indulged in surreptitious license. But even according to their faith, the public revelation of their doctrine and its adoption by the Jewish society as a whole, were dependent on a catastrophic messianic act in the future. Realistically speaking, it thus appeared even to the extreme Sabbatians that, at that time at any rate, the institutions of Jewish society could not or should not be changed. The Sabbatians do not fall in the category of practical social revolutionaries. If those who negated in their hearts the values of society were unable to establish those values on any new basis, it may be taken as an indication that the objective conditions were still not conducive to this.

By characterizing the Sabbatian movement as the actualization of the messianic belief, we imply that its emergence in 1666 constituted mere historical chance. The movement could have made its appearance at a much earlier date or not at all. There is not much basis for the attempts of historians to explain the appearance of Sabbatai Zevi as a result of the events which immediately preceded it.

There is only a remote connection between the messianic movement and the events of 1648–49. Despite clear references in Sabbatai Zevi's words to the pogroms of 1648–49, his rise should not be directly attributed to those events, of which he knew only from hearsay. The public reaction to his appearance on the scene was no different among the Jews in the countries affected by the pogroms than that among those who lived in relative peace and quiet, like the Jews of Holland, Italy, and Turkey itself. It was no specific event of the *galut*, but the consciousness of exile itself that again and again gave rise to movements like that of Sabbatai Zevi. If the latter movement was greater than all the others in its scope and in the extent of the ferment it brought about, that was the result of a number of historical circumstances, of which its proximity to the events of 1648–49 was only one.

The main reason for the deep effect of the Sabbatian movement lay in the religious stream with which many persons connected this messianism from the very first, the stream of the Safed Cabala. If the tidings of redemption represented the realization of messianism to the masses, to the leading personalities of the movement, and to wide circles of those familiar with the Cabala, the revelation of the Messiah at that time signified the consummation of the process that their system of Cabala had predicted. According to the Cabala of Rabbi Isaac Luria, the world, in his age, was entering the final stage of melioration, and needed only a slight improvement to consummate its perfection with the advent of the messianic era. The Lurian cabalist doctrine became accepted in large circles about one generation before Sabbatai Zevi, and those circles keenly anticipated the Messiah's coming. This anticipation was a direct cause of the recognition of Sabbatai Zevi as the Messiah by Nathan Ghazati. The widespread character of this feeling of anticipation constituted at least a secondary factor in intensifying the reaction among communities containing Lurianic devotees.

The link between the Messiahship of Sabbatai Zevi and the prevalent stream of Cabala explains, too, the persistence of the movement after the removal of its basis. The confusion which prevailed after the Messiah's conversion called for a reaction, but this could have taken various forms. The majority reacted by effacing the episode from its memory. But another result might have ensued: the eradication of the messianic faith and even the renunciation of Judaism and the adoption of the dominant faith. The opponents of Sabbatianism had, from the very beginning, feared such a development. If these apprehensions were not borne out to any appreciable extent—those who could not obliterate from their minds the impression left by the event reacted by creating an occult, antinomian sect—this was because the cabalist system of thought had provided for such an event. The cabalist system presented redemption as a process occurring in stages and left room for an ambiguous stage that was no longer *galut* but not yet redemption. This ambiguity implied some doubt as to whether Jewish tradition was meant to be valid for this intermediate period. Since the boundary between the *galut* and the redemption was blurred, the absolute authority of tradition was likewise undermined. The advent of Sabbatai Zevi, the redeemer, the Sabbatians believed, marked the transition between the two periods. But even before Sabbatai Zevi had appeared on the historical scene, the ingredients had existed for an antinomian deviation prompted by the internal religious development of the Cabala.

Now, the development of the Cabala itself was a religious process, whose details and stages of evolution are subject neither to an historical interpretation deriving from one-time events nor to a sociological interpretation dependent on certain social conditions and data. Yet in its general tendency, the Cabala certainly did not lack contact with historical reality; it constituted an expression of the nation's awareness of the *galut,* a consciousness which excluded all rational considerations from the shaping of the fate of the society. The self-insulation of Jewish society to the point where it avoided all contact with the world at large conditioned it to absorb a doctrine which based the future of the nation (and indirectly that of the world, as well) on an inner Jewish-religious process, i.e., the perfecting of the world through the painstaking performance of religious precept accompanied by the special cabalist devotion.

The deliberate disregard of what was happening in the outside world, and even of what the world was doing to Israel, reached its height in cabalist ethical and homiletic writings. Through these writings, the fundamentals of cabalist thought penetrated the consciousness of the Jewish people from the beginning of the seventeenth century onwards. In them, do we find not only no trace of any disputation with the faith of the other nations, but also considerable indifference to religious-national representation vis-a-vis the outside world. The process of development which was destined to effect the perfection of the world became a matter concerning only God and Israel. Although the Sabbatians deviated, to a greater or lesser degree, from the dogma and ethics accepted by the general public, even they represented no more than an extreme expression of the historical consciousness in which practically the entire nation was immersed.

The decisive influence of the Cabala on the national plane is observable not in the Sabbatian deviation, but in the over-all shift in religious values, a shift which, beginning in the latter part of the seventeenth century, went hand in hand with the social changes which manifested themselves. The shift was reflected in the new significance accorded the performance of the *mitzvot*. If, according to the conception prevailing in the literature of Halakha and *musar*, the observance of the *mitzvot* represents, first and foremost, doing the will of the Giver of the Torah, according to the cabalist view, it became a means of setting in motion the machinery of the upper spheres.

The cabalist view held that every jot and tittle of each *mitzva* was connected with a specific part of the divine order and that the observer of the *mitzva* had a direct hand in the operation of this order. It was not the fate of the individual alone, his reward or punishment, that was involved in the proper operation of the divine order, but the spiritual progression or regression of the world as a whole. The interpretation was not simply a matter of abstract theological thought; it influenced religious life in practice. In the first place, this view led to a new appreciation of the precise observance of all the minutiae of the laws and customs as they had been handed down and codified. The cabalist system of thought included an entire philosophy of the reasons for the *mitzvot*, i.e., a special explanation for each detail, through noting the influence which the performance of the particular *mitzva* exerted on the divine order. This system of motivations for the *mitzvot* was unique in that it did away almost entirely with differences of degree between one precept and another, between law and custom, between a Biblical ordinance and extra safeguards instituted by later rabbinic authority.

The flexibility of the cabalist system in creating a symbolic link between each deed and the cabalist concepts in general, facilitated not only the consolidation of the accepted ritual on the basis of the Cabala, but even the introduction of new details. The cabalist groups in Safed, as well as those who spread the doctrine—the foremost was Rabbi Isaiah Horowitz, the author of *Shnei Luhot Habrit*—were outstanding for their ritual productivity. Formally, these innovations were based on concepts of the Halakha, but the impetus to their development undoubtedly came from their attachment to a system of thought in which every movement of the hand and every motion of the lips assumed an almost metaphysical significance.

Moreover, the Cabala enriched the ritual not only with new details and new significance, but also with an entirely new dimension: *kavana* (intention, concentration, or conscious devotion). The concept of *kavana* has its source in the Talmud, and implies that in performing a *mitzva* one should concentrate one's mind on the religious purpose of the action. The Cabalist charged the concept of *kavana* with an entirely new mystic content, varying in accordance with the symbolic significance that their system attributed to the precept concerned. The symbolic significance attached to all the minutiae of the *mitzvot* had to be present in the worshipper's consciousness. The performance of a *mitzva* unaccompanied by *kavana* practically lost its religious value in cabalist eyes.

The practical effect of this development was to commit the proper observance of the *mitzvot* to a handful of persons. The great majority of people, including those possessing a basic grounding in religious law, lacked not only the knowledge but also the time and the power of concentration required for the observance of the daily ritual with such exactness and mystic purpose. The popularization of the Cabala, thus did not achieve its aim of converting the Jewish masses into adherents of this occult mode of religious practice. In fact, the result was the exact opposite of what had been intended. If until now there had been a split between the religious elite and the masses in the sphere of theoretical religious knowledge, a similar breach was now also created in the field of religious action, in the observance of the *mitzvot*.

Moreover, the split was now extended into the ranks of the elite themselves. Henceforth, traditional Jewish society comprised not one elite but two—one that had mastered halakhic knowledge and one, cabalist *kavana* and doctrine. Although these two elites had occasionally some points of contact, their principles tended to make them antagonists. The speculative character of cabalistic study competed with the straightforward learning of the biblical and talmudic texts.

Admittedly, a knowledge of religious law remained a basic prerequisite for the pursuit of the Cabala. Educational institutions were never called upon to teach the Cabala instead of the Talmud or even along with it. But the study of the Cabala did become competitive with the study of the Talmud as an ultimate goal. The individual who attained a sufficiently advanced level in Halakha was enjoined, according to the view of the cabalists, to devote his time to the occult doctrine. The latter alone, in their view, was capable of imparting a true knowledge of the Torah.

The cabalist scholar now attracted the interest of the public. The position of the Cabalist was different from that of the ordinary scholar. The latter's achievements were recognized through his public activity, as a rabbi, leader of the congregation, and yeshiva head. For the Cabalist, on the other hand, it was enough that he meditated by himself, or, at the very most, with a group of kindred spirits. A good deal of the prestige enjoyed by the scholar who pursued the study of the Torah for its own sake now passed to the man whose learning found expression not in public leadership, halakhic decisions, and the teaching of Torah, but in studying the Cabala and in performing the *mitzvot* in accordance with its dictates, a skill which only initiates were capable of appreciating. These mystic preoccupations entitled the cabalist scholar, to the same public support given to those who filled practical positions involving mastery of the Torah, such as judges in the religious courts, rabbis, and preachers.

We have traced the influence the Cabala exerted in the social sphere. In the next chapter, we shall find that this influence was spurred, in turn, by changes in the social sphere itself. If the new cabalist elite clipped the wings of the talmudic scholars, a decline in the latter's prestige had set in independently either before this or parallel to it. The rise of the new cabalist elite was facilitated through the undermining of the position of the scholarly elite. However, the new elite did not inherit the place of the old one. The attitudes of the two groups toward the public differed. The scholarly elite felt themselves set apart from the rest of the people by their knowledge, and believed that this knowledge alone invested them with the authority to teach and guide in the realm of action. However, between the cabalist elite and the masses a chasm was created in the world of deed as well. Between them there could only be created a proxy-like relationship. The few were transformed into performers of the *mitzvot* in the approved manner on behalf of the many.

Because of the extreme demands of the Cabalists, it was impossible for them to serve as an example or a source of guidance for the masses. The chasm that yawned between them became apparent in every instance where the Cabalists functioned as preachers and moralists. They applied to the public totally unrealistic criteria of conduct. To a degree which went far beyond the exaggeration customary in *musar* literature, the preachers of the period described their contemporaries as a sinful generation, rotten to the core. Undoubtedly the misfortunes of the times—wars, persecution, the acquisition of power by petty tyrants, and the internal undermining of institutions—led to deficiencies in public life. Be that as it may, it is clear from the shortcomings with which the preachers charged the public that the terrifying description they painted was partly the result of demands so extreme that they could not have been met even by the ministering angels. Even matters which had long been accepted as permissible both by custom and recognized halakhic rulings were now designated by them as irreparable iniquities.

This was simply a case of the moral and religious system of an ascetic group being turned into a criterion for judging the average man. This social rupture between the transmitters of religion and their unsophisticated charges constituted one of the signs of the crisis into which the traditional society was hurled at this stage of its development.

XXI   *The Turning Point*

$\mathcal{T}$HE EVENTS AND CHANGES DESCRIBED IN THE previous chapter may be viewed simply as variations within the framework of the traditional society. But we now come to events and processes which that designation would not fit. The two movements that arose in the second half of the eighteenth century, Hasidism in eastern Europe and Haskala in the West, served as a turning point in the history of Jewish society. The two movements cannot be considered mere variations of the existing pattern, but as definite changes in its very framework. It is necessary, at this point, to interrupt our description to ask about the nature of the distinction between a variation and a fundamental change. This distinction alone gives significance to the very concept of a turning point.

We must extend our view beyond the period on which we have based our image of the traditional society, that is, Ashkenazic Judaism between the sixteenth and eighteenth centuries. Actually, that society was only one of the varieties of the traditional Jewish society which crystallized in its "ideal" embodiment at the beginning of the period of Exile at the latest, and which from then on, underwent all sorts of modifications in the different lands of the Diaspora. The essential foundations of the society were so rigid that the principles inherent in them could unify Jewish society wherever it was exiled. These principles included the determination of its place in the gentile world; its attitudes towards economic matters, sexual life, and the other spheres of human activity; the basic functions of institutions like the family, the *bet midrash*, the synagogue, and the rabbinate. In fact, these principles themselves, so long as they were supported by a group of people who felt bound to them, constantly rebuilt Jewish society wherever its standard bearers found a refuge. There is an element of truth in Heine's witticism that traditional Judaism was the "portable homeland" of the Jews.

The ability to reconstruct Jewish society after each banishment and migration affords an excellent illustration of the sociological fact that the existence of a society is not dependent on the physical environment—on the demographic, ecological, or economic conditions—but may be the result of a common attachment of people to one another in certain spheres of activity. As is abundantly clear from this example of traditional Jewish society, it is sufficient that this mutual attachment exists in the sphere of religious and cultural values. On the basis of their fidelity to these values exclusively, the Jews constantly refounded *kehillot* and super-*kehillot* in their new places of exile. If we have succeeded in bringing out the common features of the parallel historical units of the sixteenth to the eighteenth centuries— the Jewries of Germany, Moravia-Bohemia, and Lithuania-

Poland—then we should now possess an archetype of the traditional Jewish society.

Traditional Jewish society, in this case, experienced a unique development. Instead of banishment and migration, changes now took place that left the society in the same place geographically, but that shattered, or at least distorted, its framework. This "shattered framework" image fits what happened to the traditional society in the second half of the eighteenth century in France (Alsace), Germany, Bohemia, Moravia, and, after another generation or two, in Hungary as well. These were all places where the Haskala movement was active and Jews were being granted citizenship. "Distortion of the framework," on the other hand, is the more proper term to denote the changes which took place simultaneously in Poland with the rise of the Hasidic movement.

Students of Hasidism have listed many events and phenomena as having been factors in the rise of the movement. The history of Polish Jewry in the first half of the eighteenth century reveals a process of bitter economic struggle. The economic decline is discernible in the life of the *kehillot* and their institutions, in the increase in the numbers of people without means of support, and in the inability of the institutions to fulfil their financial obligations. The relations between the Jews and the authorities went from bad to worse. The demands and pressures of the authorities constituted a primary factor in the impoverishment of the *kehillot*, but the main reason was that the political conflict within the Polish kingdom itself led both to the diffusion of political power and to unsuccessful attempts at reorganization. The result of this sequence of events was the weakening of the super-*kehilla* organizations and the subjection of the Jewish units of existence to the local nobles. The dissolution of the Council of the Four Lands in 1765 was only the finale to this sad process of decline in Jewish self-governing institutions.

The decline in the real power of the institutions was accompanied by an undermining in the moral caliber of their leaders. The exploitation of political positions for the benefit of the man in power now became an everyday occurrence. Leadership was not achieved and maintained in accordance with the people's wishes. The leaders arose and remained at the helm through the economic power concentrated in their hands or through the help of the non-Jewish authorities with whom they maintained close contact.

The crisis also affected the institutions of the rabbinate and higher education. From the end of the seventeenth century, the institutions for the teaching of Torah were in a state of decline. Owing to the troubled times, the *kehillot* were unable to maintain the yeshivot, certainly not to the degree to which they had formerly done so. We witness at this period a phenomenon which apparently had no precedent in the history of the yeshivot: the yeshiva instructors were taking payment from students seeking admission. As we have seen in Chapter IX, the prestige of the chief rabbi (*av bet din*) of the kehilla was enhanced by his occupying the position of *rosh yeshiva*. With the neglect of this function—whether through his fault or not—particularly where it was used as a source of financial gain, the rabbi was deprived of one of the main sources of his authority.

The breakdown of central government subjugated the *kehillot* to the local aristocracy. The purchase of rabbinical livings bought from the community—a long-standing irritant in *kehilla* life, was now succeeded by their purchase from the nobles. This not only represented a moral failing in itself, but it opened the door to the acquisition of office by unqualified persons. Indeed, henceforth complaints were heard not only regarding the purchase of rabbinical offices, but their being bestowed on unreliable persons or inexperienced young men. The super-*kehillot* themselves had to lower their standards for eligibility to the rabbinate. In Lithuania in 1720, twelve years of study after marriage was required for a man to serve as rabbi; in 1761, all that was demanded was that the rabbi not be under twenty years of age.

If occupying the position of rabbi ceased to be a guarantee of the incumbent's outstanding scholarship, this was even truer of the title of *moreinu*. The requirements for this title and for that of *haver* were constantly lowered from the end of the seventeenth century until they became honorary titles bearing little relation to the scholarship of the holder.

The eighteenth century can thus hardly be described as a period in which the gap between the scholars and the uneducated widened, a description which has been employed to explain the revolt of the uneducated which presumably expressed itself in the Hassidic movement. What we have here is not a widening of the gap, but a defect in the social scale that made it difficult for people to recognize their place and to admit the justice of the existing hierarchical distinctions.

The historical and social conditions which we have hitherto described must be regarded as anomic, abounding in lost souls whose attachment to existing institutions was insufficient to bind them to the common activity sponsored by those institutions. In such circumstances, the situation was ripe for the creation of new social alignments between individuals whose attachment to the old institutions had been weakened.

Even the rise of the new cabalist elite must be regarded as connected with this social process. It paralleled very closely the decline of the yeshivot and the rabbinate. These conditions also constituted the background for the new social alignment of Hasidism which went far beyond the rise of the cabalist elite. Historians were thus quite justified, in attempting to explain the rise of Hasidism, not to rest content with describing the changes in the religious field but to turn their attention to political and social developments as well.

However, after admitting the justification for linking social conditions with the rise of Hasidism, we must ask about the pos-

sible significance of this connection. Certainly it does not mean
that the conditions determined the rise of Hasidism and, at the
same time, the "distortion of the framework" of traditional society. To refute such a view, it will suffice to recall that greater
crises than that experienced by Polish Jewry in the eighteenth
century had befallen traditional Jewish society in the form of
migrations and expulsions. Society—i.e., its ideal image crystallized in the system of traditional values—managed to rebuild its
house in one of its actual historical embodiments.

Moreover, the events in this period itself tend to lead us to
the same conclusion, since the area affected by social upheaval
and that subject to Hasidic influence were not identical. Social
unrest affected all the provinces of Poland and Lithuania, while
Hasidism arose at first only in the Polish provinces of Podolia
and Volhynia. Subsequently Hasidism conquered a number of
other provinces either completely or partially; while in Lithuania,
after a difficult and protracted struggle, it was put to utter rout.
In Lithuania, as in the western provinces of Hungary, traditional
Jewish society was reincarnated.

If we thus employ the sociological method, which ascribes
the rise of Hasidism to the social factor, we should necessarily
have to distinguish between at least three different frameworks:
one which was capable of giving birth to the movement; a second
which prepared the ground for its acceptance; and a third which
prevented its complete diffusion. But there is certainly no basis
for these distinctions.

We have no choice but to come to the following conclusion:
Admittedly the rise of the new movement was facilitated by certain social conditions and it developed as a continuation of religious processes and changes which preceded it. But in its content,
values, structure, and historical course, the new movement represented such an innovation that all that went before did no more
than pave the way. The movement itself was a new "historical
creation" that displayed its true nature only after its emergence.

XXII — *The Transition to Hasidism*

$\mathcal{B}$EGINNING WITH THE THIRTIES AND FORTIES of the eighteenth century, certain individuals and groups made their debut in Jewish society in Podolia and Volhynia. They cannot be identified with, and did not identify themselves with, the type of religious conduct described in the last chapter. This new type was characterized by ecstatic behavior during prayers, their emotional restraints unfettered during divine worship. These ecstatic outbursts, however, were not limited to the occasion of prayer, but affected the entire social existence of those devotees. A feeling of release from the sphere of mundane things accompanied them even in their dealings with their fellowmen and even during their carousals. In their consciousness, this ecstatic experience represented a value which joined battle with the accepted values of the society.

According to the analysis of Gershom Scholem (to whom credit is due for citing and interpreting the sources which serve as the basis for the description given here), these groups contained both Sabbatians and adherents of traditional Judaism. In fact, it seems that the impetus for the new movement sprang from the Sabbatians, for a relaxation of restraints through an emotional surfeit was characteristic of their sectarian milieu. But the connection between the two movements soon weakened. The common experience of ecstatic religiosity was converted into a source of religious authority in itself. Although these new Hasidim absorbed many elements of Sabbatian tradition, they severed their attachment to, and freed themselves from, the trammels of the Sabbatian sects.

In their attitude towards practical religious observance, the ecstatics were like the simple people for whom the Jewish way of life was something that went without saying. Moreover, in the manner of similar religious movements, traditional rites and customs served as the occasion for attaining a high pitch of spiritual exaltation. What had undoubtedly changed was the evaluation of the rituals and the whole gamut of traditional observance. It was not the minutiae of religious precepts that mattered most, and certainly not the theoretical knowledge of them which derived from the study of Halakha. It was the religious experience which accompanied the performance of the precepts that determined their value. It is thus no wonder that in the first evidences of the appearance of the Hasidic groups, we also hear of contempt for the study of Torah, implying an additional loss of respect for those who devoted themselves exclusively to that occupation.

In the new Hasidic groups, a few personalities stood out whose historical features have been more or less preserved by tradition. Some of these, like Rabbi Nahman Kosover, Rabbi Nahman of Horodenka, and Rabbi Leib Pistiner, were not only ecstatics in practice, but were also capable of giving verbal expression to their experience. In social status, these personalities were members of the sub-intelligentsia of Jewish society—preachers, exhorters, miracle workers. These individuals became the rallying points of the movement in their localities. Rabbi Israel Baal Shem Tov (the Besht) emerged as the leading figure among them, and it was due to his intensely sensitive personality that the movement was channelled into a clearly-defined course.

The Besht was a fervid mystic who, at times of successful religious exaltation, would achieve direct contact with the realm of the divine, becoming almost completely liberated from the actual world. When he became the leader of the movement, he, and his experiences and teachings, served as an example for others. While he was still alive—and even more so after his death in 1760—he became the source of authority for all those who joined the movement.

It is not the aim of this work to trace the spread of the movement or to examine its internal diversity. The principal stages of its growth are well-known. Until the 1760's the movement did not extend beyond the provinces of Podolia and Volhynia. Thenceforth it spread westward, giving rise to offshoots throughout Poland and Lithuania. In some places, it comprised a substantial portion of the Jewish population, or at any rate, left its impress on public life. In the seventies and eighties, the counter-reaction led to a public clash. In Poland, Hasidism emerged the victor, and in some *kehillot* and provinces, it created its own milieu and dominated public life. In Lithuania, it had to retreat and occupy the position of a tolerated social minority. In any case, the movement's sociological characteristics immediately manifested themselves. It was quite obvious that it represented a separate entity amidst the other variations in traditional society.

Hasidism differed from Sabbatianism in that it rejected the messiahship of Sabbatei Zevi and checked its antinomian tendency. From a dogmatic and normative viewpoint, Hasidism thus represented a return to the mainstream of Judaism. The reactive nature of the movement may be seen in the fact that not only Sabbatian messianism, but active messianism in itself—the hopeful anticipation of redemption and the religious-magic activity on its behalf—were likewise suppressed.

In this way, Hasidism deviated not only from Sabbatianism, but from cabalist Hasidism as well. In the Hasidic conception, the positive precepts lost their magic-redemptive function. Religious ceremonies, prayer and the observance of laws and customs, were no longer motivated by the attempt to activate the upper spheres through the very act of performance. Their purpose was the religious-personal exaltation of the worshipper, who was enjoined to strive for direct mystic or contemplative contact with the divine.

Prayer and the observance of the commandments became a means to this end. Communion with God in its subjective sense was the religious end which now dominated the rituals of religion and tradition. The connection between the observance of the commandments and their subjective end—the spiritual state of communion with God—may be clearly recognized in the attitude toward the minutiae of observance, wherein the new Hasidism stood diametrically opposed to cabalist Hasidism. The new Hasidism broke away from the latter's absolute ritualistic attitude toward religious minutiae. In place of an objective, metaphysical function, the hastening of the redemption, the observance of the commandments was now assigned a new task: to serve as a preparation and a guiding force for subjective religious experience. Indeed, the connection between means and end was recognized here. A commandment that led to communion with God achieved its purpose; one that did not, failed. Human experience was likely to show that success and failure were not dependent on the strict observance of small details.

In contradistinction to Sabbatianism and cabalist Hasidism, the new Hasidism may be styled a "movement" in the full sociological sense of the word. The spokesmen of the movement, at first the Besht and later his outstanding disciples, demanded and obtained the right of leadership. This privilege was based on the personal charisma springing from the direct religious force of their personalities. These religious leaders gathered around themselves a group of followers who accepted their guidance and were prepared to be swept into the vortex of collective-religious ecstasy. In historical relation to cabalist Hasidism, we have here something in the nature of a dialectic development. Cabalist Hasidism was unable to win over the general public because of its stringent religious demands. It would seem that the new Hasidism would have appealed to an even more restricted audience since its inherent hallmark—ecstasy—could be achieved only by an extremely limited group.

In fact, and in contrast to what is generally claimed, Hasidism, in line with its basic theory, widened the gap between the *Zaddik*, the Hasidic leader, and the masses. Inasmuch as the performance of the positive precepts was for Hasidism simply a means of achieving contact with the divine, for the masses who were not capable of this achievement, even the performance of the precepts was devoid of value.

But, in practice, the very circumstances which broadened the gap between the leaders and the masses of ordinary Jews, also forged a link between them. For there was a difference between cabalist Hasidism, which could be acquired only by imitation, and rapturous Hasidism, which could be transmitted to a group of onlookers through a feeling of community. Something of the fervor of the *Zaddik* could adhere to his followers, and if they did not succeed in attaining the level of communion with God by their own power, they achieved something of this communion with the aid of the *Zaddik*.

The theory followed in the footsteps of religious-social experience. Although at first, so long as the masses remained without a leader, Hasidism denied them any justification, after the masses joined the *Zaddik*, the movement was prepared to restore to them their right to existence. The doctrine formulated in accordance with the concepts of cabalist Hasidism, that the association of the common people with the scholars—who enjoyed direct communion with God—ensured them of indirect communion, was now given actual social expression. The Hasidic sect served as a framework for direct contact between the leader and his followers, and the communion with God inherent in the *Zaddik's* enthusiasm was transmitted to his followers and, in any case, was nourished by the group's being together.

This doctrine of the dependence of the Hasid's religious communion on the direct communion of the *Zaddik* also served as a convenient justification for the economic assistance the *Zaddik* received from his followers. In itself, there was nothing new in such assistance. Itinerant and local preachers as well as scholars (including cabalist Hasidism) who devoted all their time to study, had their needs met, in full or in part, by individual patrons. But a quantitative change did take place, as might be imagined. A *Zaddik*, who had no source of livelihood in the world, relied entirely on the contributions of his followers for the support of his family. As early as the second generation, and perhaps even during the lifetime of the Besht, the *Rebbe* attracted his own particular following. He required attendants and emissaries. Guests came and went, occasionally spending Sabbaths and holidays at his home, and the *Zaddik* had to provide for them.

Even if the *Zaddik* also occupied the position of local rabbi, his salary fell considerably short of covering his expenses. The congregation of Hasidim thus quite naturally became the economic support of the *Zaddik* and his household. When *Hasidim* visited the *Zaddik*, they took along appropriate gifts. But such giving was different from the support previously extended to scholars. Supporting persons engaged in the study of Torah remained under the heading of charity, for even if regarded as the fulfillment of an obligation, which was the traditional view, it did

not fail to create value distinctions between the giver and receiver. A present to a famous scholar or yeshiva head was in the
nature of a tribute that conferred honor on the donor no less
than on the recipient.

But even here there was, at the most, only a reciprocal relation. A person who supported a scholar received, in the accepted
view, a part of the latter's reward for studying Torah. But in giving to the *Rebbe*, the relationship between giver and receiver
was altered. Since the religious justification of the Hasid was
conditioned on his loyalty to the *Zaddik*, the latter's economic
patron also became his religious beneficiary. Here, giving no
longer came under the heading of charity but served as a symbol
of the *Hasid*'s attachment to the *Zaddik*. In the changed nature
of such giving, as contrasted with giving to persons like the
itinerant preacher, we should note the tremendous social aspect
in the status of the preachers and exhorters, whom the wave of
the new religious movement raised to the high level of the *Zaddik*.

From this analysis, it will be observed that we are dealing
with a two-fold revolution, religious and social, wherein the manifestations of both realms are connected with and dependent on
one another. The transfer of the center of gravity from the actual
performance of the precept to the achievement of a particular
emotional state—ecstasy—through its medium, constituted the
main change in religious development. This change, if followed
to its logical conclusion, was calculated to subvert Judaism completely.

It is safe to say that there was no real relationship between
the internal revolution in experience and outlook and the extent
of the change in the religious way of life. The change constituted
rather a shift in emphasis. In their sermons the preachers and
exhorters did digress into purely theoretical realms and became
involved in a maze of casuistry and homily. But they eventually
returned to the theme which justified their appearance before
the congregation—exhortation and warning about the observance

of the commandments, both those between man and God and
those between man and man.

The exhortations to observe the commandments were missing
in the sermons of the early Hasidic leaders. Their concern was
with the qualitative aspect of religious worship, and they were
not concerned with respect to the general public but for the
chosen few, mainly the *Zaddikim* capable of achieving communion with God. But in any case, even as far as the masses were concerned, it was taken for granted that they followed the traditional way of life and were to be regarded as observers of the
commandments, albeit not down to the minutiae which the cabalist Hasidim considered so important. Only slight deviations in
the behavior of the masses were derived from the example and
teaching of the Hasidic leaders, and some of them, such as laxity
about the times of prayers, were a direct result of the new religiosity.

Unlike the Jews of the halakhic tradition, who regarded
prayer, above all, as the fulfilment of an obligation strictly geared
to a cycle of hours and days, the Hasidim regarded prayer as an
opportune moment to achieve communion with God. Thus, it was
obviously difficult for them to adhere strictly to the prescribed
timetable. But even in this matter they was no outright violation
of religious law. The Hasidim did not *ab initio* abolish the times
of prayer; violation of the hours of prayer was only countenanced
when it transpired that the heart was not in the right mood. The
same was true of the revision of the prayer book, where all that
was done was to replace the regular Ashkenazic version by that
of Rabbi Isaac Luria, which had been previously adopted by the
cabalist Hasidim. But socially the importance of these changes
did not lie in the principles involved; they were sufficient to mark
Hasidism as a separate entity. They served as an indication of
withdrawal from the external society and as a symbol of internal
identification. The fact that the changes pertained to the order
of prayers, where the unity of the community was given expres-

sion, considerably strengthened their power of identification and withdrawal. Moreover, to begin with, at any rate, other attempts at separation were prevalent. The most far-reaching step was the innovation in the custom of ritual slaughtering. The slaughterers of the Hasidim took pains to use only particularly well-sharpened slaughtering knives. This stringency served to camouflage their real object—to avoid eating together with non-Hasidim.

Be that as it may, the Hasidim, unlike the Sabbatian groups, could use open symbols of identification, and these served as a cohesive force in the crystallization of their society. The chief exponents of this movement, too, were members of the sub-intelligentsia; that is, preachers, scholars enjoying public support, ritual slaughterers, and teachers. Whereas Sabbatians, owing to the need for secrecy, did not bring about a change in social status, members of the Hasidic society were distinguished from the Jewish community.

As for the outstanding personalities, their membership in the Hasidic society endowed them with a position of leadership based on qualities which were diametrically opposed to the accepted basis for leadership in traditional Jewish society. Erudition in the revealed law was henceforth not an essential qualification for leadership. However, just as Hasidism did not eradicate the halakhic basis of Judaism, it did not abolish the virtue of the study of the Torah. It was, of course, convenient for a Hasidic leader to be able to top his other qualities with a reputation as a great scholar. This explains why Hasidic legend crowned even the Besht with a quality he did not really possess. In any case, it is clear that erudition in the Torah was not one of the basic accomplishments of the Hasidic leader. The ability to achieve communion with God, ecstatic contact with the divine, was the first and last condition of leadership; this was a personal trait which could not be acquired through rational study, and at times was even impeded by it.

It follows that the rise—the "revelation"—of the *Zaddik* did

not come about through election or any other rational method
similar to that employed in choosing the rabbi of the *kehilla*, for
example. It was the spontaneous attachment of Hasidim, of a
small group which expanded with amazing rapidity, that raised
the *Zaddik* to his high position. This community of Hasidim itself
bore the marks of spontaneity. Joining this movement, at least in
the first stage of its development, was a personal and voluntary
act. Not everyone who came in contact with Hasidism was attracted to it, of course. Some were disappointed in the leadership
of the *Rebbe* or in his community and rejected both; this was
true of Solomon Maimon.

However, those who did join the movement forged ties with
it of almost unlimited faith and confidence. The basis for forming
this bond was the close relationship to the *Zaddik*. This attachment to the *Zaddik* fashioned the Hasidim into a community.
They maintained the contact between themselves even when not
in his presence, when the reporting of his words of learning or
legends of his life served as a substitute. But the communal cohesion was a secondary phenomenon, and was simply the result of
the attachment each individual felt towards the head of the community. No intermediary came between the Hasid and the *Zaddik*,
and even if the *Zaddik* visited only once a year, that meeting, or
even just being in his proximity, was sufficient to sustain the
Hasid for the entire year. In this way, the community was able to
exist, though its members lived in widely separated places.

There was no such thing as a *Zaddik* who was recognized by
residents of one city alone, like the rabbi appointed by the
kehilla. So long as particular *kehillot* were not completely cap-
tured by the Hasidim, and this was true during the transition
period that interests us here, the Hasidic community and the
kehillot partially overlapped. But the members of the movement,
scattered over wide areas, were not organized in any way. Both
their membership and their contributions towards the financial
support of the *Zaddik* and his community were spontaneous.

The two-fold revolution—religious and social—inherent in the rise of Hasidism could not take place without a clash with the exponents of traditional society. It is not our task here to follow the course of the controversy, the first symptoms of which were manifested during the lifetime of the Besht and which raged violently through the two generations after his death. We shall note only the sociological basis of the struggle between the two camps. As already mentioned, Hasidism was rightly recognized by its opponents as a movement possessing charismatic religious authority and as a source of possible defection from historical-institutional Judaism. The emergence of its leaders from the sub-intelligentsia, on the one hand, and the social aloofness of their following from the *kehilla*, on the other, was sufficient to arouse the opposition of the guardians of tradition—the rabbis, yeshiva heads, and lay community leaders.

The weakening of the leadership of the *kehillot* and the dispersal of the places of settlement in the provinces of Podolia and Volhynia apparently helped Hasidism to gain a foothold. The abolition of the Council of the Four Lands, which took place around the time of the Besht's death (1765), removed the central organizational instrument which might have checked its spreading. The struggle was actually conducted by the rabbis and lay leaders of the *kehillot* and by individual personalities, headed by the Vilna Gaon, who regarded themselves as responsible for the fate and leadership of Judaism. Although the struggle was no less bitter than that waged against Sabbatianism, it did not result in an outright communal split. The amazing moderation of Hasidism prevented this. Since Hasidism did not eradicate the halakhic basis of Judaism nor even abrogate the value of Torah study, there was no unbridgeable gap between the two camps.

The result of the struggle was the co-existence of the two institutions, *Rabbanism* and *Zaddikism*, the study of the Torah and Hasidism. In other words, there evolved a sphere of activity neither entirely intellectual nor yet completely emotional, with preference given to the value of *Zaddikism* and Hasidism over ordinary study of the Torah and *Rabbanism*. It will be recalled that even among the early Hasidism there were outstanding halakhic scholars. But it is clear that even they ceased to regard this ability as a primary attribute.

For the most part, something like a division of labor between the rabbi and the *Zaddik* actually emerged; the former was the religious functionary, an expert, as it were, in the halakhic rulings needed for formal leadership, and the latter was the mentor of his fold. Although the authority of the rabbi was apparently preserved in the field designated to him, his position shrank and his influence declined. In the traditional period, it was the halakhic scholar who represented the religious objective—the observance of the precepts as prescribed—while the preacher, the master of *aggada,* and moralist, assisted him. Now the relationship was changed. The object had become the achievement of a certain standard of piety, embodied by the *Zaddik,* who helped his followers achieve it. The rabbi, who merely issued halakhic rulings, dropped to the rank of an auxiliary.

Parallel to the appearance of the new leadership was the formation of the new community of Hasidism. This community came together, as we have seen, from widely separated areas; membership in it was voluntary; and, in the beginning at least, it was not general but individual and selective. The emergence of this community split the *kehilla,* part of which now owed loyalty to an extraneous body. The weakening of the *kehilla* organization in the period which preceded Hasidism probably facilitated the movement's taking root. But the influence exerted in the opposite direction was also strong. The penetration of Hasidism tended to weaken the governing power of the *kehilla.* It would seem that for the first time in the history of the *kehilla,* a principle appeared that was also likely to serve as the basis for political cohesion in the internal struggle for power. The victory of Hasidism over the length and breadth of Poland also meant the conquest of the *kehilla* organizations by the Hasidim.

The same was true of the family. The individual joined the Hasidim after undergoing something resembling conversion, a personal experience which did not take in all the members of the family at once. The person attracted to Hasidism sometimes regarded himself as distinguished from the rest of his family, and, if they were sworn opponents of the "sect," this distinction was likely to reach the point of estrangement. But even the family which embraced Hasidism as a body became different from the ordinary traditional family. Owing to the Hasid's visits to the *Zaddik*, especially on Sabbaths and festivals, the chief basis of family unity—the celebration of the holidays together—disappeared or was weakened. Moreover, membership in the emotion-packed Hasidic congregation and the strong attachment of the Hasid to his mentor served to some extent as a substitute for family ties. In extreme cases, even grief over the death of a member of one's family took second place to that felt for the loss of the *Zaddik*.

The spiritual revolution in Hasidism penetrated the depths of erotic life. The diligence with which religious devotion was practiced diminished erotic tension. Although Hasidism did not bring about a movement of celibacy, there was a clearly discernible tendency to depreciate erotic life, as well as to lower the status of women. The Hasidic congregation was a man's world; in it, there was no place for women, as there was in the family. Not even a parallel women's community was organized, as in the *kehilla* associations. The community of Hasidim was built, if not on the ruins, at the expense of the traditional institutions of society.

A religious revolution like that of Hasidism does not change only the institutions of the society's existence. It also influences the mental outlook of its adherents. In this sphere, too, it is more important to fix our attention on the psychological results of the initial religious revolution than to seek the reason for the emergence of Hasidism in earlier psychological data. There is no doubt that Hasidism transformed Jewish mentality, or in any case, exerted a tremendous influence on it. The rationalistic course in daily conduct gave way to the passive expectation of a miraculous occurrence. To resort to rational means, such as medical science, was to invite suspicion of lack of trust in God; in one stream of Hasidism—the Brazlaver—this was carried to the point where an outright prohibition was issued on consulting a physician. The same was true in other fields. The rational use of time, that is, its division and fullest exploitation for practical purposes and for the realization of religious values, was basically impaired by making a virtue out of waiting hours until the opportune moment arrived for communion with God. It is no exaggeration to call this the sanctification of indolence, for which social conditions prepared an actual basis and the religious movement gave its solemn approval. The deep split which was felt in the post-Hasidic period between Hasidic Jews and those of the non-Hasidic areas was the result of the religious revolution brought about by Hasidism.

XXIII
The Emergence of
the Neutral Society

OUR ANALYSIS OF HASIDISM REVEALED THE EX-
tent of the transformation which took place in traditional Jewish society during and after the days when that movement flourished. But all these changes applied only to the internal structure
of society—to the mode of organization, the sources of authority,
and the criteria of stratification within society itself. In relation
to the world outside, no change at all took place. Disintegration,
in the full sense of the word, implies the breakdown of the institutions of society and the dispersion of its members.

The prospect of outright disintegration is faced by the type
of society whose existence is based on deliberate circumscription
and withdrawal from the surrounding milieu. The Jewish society

we are discussing was such a community. If this circumscription and withdrawal were to end, conceivably, not only would the institutions break down but even their reconstruction would be renounced. The individuals in the Jewish society would then be absorbed by the surrounding society and their needs would be met throught the institutions operating there. Jewish society, as the reader is aware, never went to that extreme, even where it was apparently given the opportunity to do so. But tendencies to disintegrate and self-liquidate were seen occasionally, and the Haskala and emancipatory movement, the emergence of which we shall now describe, affords an outstanding example.

The social turning point to which we have alluded is revealed in the emergence of a new type, the *maskil*, who added to his knowledge of the Torah a command of foreign languages, general erudition, and an interest in what was happening in the non-Jewish world. This type became increasingly numerous beginning with the 1760's, and it soon constituted a subgroup in Jewish society. It demanded for itself not only the right of existence but also the privilege of leadership.

After the emergence of the *maskilim*, new ideals pertaining to daily living, the organization and leadership of society, and the methods of education came to be formulated in a programmatic manner. When the *maskilim* began to gather strength, a feeling of crisis arose in the consciousness even of those who continued to adhere to the values of the tradition in which they were reared. An awareness of the crisis forced itself on the people by dint of changes in the objective data that had hitherto determined the framework of Jewish life. Where the abandonment of the accepted and the traditional was carried to extremes, the consciousness of crisis became a conviction that ultimately the utter eclipse of Jewish society would come about. This conviction sanctioned the individual, and perhaps even charged him, to seek a refuge outside the framework of his disintegrating society.

The feeling of dissolution can be described as an internal

Jewish manifestation. But it was prompted by processes which affected both Jewish society and the external environment. We must therefore broaden our field of vision to include the factors which brought about the change in relations between the two societies.

Our discussion in the early chapters of this book has taught us to recognize that the erection of the political and social boundaries of the Jewish society was dependent on the institutions of the surrounding society. From a formal point of view, the governing institutions of the state determined the Jewish sphere of existence. So long as the state was divided on a class basis, the Jews were fitted into this type of subdivision, though they represented a special category. Jewish residence in a given place was conditional on a formal agreement or at least on the wishes of the rulers. Functionally, however, the community was integrated into the life of the state as one class among others.

The class structure itself underwent changes during the period we are discussing. The changes were the result of a complicated development which we cannot detail here. For our purpose, it will suffice to note the results of these changes. They can be summed up as follows: the absolute ruler—the emperor, the king, or the prince—tried to concentrate the government with the aid of an administrative organization. Under such a regime, the different classes were gradually shorn of their autonomy; the absolute ruler converted the members of the different estates into citizens. However, the organizational framework of the classes was not destroyed, and the differences in the privileges enjoyed by members of the various classes were by no means abolished.

The affairs of each class were transferred to the central authority of the ruler, whose orders determined the functions of the respective members, their duties, and their privileges. These were based on the traditional place the class had occupied in the state, but the right of the members of the respective estates to decide for themselves was now repudiated. The central government was,

in theory, required to direct the activities of all the classes so
that they complemented one another for the good of the state,
which was now held to be the political unit of supreme value and
responsibility.

These changes in the structure of the state had repercussions
in the life of the Jewish community. In the economic-occupational
area, this influence was less than it might seem to have been on
the surface. Some broadening of the fields of employment occurred when Jews were granted permission to study medicine in
German universities in the last third of the seventeenth century;
this was an opportunity of which a number of Jews took advantage.
But even in the absolute state, most Jews continued to earn their
livelihood by the employment of the financial capital belonging
to themselves or others. Only methods of investment changed to
keep pace with economic developments.

Economic organization was also connected with the new form
of government. The concentration of political leadership in the
hands of the ruler and his advisers, the existence of a national
army and a bureaucratic organization, the search for new financial sources through the expansion of the network of taxes and
customs, the initiation of economic activity by the rulers—in
short, the dovetailing of political and economic activity typical
of this stage of the development of the modern state—turned
the place of government not only into the political center, but
also into the locus of economic and financial activity.

So long as the absolute state did not influence Jewish communal life there was no functional curtailment of the activities of
its institutions. Such curtailment did occur, however, when the absolute state directly interfered in the affairs of the Jewish "class,"
as it did in the life of the other classes. From then on—from the
first quarter of the eighteenth century at the very latest—serious
breaches were made in the autonomous internal government of
the *kehilla* and super-*kehilla*. The authorities no longer contented
themselves with the fulfillment of the conditions required for the

enjoyment of the rights of domicile—payment of taxes, strict obedience to the laws of the state, etc. The ruler and the administrative organs of the state were interested in the internal financial and organizational management of the *kehillot* and the super-*kehillot*. They wished to exercise some form of control over communal affairs. Functions which had previously been imposed on institutions of the *kehilla*, such as the collection of promissory notes and the liquidation of businesses because of bankruptcy, were now transferred to government officials. In this way, the *kehilla*'s hold on its members was weakened.

The direct means of compulsion were also curtailed. The imposition of the ban (*herem*) was either completely forbidden or made dependent on the special approval of the authorities. If the *kehilla* leadership did exert compulsion on a member, the person punished could find a sympathetic ear among the authorities and induce them to review the action of the internal Jewish court. Though the authorities of the absolute state did not disband the accepted institutions of the *kehilla*, they interfered in their activities on the slightest pretext.

The task of curtailing Jewish autonomy was easier for the absolute state than was the struggle against the other classes. The latter were supported by rights which were in the nature of an historical heritage, but the autonomy of the Jewish community had, from the very first, been a free concession on the part of the rulers, a concession that could be granted or revoked at will. Though the Jewish community tried to combat with all means at its disposal the haphazard intervention of the states on behalf of one party or another in internal Jewish disputes, we find no attempts to oppose the more far-reaching intervention of the absolute state affecting the very basis of Jewish autonomy. Some *kehillot*, from the moment of their formation, were established on the limited basis that the absolute state was prepared to grant to the Jewish community. Even where the limitation came after some time, it took place gradually. There is no evidence that the members of the *kehillot* regarded the changes as decisive turning points in their lives. Furthermore, even from a historical perspective, it is doubtful whether these changes were of decisive social significance.

The curtailment of the basis of activity of the *kehilla* loosened the bond between the individual and his community. However, this loosening was neither preceded nor immediately followed by the individual's adherence to another society. The social-religious barrier between Jewish and non-Jewish society still stood. Admittedly, the court Jews did have intercourse with members of the non-Jewish society, even in matters not connected with business. Kings and princes occasionally accepted invitations from their Jewish officials to attend the weddings of their children, and they sometimes even stayed over in their homes. But such an appearance of a distinguished Christian at a Jewish celebration was more an act of condescension than a social mixing on a basis of equality and reciprocity. As for the Jew himself, such meetings represented a signal honor which demonstrated his achievements to the members of the Jewish and non-Jewish societies. But the receipt of such honors, which were isolated occurrences in the life of the Jew, did not represent any shift in his social position. At the most, personal ties were formed between the court Jew and his lord, whom he served out of a feeling of loyalty and personal attachment. Social life and, even more, cultural and religious life, remained bound to the inner Jewish circle. Even the individuals who gained power and influence through their economic achievements in the non-Jewish world exercised their social prestige in the internal life of the Jewish community.

The non-Jewish world, although it lost something of its hostile nature, remained foreign territory that could be entered only by the way of conversion. If the frequent and varied contact of the court Jews in this period increased the number of converts to Christianity, particularly among the children and grandchildren of those who had achieved greatness, this did not affect the existence of the traditional society, which was capable of preserving its principles and its special character despite these defections.

A decisive turning point in the history of the Jewish society occurred only when its individual members transferred their social goals to the context of the surrounding non-Jewish milieu. This took place when individuals began to regard the non-Jewish society not only as a framework for economic activity, but also as a source of social gratification. Up to this time, if such a change in social goals took place, it led the individual to a transfer from Jewish society to the non-Jewish. The outward diversion of the social ambition of the Jew unaccompanied by the necessity that he become converted to Christianity was conditioned on the emergence of a non-Jewish class for which the difference of religion had lost its circumscribing function.

Originally, such a class did not exist even in the absolute state, but it gradually emerged as a new elite, the elite of independent commonalty. This commonalty itself came as a consequence of the economic activity directed at the free market, an activity which the absolute state tolerated and sometimes even encouraged. The absolute state aimed to divest the classes of their political content, but unintentionally it also encouraged the weakening of their social framework.

To a greater and greater extent, individuals were unable to find satisfaction in their traditional niche in the social framework—merchants and artisans in their guilds and associations and the nobility in their traditional occupations and in public life. These individuals found support in the free economic activity based on the rational calculation of the prospects of the market. The emergence of the free market and individual class defection were mutually interconnected. These two phenomena were conditioned on numerous and complicated political and technical factors beyond the scope of this study.

This historical process affected Jewish society at a later stage, when the fluctuations in the economic-social area were no longer isolated phenomena. The economic-social independence then became a primary condition of an entire class, and it sought expression and justification for itself in theoretical doctrines and demands.

The ideological basis for these doctrines and demands was to be found in various sources. From "natural law" they learned to claim that every person possessed the right to unlimited independence. Rationalist philosophy authorized the individual to support his deeds on the basis of his reason alone and to sweep away the restraints imposed by the cultural and religious tradition. Utilitarian ethics identified the good with the useful and gave moral sanction to the individual's efforts to achieve his own practical ends. All the principles of rationalism or enlightenment were mobilized in order to paint the picture of a new world that differed from that shown by historical reality. In this picture of the future, class and religious differences disappeared, and all that remained was the direct bond between one rationalist and another. No wonder the Jew was also included in this rationalist's dream of human society, not as a member of a specific religion or nation, but simply as a human being.

The rationalist vision of the future began to take shape in the middle of the eighteenth century. The inclusion of Jews in the picture was delayed, however, until the last third of the century. Their inclusion, however, did not alter their position in the current social reality. A typical feature of the period of rationalism in France and of *Aufklaerung* in Germany was that the rationalists were swept into theorizing on matters that they were unable to bring into concrete existence.

The acknowledgement of rationalist principles resulted only in a sort of auxiliary phenomenon: here and there it created a new basis for the social grouping of the bearers of the new ideology. The rationalists who identified themselves with the vision of the marvelous new world of the future formed a distinct social unit. Whereas in the class society, the intellectuals had attached themselves to their respective classes—writers and lawyers to the courts of kings, priests and teachers to the commonalty organized in guilds, and talmudic scholars to their corresponding niche in Jewish society—there now appeared a stratum of intelligentsia who presumed to be above and beyond all classes.

This stratum was defined as a "spiritual elite," a social unit membership in which demanded the fostering of spiritual values. The formation of this elite was a by-product of the rise of the independent commonalty, but the two were not identical and the members of the elite were not drawn exclusively from this class. After the ideas were formulated and given concrete expression, they attracted adherents by the power of persuasion alone—by the internal consistency of their system, by satisfying the demands of justice, and by the guarantee of a better world. Once established, the ideals of the Enlightenment also attracted persons who were not commoners, such as nobles and priests and even princes and kings, the very ones who, until then, had been responsible for the accepted class division of society.

This development first influenced Jewish society through the creation of a sort of social identification between enlightened Jews and their non-Jewish counterparts. For these individuals there was a clear distinction between the non-Jewish masses, towards whom they held a disparaging attitude, and the enlightened non-Jews, whom they admired and whose views they respected. But this was an ideological identity alone; it achieved no practical social results.

A social turning point was reached only where the Enlightenment came to serve as a basis for social grouping. This began in the middle of the eighteenth century, particularly in the German states, when "intellectual" changed from a mere label to an appellation of a well-defined social group. Ties were formed between individual rationalists in different ways—by reading the same books and periodicals, by chance or arranged meetings, and finally by the creation of circles designed to foster the values of the Enlightenment within a single social framework.

From the point of view of our subject, this new social form possessed a particular significance. In consequence of the sociological nature of this new grouping, the way was paved for a further innovation—that even Jews would be accepted as equals. An association formed on the basis of an acknowledgement of the values of the Enlightenment would have to discard all rules of selection under which it would have been possible to restrict membership to adherents of a single religion. The rationalist creed recognized no class or religious divisions. The exclusion of the Jews from membership would have struck at the very basis of their principles.

Although, as a matter of principle, the admission of Jews into these associations of rationalists practically went without saying, this represented, from the Jewish viewpoint, an unparalleled departure. The innovation lay, of course, not in the actual encounter between Jews and non-Jews, but in its new sociological basis. Hitherto, the two groups had come together only with some extraneous, practical end in mind. Now, the meetings between members of the societies were designed for their own sake, to give the participants a feeling of belonging to a primary, intimate group. It is safe to assume that those who joined the new social group did so because they had cut themselves off from their class and felt relatively isolated. Be that as it may, they found their chief satisfaction in the meetings themselves, and, if clearly defined purposes—such as the fostering of learning or mutual assistance—were connected with the existence of the societies, these were simply secondary aims. The principal function and justification for these meetings was in the pleasure of the contact with kindred souls that they afforded. This was the surprising fact as far as the Jewish society was concerned—that some of its members were, in some aspects of their existence, transplanted to a common socio-cultural milieu with non-Jews.

The social manifestation outlined here served as the background for the development of the personality of Moses Mendelssohn and many others of lesser ability and character. Mendelssohn fell in with a group of rationalists in Berlin, and there he remained until his entire spiritual being and social activity were conditioned by the double connection—to his religious community and thus to traditional Jewish society on the one hand, and to groups of rationalists and, consequently, to the neutral European society, on the other.

Mendelssohn's tarrying in two social units, which most people in both camps still regarded as two separate worlds with only a utilitarian connection, amazed those who observed him. Repeated attempts were made to convince Mendelssohn of the necessity of choosing between the Jewish and the Christian worlds. The best known of such attempts is Lavater's public challenge to Mendelssohn to admit or refute the truth of Christianity. As a matter of fact, appeals of this sort missed the point, for the essence of the rationalists' social achievement lay precisely in their creation of a neutral basis above religious differences. The human-universal was transformed into an intrinsic value, and it served as a unifying principle for all who accepted it. The insistence on a verdict in favor of either Christianity or Judaism blunted its urgency and acuteness. From this point on, there was a third sphere—the neutral, human one—to which members of both religions could belong. In the ideological field, this sphere evolved out of the universal values of the Enlightenment, and in the social, from the framework of neutral associations of rationalists. On the basis of conclusive historical evidence, it can be asserted that in the German states this third sphere steadily gained in strength, particularly in the decade from 1770 to 1780.

The rationalists were not isolated from their original social spheres by belonging to the third sphere. In most cases, the new framework embraced only part of their being. In a number of walks of life, Christians remained Christians and Jews, Jews.

Mendelssohn and other *maskilim* like him preserved their attachment to the life and principles of their original culture. They divided their lives between the two worlds. But this dualistic position was not easy to maintain. For many Jews, the neutral contact with non-Jews resulted in their complete divorcement from Judaism. The supposedly neutral rationalist groups sometimes served only as an intermediate stage in the journey of the Jewish *maskilim* to Christianity.

This process of divorcement gained in momentum in the famous salons of Jewish women in the generation after Mendelssohn's death. The salons of both Rachel Varnhagen and Henriette Herz in Berlin and of Fanny Arnstein and Zipporah Eskeles in Vienna were ostensibly neutral meeting grounds where Jews and non-Jews could spent time in one another's company, with their differences of origin forgotten. However, since the unifying feature of the salons was social amusement for its own sake, they established a style of behavior which clashed with the traditional way of life to a far greater degree than did the rationalist circles in which Mendelssohn participated. The salons became parts of an assimilating social framework dominated by non-Jewish culture. Participation in salon life generally led Jews to join the non-Jewish society outright, an act that meant embracing its religion and its church.

If the new converts required ideological backing for their decision, this was forthcoming in the theory of the positive nucleus common to all religions that discredited completely the claims to uniqueness of each religion. A person who accepted this theory could believe that in changing his religion he was simply altering the external trappings, which were unimportant in any case. On the basis of this theory, one public figure, David Friedlaender, thought it possible for the entire Jewish community to be absorbed into Christianity without having to renounce what really constituted their fundamental beliefs. For those individuals who were enticed by social inducements to accept the prevailing religion, this theory no doubt served to soothe their conscience and remove psychological inhibitions.

Thus, to no small extent, the neutralization between the Jewish and non-Jewish societies led portions of Jewish society to become absorbed by the Christian world. But if this had been the only result of the process, it would not have constituted a turning point in the life of the Jewish society as such. In other periods, an even greater number of Jews had deserted the traditional society, but the society itself had stood fast.

Abandonment of the Jewish society was only one kind of reaction to the conditions of neutralization. Mendelssohn himself, it may be recalled, did not take this course. But neither was he capable of maintaining his dual role based on the division of life into Jewish and neutral spheres. From the time of his debate with Lavater in 1770 and in the light of increasing indications of impending changes in the system of the class state in general and of the status of the Jews in particular, Mendelssohn was drawn further and further from his dual position. Out of a sense of responsibility for the fate of Jewish society, he agreed to undertake tasks which more or less delineated its course. From then on, this was the position of all those *maskilim* whose identification with the values of the neutral society set them apart from the members of the traditional society but whose attachment to the values and the culture of their original milieu did not allow them to divorce themselves completely from it.

In the lives of many Jews of that generation, we witness a struggle with the decision of whether to preserve the link with their Jewish origin or to choose the path of conversion. Precisely because decision was one that had to be made by the individual, the point at which various psychological and social factors converge, it was inconceivable that the outcome would always favor conversion. There were, of course, *maskilim* whose attachment to Judaism was so deep that the idea of conversion never even entered their minds even as a theoretical possibility.

On the other hand, not all the *maskilim* had equal prospects of being absorbed into Christian society. Wealthy Jews had an advantage, and their children an even greater one, since they capped their wealth with education and a style of living that put them on an equal footing with their Christian contemporaries. But *maskilim* in reduced circumstances, and particularly those who still bore evidence of their origins in speech and manner, had difficulty in finding their way not only to the salons, but to the neutral associations as well. Despite the principle which called for the removal of the barriers between the Jewish and non-Jewish societies, they associated only with one another. This is why, insofar as it was not the individual but the overall society that was concerned, the continued existence of this intermediate class was ensured.

This stratum of *maskilim* was now defined by its identification with the society of its origin, and its reservations about the traditional system of values. If the members of this group did not actually join the neutral associations, they cast envious glances at their brethren who did. In sociological terms, it may be said that the neutral associations became the group of orientation for the *maskilim*. It was from the neutral associations and their doctrines that these *maskilim* derived their criteria for appraising Jewish society itself. In any case, tradition as such could no longer serve as the justification for what existed. The *maskilim* now held up the institutions of traditional society to the test of reason, intelligence, and nature—terms that were practically interchangeable as used in that period.

Most important of all is the fact that the *maskilim* pictured the future of Jewish society on the basis of their identification with the values of the neutral society. In their aspiration to be the shapers of the future of their society, they assumed the right to serve as mentors to the entire nation. For although diehard traditionalists regarded the *maskilim* as deviators and violators of religious propriety, in their own eyes, they constituted the pioneers and heralds of the future. From the 1780's onwards, the *maskilim* emerged as a group with a clear-cut social-ideological character, laying claim to the leadership of society as a whole, just like any other social elite. The rise of this new elite beside the traditional groupings constituted the decisive event in Jewish social history of the period.

XXIV   *The Haskala's Vision*
of the Future

*I*N A FORMAL SENSE, THE HASKALA MOVEMENT
was like the parallel non-Jewish Enlightenment movement in that
both, when they first emerged, envisioned a new future contra-
dicting the obvious reality. This vision of the future originally
developed against the background of the breakdown of reality.
But when it became a clear ideological concept with well-defined
doctrines and demands, it became an ideal that aimed not at
reforming the evils of reality but at setting up a new reality in
its place.

Henceforth, the ideal did not derive its impetus directly from
dissatisfaction with the existing situation. The logical consistency
of the doctrines and the justice of its demands proved to its sup-

[260]

porters the rightness of the ideal and endowed it with moral authority. The ideal served as a criterion for the appraisal and criticism of reality. In this manner, it became a decisive factor advancing the historical process. It is not our task to trace the development of the Haskala movement through the entire period in which the ideal retained its validity and continued to perform its historical function. We shall describe, as we did with Hasidism, the rise of the vision of the new future to reveal the direction of the breakdown. Its criticism overlooked no institution of traditional Jewish society. Let us consider these institutions as they appeared to the critical eye of the *maskilim*.

Jewish and non-Jewish rationalists found the economic structure of Jewish society to be faulty and illogical. This was only natural. Admittedly, its occupational one-sidedness was justifiable only as long as Jewish society was regarded as a class performing a specific function among the other classes. But when human society began to be regarded as composed of individuals enjoying freedom of social movement, Jewish attachment to a few special occupations seemed an anomaly. The appraisal of this phenomenon differed. Hostile critics reproached the Jews for sticking to trade and financial transactions and avoiding the crafts and manual labor in general. The disrepute in which all merchants and money-lenders were held applied to the Jews with even greater force.

It was a sign of the social proximity of the *maskilim* to their non-Jewish counterparts that they now identified themselves with this evaluation of occupations. However, they tended to take the moral sting out of the criticism by attributing the occupational one-sidedness to the vocational restrictions imposed on the Jews by state laws. Moses Mendelssohn even justified commercial transactions on the basis of an economic theory which ascribed productive value even to the transfer of goods from place to place. But as for the future, even Mendelssohn saw the need of broadening the areas of Jewish employment, particularly in the direction of the free professions. The *maskilim* tended to believe that a sweeping occupational redistribution would take place among the Jews that would lead to the emergence of artisans, farmers, and soldiers. This would come about if only they were given the necessary permission by the laws of the state. In any case, all agreed that the Jewish occupational singularity could not persist in the envisioned society with unlimited mobility. The *maskilim* included vocational dispersal in their theory, not as a mere prospect or possibility but as an inexorable moral demand.

Of a similar nature was the *maskilim's* criticism of Jewish organizations that continued to operate along traditional lines. In this matter, Mendelssohn was not only the chief spokesman, but also the one who took the strongest line in repudiating the existing state of affairs. In his opinion, all the powers of compulsion which the Jewish organizations had taken into their hands had come about through imitation of the Christian Church. To such an extent was the historical judgment warped in a man who was still in a position to see the ancient *kehillot* engaged in their broad public activities. On this assumption, it is easy to understand the conclusion that, in the future, only those Jewish organizations that were voluntary associations of individuals whose formation stemmed from the similarity of the faith and ritual to which they adhered, should be formed.

The function of the Jewish *kehilla*, like that of any other religious organization, was to serve as a framework for the advancement of an appropriate religious object. This object was the fostering of the good intention which leads to the good deed, whereas the state is entitled and obligated to impose the deed without being in a position to examine the nature of the motive behind it. Only with difficulty and by compromise with tradition did Mendelssohn allow a place for internal Jewish administration of justice—on condition that the parties involved voluntarily accept the jurisdiction of the Jewish court. But the power of compulsion to the extent that human society required it was exclusively vested in the state. Religion and the state were different in nature and should also be distinct in their activities. Only after such separation would the activities of religion and state complement one another.

Needless to say, this theory was far removed from the realities of 1783, the year in which Moses Mendelssohn formulated it in his book, *Jerusalem*. Here, too, principles and demands were set forth. The vision of the future is described with such moral pathos that the hoped-for order does not seem to be the fruit of unavoidable adjustment to reality, but the realization of values possessing absolute validity.

A decisive change also took place in the position of the *maskilim* in the social sphere. The *maskilim*, who had their reservations as to the values of the traditional society and its institutions, were unable to find social satisfaction in the existing traditional associations. However, as we have seen in the previous chapter, even the neutral associations did not absorb all the *maskilim*. To the extent that the *maskilim* tried to perform the function of an elite and to point the way to the entire Jewish public, the neutral associations could not serve their purpose. Only in the framework of special Jewish associations could they foster the rationalist values in their special Jewish coloration, and only through public cohesion could they hope to influence or even join battle with the Jewish community that still stood apart from the Haskala.

These conditions formed the background for the emergence of the associations of *maskilim* which began to make their appearance in the 1780's. *Hevrat Dorshei Leshon Ever* (Society of Students of the Hebrew Language) in Koenigsberg in 1784 (its name was changed two years later to *Die Gesellschaft zur Befoerderung des Guten und Edlen*—Society for the Furthering of the Good and the Noble) and the *Gesellschaft der Freunde* (Society of Friends) in Berlin in 1927 will serve as examples. The Koenigsberg society decided to publish a Hebrew monthly, *Ha-*

measef, to spread Enlightenment among the Jews. The Berlin society organized its members in order to impose on the local burial society their wish not to be buried immediately after death, but only after a few days—a demand which became a watchword in the battle of the innovators against the conservatives, as representing the victory of common sense and science over the blind adherence to tradition. These associations thus fulfilled tasks which constituted the essential program of the *maskilim.* But they also performed such auxiliary duties as giving mutual aid, extending support to the needy, caring for the sick, and preparing the dead for burial. They also provided their members with opportunities for amusement. In all, these activities are apparently reminiscent of the practices of the holy associations in the traditional Jewish society. But the resemblance was only superficial.

In the first place was the difference in the values which the new societies were meant to further. Their aim, from the very start, was not to promote the observance of religious precepts but to disseminate Enlightenment and achieve rationalist goals. Second, social amusement no longer sought the warrant of religion. It was demanded and indulged in *per se,* as an expression of the sociability of man, one of his innate virtues in the Haskala view. It should occasion no surprise to learn that henceforth in *maskilim* circles attempts were made to abrogate or reduce the scope of some of the customary religiously prescribed banquets (*se'udot mitzva*). The reason they gave for abrogating the *zakhor* (the traditional festivities on the Friday night after the birth of a son) and the feast which immediately followed the circumcision ceremony was hygienic, to protect the health of the mother. But we may ascribe this tendency to the fact that the *maskilim* no longer needed the protection of religion in order to satisfy their social needs. This rejection of religious values and the supplanting of the traditional institutions came about almost unpremeditatedly and without attracting particular attention.

It was in the field of education that an open clash first took place between the old and the new. In non-Jewish society, an educational philosophy was now being expounded which advocated a uniform education for children of all religions. This was put into practice in the philanthropic pedagogic trend in places such as the school of Basedow in Dessau, where children of different religions were taught side by side. The pupils of various religious faiths were given the opportunity to take part in the rituals of their respective churches. But within the confines of the schools, which were all-day institutions, the presence of children of different religions precluded the possibility of fostering the attachment of the pupils to the religion of their fathers.

From the educators' point of view, this did not represent an unavoidable compromise but a deliberate intention. The Philanthropists actually did want to shunt the historical religions off into a corner, supplanting them by natural religion and teaching its deistic tenets and ethical principles jointly to the members of all religions.

In the Philanthropist schools, we again encounter the neutral society in its educational metamorphosis. The *maskilim* who accepted the idea of the neutral society had difficulty in disassociating themselves even from its most extreme expression, where what was involved was not tolerant intercourse between members of different religions, but the rearing of a new generation on an entirely neutral basis. Nevertheless, it was unlikely that this type of joint education would replace the traditional educational institutions. It was obvious that children educated in the neutral atmosphere of these general institutions would lack all attachment to Judaism. For this reason, these institutions could serve only those parents who themselves were on the verge of deserting Jewish society. But, as we have seen, the foundations of the traditional Jewish society were undermined precisely by the *mas-*

kilim who retained their connection with the Jewish community as such and wished only to modernize its system of values.

As a matter of fact, the program of the *maskilim* was systematically propounded by a man who was himself firmly rooted in the world of traditional values and inspired by a constructive rather than destructive approach. The proposal expressed in the propagandist pamphlet of Naphtali Herz Wessely, *Divrei Shalom Ve'emet* (Words of Peace and Truth), was written in 1782 on the occasion of the publication of the Edict of Toleration by the Emperor Joseph II of Austria. The Emperor's proposition provided a suitable opportunity for advancing the educational program that had already crystallized in the circles of the *maskilim*. Identification with the values of the neutral society is clearly evident both in the overall program and in its details. The basis of this educational philosophy was "the teachings of man," that is, educational values common to all human beings. "The teachings of God," or the content of Jewish religious tradition, was merely a special supplement for the education of the Jew, and its worth was dependent on the prior mastery of the foundations of universal knowledge. In its details, the identification with the neutral society is reflected in the pride of place given to such subjects as the language of the country, geography, and history, which were then considered the foundation for general knowledge.

Even in the content of the Jewish studies themselves, preference was given to elements that could be regarded as containing values common to the members of the non-Jewish society— Bible and Hebrew grammar, but not the Talmud, application to which was said to put a man out of touch with his fellows. What we have here is not a slight adjustment of the curriculum to contemporary needs. The real significance of the program lay in the fact that it accorded the status of ends in themselves to studies which, at best, had hitherto been tolerated merely as means and handmaidens of sacred pursuits. Indeed, Wessely did not base his program mainly on the grounds of expediency, but presented it as the most desirable method of achieving the perfection of the individual Jew. Wessely resorted to the same moral pathos with which Mendelssohn urged his political program in presenting his educational blueprint.

The representatives of the old system of values realized the implications of the new educational program even more than the circles which had advanced it. The appearance of Wessely's pamphlet was the main reason for the conservatives' sounding the alarm to warn of the danger threatening the foundations of the entire society. Wessely himself tended to play down the conclusions implied in his words. But the course of events indicates that his program expressed not so much the ideas of a single individual as the change in values that had taken place in the consciousness of an entire community.

Institutions began to be founded to carry out programs similar to Wessely's. They received public sympathy and support and were able to compete with the educational institutions of the traditional society. The latter began to disappear from the *kehillot* during the generation after Mendelssohn. Political factors also speeded their disappearance: namely, the desire of the authorities to equate Jewish educational facilities with those of other citizens. The authorities were able to rely on Jewish public opinion in this context, and the only opposition was voiced by some survivors of the old generation whose influence had waned. With the disappearance of the traditional educational institutions, traditional Jewish society lost the basic instrument for ensuring its survival.

The changes in the vocational, political, and educational spheres can easily be attributed to the feeling of identification with the surrounding non-Jewish society, a feeling that loomed increasingly larger in the consciousness of the *maskilim*. Conformist and traditional standards were abandoned in favor of behavior conducted on rationalist principles.

Changes also took place in the institution of the family, but their nature and direction were completely different. The erotic experience was given preference over rational considerations in the founding of a family. The innovation did not, of course, lie in the presence of erotic experience in itself, but in raising it to a prerequisite for the social suitability of the marriage. Whereas in the traditional society, a couple who fell in love before getting married needed some moral-rational camouflage to justify their union, it was now the other way round; even marriages contracted solely on the basis of objective considerations were made to appear as if they had come about through the personal attraction of the couple to one another.

Mendelssohn himself was the outstanding example of this change in Jewish society. He apparently was introduced to his future wife by mutual friends, but he later tried to give the impression that the match had come about entirely spontaneously. In seemingly trivial matters, such as refusing to undertake to give his bride gifts formally stipulated in advance and in ignoring the set style in writing to his betrothed, he wished to stress the personal element in everything pertaining to the marriage institution. In displaying this attitude, he departed, in any case, from accepted practice and rejected it in principle. In this, Mendelssohn was simply expressing the growing trend. Almost overnight marriages arranged by matchmakers lost their social propriety. They did not disappear, but they had to adapt themselves to the new ideal. The matchmaker had to do his work unobtrusively. The dowry became a matter negotiated behind the scenes, and the couple pretended to be a pair of lovers whom fate had thrown together. In some cases, the erotic impulse was given a completely free rein. Mendelssohn's daughter Dorothea left her husband and children out of a feeling that she must not remain deaf to the call of love. Here the romantic ideal reached its extreme, and the institution of the Jewish family was razed to its foundations. In less sophisticated circles, the ideal functioned less intensively, but here, too, it gave force to the new norm of marriage by free choice.

Romantic love became the rule in both Jewish and non-Jewish societies in the very period when the walls dividing the two began to be breached—and the same historical root will explain both. The undermining of the rigid class system forced the individual to stand on his own two feet. A consciousness of isolation prepared individuals for social grouping along lines other than the customary class basis, impelling them to seek the experience of intimacy in the sphere of friendship and love. Admittedly, romantic love with all its dynamic qualities represented only a transitional phase. Nevertheless, both the rationalist ideals and erotic experience emerged against the background of class dissolution and the deliverance of individuals from its grip; they are two sides of the same coin.

The bearers of the new spirit maintained that no single Jewish institution remained whose foundations had not been destroyed and which had not lost its validity—at least in its customary forms. This assertion was meant to include religious institutions as well as the national ideals they represented. "Natural religion," that is, the principles of faith which harmonized with the rationalist conception of the *maskilim*, became the criterion for evaluating the historical religions, Judaism included. The conclusions reached by different rationalists on their relationship to historical religion, as it then existed, ran the gamut from outright dissociation to complete harmonization with its doctrines in theory and acceptance of its yoke in practice. Between these two extremes, was every nuance among both Jewish and non-Jewish rationalists.

Moses Mendelssohn identified Judaism with the essential principles of natural religion, which were safeguarded by the ritual observances incumbent on the Jew. But even Mendelssohn's contemporaries argued that this rationalization in itself destroyed the absolute validity of these observances. For if the essentials of Judaism were really identical with those of natural religion, the latter had, for some time, been prevalent among the rationalists of all nations, and there no longer existed any real purpose in ritual observance even for the Jewish rationalist. Such reasoning was likely to pave the way for the repudiation of religious observances. Indeed, even those *maskilim* who did not divorce themselves completely from Judaism ceased to acknowledge the absolutely binding nature of religious precepts. It was precisely among this group that confusion prevailed regarding the shape to be assumed by this new Judaism which, in their view, had in any case been divested of its traditional character.

This divestment led to the fact that, as far as these *maskilim* were concerned, the halakha had ceased to serve as the final authority on the question of what was permissible and desirable. Admittedly, in debates over details they continued to marshal arguments from the treasury of the halakha. Halakhic literature itself became an arsenal for those who were familiar with its byways. But rabbinic authority lost its hold as the final word and arbiter in all situations. As far as a large part of the Jewish community was concerned, this development involved an abrogation of one of the basic foundations of traditional Judaism.

In the transition from the traditional society to the new social forms, the position of the synagogue seems to have been less shaken than that of any of the other institutions. Those who admitted the Jewish religious community's right to existence tied this up with the prayer ritual peculiar to it. In the traditional society, as we have seen, the synagogue fulfilled various secondary administrative and social functions. But when the *kehilla* itself ceased to exercise the functions of government and social life found independent frameworks for the fulfillment of its needs, the synagogue began to devote itself exclusively to the performance of its primary function, the assembly of the faithful for common prayer. The obligation to participate in public prayer was not questioned, but its frequency was reduced and the attitude towards it changed.

Even in this domain, however, tradition ceased to be the ultimate arbiter of the permissible and desirable. The content and language of the prayers, the architecture of the synagogue, and the form of the ritual were now measured by the criteria of contemporary feeling and taste. As we shall see, even Mendelssohn noted an inconsistency between the content of the prayers—the longing to return to Zion—and the conscious aspiration of his contemporaries to make their permanent abode in their countries of residence. Owing to his formal conservatism, Mendelssohn refrained from suggesting changes in the wording of the prayers. His successors, however, had no such compunctions, and in the clash between the traditional and what seemed reasonable to them, they decided against tradition.

The same was true of questions pertaining to beauty and esthetic appearance. The structure of the synagogue, the style of the prayers, and even the melodies and cantillation of the scriptural readings suddenly struck the *maskilim* as odd and offensive. This was simply because their self-identification with outside groups planted reservations in their hearts about their social heritage—even in the sphere not subject to rational decision.

Adherence to Judaism also involved a national attachment—that is, a consciousness of belonging to the Jewish community, past and future, and a feeling of solidarity with one's coreligionists in the present. The disintegration of traditional society led henceforth to a dichotomy between the religious and the national bond. This development took a different direction from the parallel process in the non-Jewish society. The extremists of the other religions, even if they severed their ties with their church, did not thereby divorce themselves from their national culture. Though the national cultures of the other peoples were also woven into the fabric of medieval religious tradition, they were not so intimately tied to it as was the Jewish culture.

The disintegration of medieval religious institutions that accompanied the dissolution of the class structure did not do away with nationalist feeling. On the contrary, it prepared the ground for the new social formation on the basis of modern nationalism. This process could take place where the primary elements of nationalism—common language and common country—actually existed. Jewish nationalism, however, as we saw in our analysis of the traditional society, was built principally on substitutes for actualities—an attachment to an unspoken language, an attachment to the memory and hope of an unattained homeland, and bonds of religious and historical consciousness which flowed through the literary and institutional channels of tradition.

A Jew who did not confine himself to the framework of the Jewish class, and, more particularly, a Jew who cut himself off from the Jewish faith, found it easy to divest himself of the trammels of nationalism. The severance of ties with one's class of origin was more fundamental and rapid in Jewish than in non-Jewish rationalist circles. The latter, even if they weakened their ties with their place of origin, did not replace them by ties to the neutral society, which, after all, was nothing more than a temporary social grouping or a utopian vision of the future. The *maskilim* were sometimes left with nothing more than this illusory world, in which they had difficulty sustaining themselves for any length of time.

Those who persisted in their general attachment to Judaism nevertheless wished to divest themselves of its national ingredients. Both Mendelssohn and Wessely attempted to eliminate the use of Yiddish between Jews and to limit Hebrew to sacred use. Civic integration into the surrounding society demanded the relinquishment of the attachment to the hope of the national Jewish future in the land of its origin even at this period when the nationalism of the European nations had not yet reached its dynamic power. Admittedly, Mendelssohn, in his typically compromising way, left unchanged the wording of the prayers that mention the return to Zion, but he asserted that these prayers possessed no real significance in the worshippers' consciousness. Here, too, the decline of national feeling operated in full force.

As the symbols of national attachment lost their validity, the feeling of unity with Jews in all other countries also began to weaken. One of the first indications of this was the call for linguistic assimilation. When Yiddish was disqualified as an internal Jewish language, a barrier was created between the Jews of the West and the celebrated standard-bearers of Yiddish from Poland. The latter were the principal targets of the critics of the old educational system. Those critics attributed the cultural backwardness of the Jews of the West to the activities of the schoolmasters who came from Eastern Europe. Their desire to adapt themselves to the surrounding environment turned them, quite consistently, against the linguistic foundation which had hitherto served as the basis for the unity of traditional Jewish society within the territory of greater Ashkenazi Jewry. The possibility of interchange between leading personalities of East and West became increasingly remote. Henceforth, Western Jewry aspired to a cultural autonomy that would make it quite distinct from eastern European Jewry.

The disintegrative process described here was originally pioneered by a minority that demanded for itself the right to lead the society. But the activity of this minority gave rise to a general feeling of crisis, a consciousness that the foundations of society were crumbling. Even those who persisted in their attachment to the old underwent a change of outlook. The guardians and leaders of society became a class on the defensive.

The change in the conservatives' position coincided with a change in that of the innovators. Until the 1770's, not even the most perspicacious, like Rabbi Jacob Emden, were aware that real changes were about to occur in the life of the Jewish society. On the contrary, even those who were later to pronounce the ban on the innovations were themselves subject to the influences that were destined to turn into forces of disintegration and destruction.

It was only in the 1770's or 1780's, when the forces of change crystallized into tangible doctrines and demands, that the conservatives began to realize their significance. They resorted to the time-honored weapons for suppressing deviators and rebels in the traditional society—denunciation, punishment, and excommunication. They did not realize at first that here was an adversary of a different caliber. No longer was he a deviator and a sinner by his own standards; he was an opponent who felt that his deeds were justified by his own system of values. The battle of the communal leaders and the rabbis thus turned, at times, into a grotesque spectacle. Their weapons had gathered rust, but they seemed completely unaware of the fact. Although the *maskilim* were at first an insignificant minority, they had the upper hand. At this decisive juncture, the God of History was on their side.

Index